THE LIGHT
THAT FAILED

THE LIGHT THAT FAILED

Why the West Is Losing the Fight for Democracy

IVAN KRASTEV AND **STEPHEN HOLMES**

PEGASUS BOOKS
NEW YORK LONDON

The Light That Failed

Pegasus Books, Ltd.
West 37th Street, 13th Floor
New York, NY 10018

Set in 10.5/14 pt Sabon LT Std
Typeset by Jouve (UK), Milton Keynes

First Pegasus Books hardcover edition January 2019

ISBN: 978-1-64313-369-0

10 9 8 7 6 5 4 3 2 1

Printed in the United States of America
Distributed by W. W. Norton & Company

Contents

Imitation and its Discontents

We are all born originals – why is it so many of us die copies?
Edward Young

The future was better yesterday. We used to believe that the year 1989 divided 'the past from the future almost as clearly as the Berlin wall divided the East from the West'.[1] We had 'trouble imagining a world that is radically better than our own, or a future that is not essentially democratic and capitalist'.[2] That is not the way we think today. Most of us now have trouble imagining a future, even in the West, that remains securely democratic and liberal.

When the Cold War ended, hopes for liberal capitalist democracy spreading globally were high.[3] The geopolitical stage seemed set for a performance not unlike George Bernard Shaw's *Pygmalion*, an optimistic and didactic play in which a professor of phonetics, over a short period of time, succeeds in teaching a poor flower girl to speak like the Queen and feel at home in polite company.

Having prematurely celebrated the integration of the East into the West, interested observers eventually realized that the spectacle before them was not playing out as expected.[4] It was as if, instead of watching a performance of *Pygmalion*, the world ended up with a theatrical adaptation of Mary Shelley's *Frankenstein*, a pessimistic and didactic novel about a man who decided to play God by assembling replicas of human body parts into a humanoid creature. The defective monster felt doomed to loneliness, invisibility and rejection. And envying the unattainable happiness of its creator, it turned violently against the latter's friends and family, laying their world to waste, leaving only

I

remorse and heartbreak as legacies of a misguided experiment in human self-duplication.

How liberalism ended up the victim of its heralded success in the Cold War is the story this book aims to tell. Superficially, the fault lay with a series of profoundly destabilizing political events: the 9/11 attack on the World Trade Center in New York, the second Iraq War, the 2008 financial crisis, Russia's annexation of Crimea and intervention in Eastern Ukraine, the impotence of the West as Syria descended into a humanitarian nightmare, the 2015 migration crisis in Europe, the Brexit referendum, and the election of Donald Trump. Liberal democracy's post-Cold War afterglow has also been dimmed by the Chinese economic miracle, orchestrated by a political leadership that is unapologetically neither liberal nor democratic. Attempts to salvage the good name of liberal democracy by contrasting it favourably with non-Western autocracy have been undercut by the feckless violation of liberal norms, as in the torture of prisoners, and the evident malfunctioning of democratic institutions inside the West itself. Tellingly, how democracies atrophy and perish has become the question that most preoccupies liberal scholars today.[5]

The very ideal of 'an open society', too, has lost its once-fêted lustre.[6] For many disillusioned citizens, openness to the world now suggests more grounds for anxiety than for hope. When the Berlin Wall was toppled, there were only sixteen border fences in the world. Now there are sixty-five fortified perimeters either completed or under construction. According to Quebec University expert Elisabeth Vallet, almost a third of the world's countries are rearing barriers along their borders.[7] The three decades following 1989 turned out to be an 'inter-mural period', a brief barricade-free interval between the dramatic breaching of the Berlin Wall, exciting utopian fantasies of a borderless world, and a global craze of wall-building, with cement and barbed-wire barriers embodying existential (if sometimes imaginary) fears.

Most Europeans and Americans today also believe that the lives of their children will be less prosperous and fulfilling than their own.[8] Public faith in democracy is plummeting and long-established political parties are disintegrating or being crowded out by amorphous political movements and populist strongmen, putting into question the willingness of organized political forces to fight for democracy's survival in times of crisis.[9] Spooked by the phantom of large-scale migration, elect-orates in parts of Europe and America are increasingly drawn to xenophobic rhetoric, authoritarian leaders and militarized borders. Rather than believing that the future will be uplifted by the liberal ideas radiating out of the West, they fear that 21st-century history will be afflicted by the millions of people streaming into it.[10] Once extolled as a bulwark against tyranny, human rights are now routinely accused of limiting the ability of democracies to fight terrorism effectively. Fears for liberalism's survival are so acute that references to William Butler Yeats's 'The Second Coming', written in 1919 in the wake of one of the deadliest conflicts in human history, became an almost obliga-tory refrain for political commentators in 2016.[11] A century after Yeats wrote them, these words are now the mantra of apprehensive defenders of liberal democracy worldwide: 'Things fall apart; the centre cannot hold; / Mere anarchy is loosed upon the world.'

In his memoir *The World as It Is*, Ben Rhodes, Barack Obama's closest aide and personal friend, confides that, on the day Obama left the White House, the worry that haunted him most was: 'What if we were wrong?'[12] The uncertainty was not 'What went wrong?' or 'Who acted wrongly?' Nor was Hillary Clinton's 'What happened?' the most urgent mystery to solve. Obama's more troubling query was: 'What if we were wrong?' That is, what if liberals had misinterpreted the nature of the post-Cold War period? 'What if we were wrong?' is the right question and the one we have set out to answer in this book.

For the two of us, it is also an acutely personal question. The older of the two, the American, was born a year after the Cold War began and learned in high school that the just-erected Wall was an incarna-tion of intolerance and tyranny. The younger one, the Bulgarian, was born on the other side of the East–West divide some four years after the Wall went up, and grew up believing that tearing down walls was a pathway to political liberty and individual freedom.

While our backgrounds are different, both of us lived for years in the shadow of the Wall and its dramatically televised demolition turned out to be the defining moment in our political and intellectual lives. First the Berlin Wall and then its absence have indelibly marked our political thinking. The illusion that the end of the Cold War was the beginning of an Age of Liberalism and Democracy was our illusion too.

This book represents our attempt to understand not only why we were once ready to embrace this illusion but also how to think about a world onto which a high tide of illiberal and anti-democratic 'anarchy' has now been so ominously loosed.

THE SENSE OF AN ENDING

Three decades ago, in 1989, a US State Department official pithily captured the spirit of the time. Writing a few months before the Germans would joyfully dance on the sledge-hammered remains of the Berlin Wall, he proclaimed the Cold War effectively over. The comprehensive victory of liberalism over communism had been sealed by a decade of economic and political reforms initiated in China by Deng Xiaoping and in the Soviet Union by Mikhail Gorbachev. The elimination of 'the Marxist-Leninist alternative to liberal democracy', Francis Fukuyama argued, signalled 'the total exhaustion of viable systematic alternatives to Western liberalism'. Having been crowned by Marxists as the culmination of 'History' in the Hegelian sense, communism was suddenly demoted to 'history' in the American sense of something of negligible significance. 'Western liberal democracy', under these circumstances, could be called 'the end point of mankind's ideological evolution'. After the downfall of 'the fascist and communist dictatorships of this century, the only form of government that has survived intact to the end of the twentieth century has been liberal democracy'. Because 'the basic principles of the liberal-democratic state' were 'absolute and could not be improved upon', the sole task left to accomplish for liberal reformers was 'extending those principles spatially, such that the various provinces of human civilization were brought up to the level of its most advanced outposts'. Fukuyama maintained that liberalism 'would eventually become victorious throughout the world'. But his real point was that no 'ideologies which claimed to be more advanced than liberalism' could hereafter arise.[13]

What did the recognition of capitalist democracy as the final stage of mankind's political development mean in practice? Fukuyama was somewhat evasive on this point. But his argument undoubtedly implied that Western-style liberal democracy was the only viable ideal towards

4

which reformers everywhere should strive. When he wrote that the last 'beacon for illiberal forces' had been extinguished by Chinese and Soviet reformers, he meant that America's liberal beacon alone was lighting mankind's pathway to the future.[14]

This denial that any globally appealing alternative to the Western model existed explains why Fukuyama's thesis not only appealed to American self-love but also felt self-evident to dissidents and reformers living behind the Iron Curtain.[15] A short year earlier, in 1988, some of the most ardent proponents of democratic pluralism in the Soviet Union had published a collection of articles under the title *Inogo ne dano*,[16] which can be roughly translated as 'There Is No Other Way'. The Bible of Soviet reformism, too, was a book arguing that there were no sustainable alternatives to Western capitalist democracy.

Formulated in our terms, 1989 heralded the onset of a thirty-year Age of Imitation. The Western-dominated unipolar order made liberalism seem unchallengable in the realm of moral ideals. After initially high hopes of exporting the West's political and economic model began to fade, however, revulsion at the politics of imitation gradually spread. An anti-liberal backlash was arguably an inevitable response to a world that had been characterized by a lack of political and ideological alternatives. This absence of alternatives, we submit, even more than the gravitational pull of an authoritarian past or historically ingrained hostility to liberalism, best explains the anti-Western ethos dominating post-communist societies today.[17] The very conceit that 'there is no other way' provided an independent motive for the wave of populist xenophobia and reactionary nativism that began in Central and Eastern Europe and is now washing across much of the world. The lack of a plausible alternative to liberal democracy became a stimulus to revolt because, at some elemental level, 'human beings need choice, even just the illusion of it'.[18]

Populists are rebelling not only against a specific (liberal) type of politics but also as against the replacement of communist orthodoxy by liberal orthodoxy. The message of insurgent movements on both the left and the right, in effect, is that a take-it-or-leave-it approach is wrong and that things can be different, as well as more familiar and more authentic.

Obviously, no single factor can explain the simultaneous emergence of authoritarian anti-liberalisms in so many differently situated countries in the second decade of the twenty-first century. Yet resentment at liberal democracy's canonical status and the politics of imitation in general has, we believe, played a decisive role, not only in Central Europe, but in Russia and the United States as well. To begin making this case, we call two of Central Europe's most articulate critics of liberalism as our opening witnesses. A Polish philosopher and conservative member of the European Parliament, Ryszard Legutko, is irate that 'liberal democracy has no alternative', that it has become 'the only accepted course and method of organizing collective life' and that 'the liberals and the liberal democrats have managed to silence and marginalize nearly all alternatives and all nonliberal views of political order'.[19] An influential Hungarian historian concurs: 'We don't want to copy what the Germans are doing or what the French are doing,' announced Maria Schmidt, Viktor Orbán's intellectual-in-chief. 'We want to continue with our own way of life.'[20] Both statements suggest that a stubborn unwillingness to accept 'the total exhaustion of viable systematic alternatives to Western liberalism' helped turn the West's soft power to inspire emulation into weakness and vulnerability rather than strength and authority.

A refusal to genuflect before the liberal West has become the hallmark of the illiberal counter-revolution throughout the post-communist world and beyond. Such a reaction cannot be casually dismissed with the trite observation that 'blaming the West' is a cheap way for non-Western leaders to avoid taking responsibility for their own failed policies. The story is much more convoluted and compelling than that. It is a story, among other things, of liberalism abandoning pluralism for hegemony.

NAMING AND NECESSITY

During the Cold War, the most politically consequential schism in the world ran between communists and democrats. The earth was divided between the totalitarian East and the West's free world, and societies populating the periphery of the main conflict had, or imagined they had, the right and the power to choose sides. After the fall of the Wall, this constellation changed. Henceforth, the most consequential split in the geopolitical firmament separated imitators from the imitated, established democracies from countries struggling to complete the transition to democracy. East–West relations morphed from a Cold War stand-off between two hostile systems into a strained relationship between models and mimics inside a single unipolar system.

The striving of ex-communist countries to emulate the West after 1989 has been given an assortment of names – Americanization, Europeanization, democratization, liberalization, enlargement, integration, harmonization, globalization, and so forth – but it has always signified modernization by imitation and integration by assimilation. After the communist collapse, according to Central Europe's populists, liberal democracy became a new, inescapable orthodoxy. Their constant lament is that imitating the values, attitudes, institutions and practices of the West became imperative and obligatory. As the Polish philosopher cited above has also written, ridiculing the mindset of many of his countrymen after 1989:

> the deeper wisdom was to copy and to imitate. The more we copied and imitated, the more we were glad of ourselves. Institutions, education, customs, law, media, language, almost everything became all of a sudden imperfect copies of the originals that were in the line of progress ahead of us.[21]

This fraught asymmetry between those morally ahead and those morally behind, that is, between the imitated and their imitators, became a defining and painful feature of East–West relations after 1989.

After the fall of the Wall, across-the-board imitation of the West was widely accepted as the most effective way to democratize previously non-democratic societies. Largely because of the moral asymmetry it implied, this conceit has now become a pre-eminent target of populist rage.

STRAINS OF IMITATION

That imitation is ubiquitous in social life goes without saying. The renowned nineteenth-century social theorist Gabriel Tarde went so far as to claim that 'society is imitation'.[22] He even referred to 'contagious imitation' as a kind of 'somnambulism', meaning that human beings copy each other spontaneously, without any strategic purpose or plan, as in copycat crimes, and without being forced or compelled in any way.[23]

When Central Europe's populists rail against a perceived Imitation Imperative as the most insufferable feature of liberalism's hegemony after 1989, they obviously mean something less generic and more politically provocative. The form of comprehensive institutional imitation at issue involves, first, the acknowledged moral superiority of the imitated over their imitators, second, a political model that claims to have eliminated all viable alternatives, third, an expectation that the imitation will be unconditional rather than adapted to local traditions, and, fourth, a presumption that representatives of the imitated (and therefore implicitly superior) countries could legitimately claim a right to monitor and evaluate the progress of imitating countries on an ongoing basis. Without pressing the analogy too far, it's interesting to observe that the style of regime imitation that took hold after 1989 bears an eerie resemblance to Soviet-era elections where voters, overseen by Party officials, pretended to 'choose' the only candidates who were running for office.

To describe better what is at stake, we need to draw a few preliminary distinctions. We need to distinguish, as already suggested, between the full-scale imitation of a single orthodox model, monitored (not imposed) by judgemental foreigners, and the ordinary learning by which states vicariously profit from each other's experiences.[24] The former engenders resentment, while the latter, usually ascribed to the demonstration effect of perceived successes and failures, does not.

Second, and even more importantly, we should separate the imitation of means from the imitation of goals. We call the former *borrowing* rather than imitation. A classic formulation of this distinction was articulated by the great economic sociologist Thorstein Veblen, who wrote at the beginning of the twentieth century that the Japanese had borrowed 'the industrial arts' of the West but not the West's 'spiritual outlook' or its 'principles of conduct and ethical values'.[25] Borrowing technical means does not affect identity, at least not in the short term, while imitating moral ends cuts deeper and can initiate a much more radically transformative process, veering close to a 'conversion experience'. In rebuilding their societies after 1989, Central Europeans strove to replicate the lifestyles and moral attitudes which they observed in the West. The Chinese, by way of contrast, have taken a path not unlike the one identified by Veblen, adopting Western technologies to drive economic growth and boost the prestige of the Communist Party for the explicit purpose of *resisting* the siren song of the West.

The imitation of moral ideals, unlike the borrowing of technologies, makes you resemble the one you admire but simultaneously makes you look less like yourself at a time when your own uniqueness and keeping faith with your group are at the heart of your struggle for dignity and recognition. The prevailing cult of innovation, creativity and originality at the core of liberal modernity means that, even for the inhabitants of economically successful countries such as Poland, the project of adopting a Western model under Western supervision feels like a confession of having failed to escape Central Europe's historical vassalage to foreign instructors and inquisitors.

This self-contradictory request to be both an original and a copy was bound to be psychologically stressful. A feeling of being treated disrespectfully was also fomented by what can be reasonably identified as the central irony of post-communist democracy-promotion in the context of European integration: the Central and East European countries ostensibly being democratized were compelled, in order to meet the conditions for EU membership, to enact policies formulated by unelected bureaucrats from Brussels and international lending organizations.[26] Poles and Hungarians were told what laws and policies to enact, and simultaneously instructed to pretend that they were governing themselves. Elections started looking like 'a trap for fools', as Rudyard Kipling would have said. Voters regularly threw the incumbents out, it is true, but the policies – formulated in Brussels – didn't substantially change. Pretending to rule themselves while being ruled by Western policy-makers was bad enough. The last straw was being disparaged by visiting Westerners, who accused them of merely going through the motions of democracy, when that was exactly what political elites in the region thought they were being asked to do.

The collapse of communism kindled a psychologically problematic and even traumatic transformation of East–West relations because, for various reasons, it created the expectation that countries exiting from communism needed to imitate not means but ends. Those Eastern political leaders who pioneered the importation of Western models in this strong sense wanted their fellow citizens to internalize the model's goals and adopt the model's preferences in a holistic rather than piece-meal fashion. The core complaint motivating anti-liberal politics in the region today is that the attempt to democratize formerly communist countries was aiming at a kind of cultural *conversion* to values, habits and attitudes considered 'normal' in the West. Unlike grafting a few foreign elements onto indigenous traditions, this political and moral 'shock therapy' put inherited identity at risk. Because it was inevitably partial and askew, copycat liberalism made many of those who had originally embraced the changes feel like cultural impostors, a malaise that, in turn, excited politically exploitable longings for a lost authenticity.

Admittedly, attempts by the weak to imitate the strong and successful are nothing exceptional among states and nations. But imitation usually resembles shallow parroting rather than the psychologically and socially stressful transfiguration that was attempted in Central Europe after 1989. Louis XIV's France, as the dominant power in seventeenth-century Europe, inspired many imitators of this superficial kind. As political scientist Ken Jowitt has pointed out, replicas of Versailles were built in Germany, Poland and Russia, French manners were copied, and French became the language of far-flung elites. In the nineteenth century, it was the turn of the British parliament to become the focus of perfunctory and ornamental imitation, while 'after World War II a number of Stalinist regimes were created in Eastern Europe, from Albania to Lithuania, all stamped with iden-tically ugly Stalinist architecture – political and physical.'[27] An important reason why cosmetically imitative behaviour is so common in political life is that it helps the weak appear stronger than they are – a useful form of mimicry for surviving in hostile environments. It also makes the imitators seem legible to those who might otherwise help, hurt or marginalize them. In the post-Cold War world, 'learning English, displaying copies of the *Federalist Papers*, wearing Armani suits, having elections' – and, to recall Jowitt's favourite example, 'playing golf'[28] – enable non-Western elites not only to put their powerful Western interlocutors at ease, but also to make economic, political and military claims upon them. Mimicking the powerful allows a weak country to share vicariously in the enormous stature and prestige of an authentic 'Versailles', without necessarily becoming a source of national humiliation or a grave threat to national identity.

When we speak of the unintended consequences of the unipolar Age of Imitation and describe a perceived post-1989 Imitation Imperative as an important reason why the liberal dream turned into a liberal nightmare, we are referring to patterns of mimetic behaviour and mimetic intoxication that are more emotionally taxing and transformative than glib simulation. At issue is the kind of comprehensive political makeover that, partly because it is orchestrated not at the West's command but 'under Western eyes', evokes feelings of shame and resentment and stokes fears of cultural erasure.

Some of Central and Eastern Europe's most influential political leaders eagerly embraced copycat Westernization as the shortest path to reform in the immediate aftermath of 1989. Imitation was justified as a 'return to Europe', and that meant a return to the region's authentic self. In Moscow, of course, the situation was different. Communism there was never experienced as foreign domination, and thus imitation of the West could not be plausibly presented as a recovery of the country's authentic national identity.

However earnestly or disingenuously embraced at the outset, Western models eventually lost their charm even for their originally most hopeful Eastern imitators. Reform along liberal-democratic lines began to feel less agreeable for many reasons besides those already suggested. For starters, even the best-intentioned Western advisors were unable to conceal the implied superiority of the model over the mimic. Making things worse, foreign promoters of political reform in the East continued to hold up an idealized image of liberal democracy even after the signs of the latter's internal dysfunction became too obvious to ignore. It was in this context that the global financial crisis of 2008 gave liberalism's good name its final *coup de grâce*.

The French philosopher René Girard argued voluminously that

imitation's centrality to the human condition has been misleadingly and dangerously neglected by historians and social scientists. He devoted his career to studying how imitation can breed psychological trauma and social conflict. This happens, he claimed, when the model imitated becomes an obstacle to the self-esteem and self-realization of the imitator.[29] The form of imitation most likely to generate resentment and conflict, according to Girard, is the imitation of desires. We imitate not just means but also ends, not just technical instruments but also targets, objectives, goals and ways of life. This, in our opinion, is the inherently stressful and contentious form of emulation that has helped trigger the current sweeping anti-liberal revolt.

According to Girard, human beings want something not because it is inherently appealing or desirable, but only because somebody else wants it, an observation that makes the ideal of human autonomy seem illusory. The hypothesis can be tested by observing two small children in a room full of toys: the 'most desirable' toy is usually the one in the other child's hands.[30] Imitating the goals of others is also associated, Girard argues, with rivalry, resentment, and threats to personal identity. The more confidence that imitators have in those they imitate, tellingly, the less confidence they have in themselves. The model being imitated is inevitably a rival and a threat to self-respect. This is especially true when the model you are supposed to imitate is not Jesus Christ in heaven but your neighbour to the west.

Arguments from etymology are notoriously weak. But it is probably worth recalling that 'emulation' originally signified not deferential admiration but ruthless competition. The son wants to be like his father, but the father conveys the subliminal message that the boy's ambition is unachievable, causing the son to hate the father.[31] This pattern is not far from what we observe in Central and Eastern Europe where, according to the populists, the Western-inspired Imitation Imperative made it seem like destiny for countries to shed their hallowed pasts and adopt a new liberal-democratic identity which, if truth be told, would never be fully theirs. Shame at reshaping one's preferences to conform to the value hierarchies of foreigners, doing so in the name of freedom, and being looked down upon for the supposed inadequacy of the attempt – these are the emotions and experiences that have fuelled the anti-liberal counter-revolution that began in post-communist Europe, specifically in Hungary, and that has now metastasized worldwide.

Girard's insight into the persistent tendency of imitation to breed resentment, while based almost exclusively on the analysis of literary texts, is nevertheless highly pertinent to understanding why a contagious uprising against liberal democracy began in the post-communist world.[32] By drawing attention to the inherently conflictual nature of imitation, he helps us to see democratization after communism in an entirely new light. His theory suggests that the problems we face today arise less from a natural relapse into bad habits of the past than from a backlash against a perceived Imitation Imperative promulgated after the fall of the Berlin Wall. While Fukuyama was confident that the Age of Imitation would be endlessly boring, Girard was more prescient, foretelling its potential for incubating the kind of existential shame that can fuel explosive upheaval.

THE FLOWERS OF RESENTMENT

The origins of today's worldwide anti-liberal revolt lie in three parallel, interconnected and resentment-fuelled reactions to the presumptively canonical status of Western political models after 1989. That is the thesis we wish to explore and defend, with all due awareness of its one-sidedness, incompleteness and empirical vulnerabilities. Our aim is not to produce a comprehensive and definitive account of the causes and consequences of contemporary anti-liberalism but to emphasize and illustrate one specific aspect of the story that has yet to garner the attention that we believe it deserves. To highlight the sometime hidden affinities among our three cases of reactionary nativism and authoritarianism, we have relied on a flexibly articulated and admittedly speculative but, we hope, coherent and revealing concept of political imitation. With this purpose in mind, we have structured the book as follows.

We begin by examining the intolerant communitarianism of Central European populists, especially Viktor Orbán and Jarosław Kaczyński, attempting to explain how a significant swathe of the electorate, in countries where a liberal elite had only recently embraced the imitation of Western models as the quickest path to prosperity and freedom, began to view such imitation as a road to perdition. We examine how an anti-Western counter-elite, with predominantly provincial origins, began to emerge in the region and to attract considerable popular support, especially outside the globally networked metropolitan centres, by monopolizing the symbols of national identity that had been neglected or devalued in the process of 'harmonization' with the European Union's post-national standards and regulations. And we aim to show how the process of depopulation in Central and Eastern Europe that followed the fall of the Berlin Wall[33] helped populist counter-elites capture their public's imagination by denouncing the universalism of human rights and open-border liberalism as expressions of the West's lofty indifference to their countries' national traditions and heritage.[34] We do not contend that the Central European populists are blameless victims of the West, or that resisting what they experienced as an Imitation Imperative is their sole agenda, or that their illiberalism was the only possible response to 2008 and other crises in the West. Nor are we unmindful of the heroic fight against illiberal populism that is under way in the region. What we argue, instead, is that populism's political rise cannot be explained without taking account of widespread resentment at the way (imposed) no-alternative Soviet communism, after 1989, was replaced by (invited) no-alternative Western liberalism.

We turn next to Russia's sense of grievance in the face of what they saw as yet another round of imperative Westernization. For the Kremlin, the disintegration of the Soviet Union signalled Moscow's loss of its superpower status and therefore of its global parity with its American adversary. Russia was transformed virtually overnight from a formidable peer competitor to a basket case begging for support and forced to feign gratitude for the advice delivered by well-meaning but poorly prepared American consultants. For Russia, imitation was never going to be synonymous with integration. Unlike Central and Eastern Europe, it wasn't a serious candidate to join NATO or the European Union. It was too large, possessed too many nukes, and had a sense of its own 'historical greatness' that would not allow it to become a junior partner in a Western alliance.

The Kremlin's first response to the global pre-eminence of

liberalism was a form of *simulation* of the sort adopted by relatively weak prey to avoid being attacked by dangerous predators. Russia's political elite, in the immediate aftermath of the Soviet collapse, was by no means uniform. But most of them found faking democracy perfectly natural since they had been faking communism for at least two decades before 1991. Russia's liberal reformers, such as Yegor Gaidar, genuinely admired democracy, but they were convinced that in the vast reaches of the country, and given the authoritarian tradition that had shaped society for centuries, creating a market economy was impossible under a government genuinely responsive to the popular will. The creation of 'imitation democracy' in 1990s Russia involved none of the arduous work of real political development. It was essentially a matter of erecting a Potemkin façade with a superficial resemblance to democracy only. The masquerade was effective to the extent that, during a difficult transition period, it reduced Western pressure to engage in political reforms that, while not creating accountable government, might have put the inherently traumatic and inevitably corrupt process of economic privatization at risk.

By 2011–12, this democratic charade had outlived its usefulness. Russia's leaders then switched to a resentment-fuelled policy of violent parody, a style of imitation that is brazenly hostile and intentionally provocative. It certainly cannot be captured by bland analyses of foreign policy imitation as 'observational learning'.[35] We call it *mirroring*. Rankling under what it saw as the imperious and futile demand that Russia imitate an idealized image of the West, Kremlin insiders decided to imitate what they perceived as the most odious behavioural patterns of the American hegemon in order to *hold up a mirror* to the West and to show these would-be missionaries what they really look like when their self-flattering pretences are stripped away. Mirroring is a way for erstwhile imitators to avenge themselves on their would-be models by revealing the latter's unattractive defects and irksome hypocrisy. What makes this rage for unmasking significant is that the Kremlin often pursues it as an end in itself, apart from any collateral benefits the country might hope to reap, and even at considerable cost.

Russia's interference in the American Presidential elections in 2016, to come to the most salient example of this tauntingly ironic

'mirroring' approach, was understood by its organizers and perpetra-
tors as an attempt to duplicate what the Kremlin considered the
West's unwarranted incursions into Russia's own political life. The
explicit purpose was less to elect a Kremlin-friendly candidate than
to teach Americans what foreign interference in a country's politics
looks and feels like. Alongside this pedagogical objective, such mirroring was meant to expose the ricketiness and vulnerability of a
supercilious democratic regime.

Having simulated the accountability of politicians to citizens in the
1990s, we argue, the Kremlin today has lost all interest in democratic
charades. Instead of pretending to imitate America's domestic political
system, Putin and his entourage prefer to imitate the way America illicitly interferes in the domestic politics of other countries. More generally,
the Kremlin aims to hold up a mirror in which America can contemplate its own proclivity to violate the international rules it pretends to
respect. And it does so condescendingly, with the aim of humiliating
the Americans and cutting them down to size.

Resentment of Americanization provides a powerful (if only partial) explanation for Central Europe's domestic illiberalism and
Russia's foreign-policy belligerence. But what about the United States?
Why would so many Americans support a president who sees America's commitment to the liberal world order as its main vulnerability?
Why would Trump's supporters implicitly accept his eccentric idea
that the United States should stop being a model for other countries
and perhaps even remake itself in the image of Orbán's Hungary and
Putin's Russia?

Trump won both popular and business support by declaring the
United States to be the greatest loser from the Americanization of
the world. Significant public acceptance of this deviation from the
boastful mainstream of American political culture cries out for an
explanation. Because Russians and Central Europeans reject imitation as bad for the imitators and good only for the imitated, it is at
first puzzling that some Americans would reject imitation as bad for
the imitated and good only for the imitators. Indeed, Trump's resentment against a world full of countries that seek to emulate America
seems anomalous until we realize that, for his American supporters,
imitators are threats because they are trying to replace the model they

imitate. This fear of being supplanted and dispossessed has two sources: immigrants, on the one hand, and China, on the other.

The far-fetched image of America as an abused victim of its admirers and imitators was not taken seriously by the business community or the public when Trump first made it his signature idea in the 1980s. So why did it begin to speak loudly to both in the second decade of the twenty-first century? The answer lies in the travails of middle- and working-class white Americans and the emergence of China as a much more dangerous economic competitor to the US than either Germany or Japan had been. The white voter's perception that China is stealing American jobs and the business community's perception that China is stealing American technology helped Trump's eccentric message of American victimization – despite its being a radical break from the country's traditional self-image – gain a crude plausibility that it had never previously enjoyed.

This preliminary example illustrates how the model and not only the mimics can come to resent the politics of imitation and, in this case, how the leader of the country that built the liberal world order could decide to do everything in his power to tear it down.

China also provides a natural finale to our argument because the rise of an internationally assertive China, ready to contest US hegemony, signals the end of the Age of Imitation as we understand it. In his December 2018 resignation letter to the US President, Secretary of Defense James Mattis wrote that Chinese leaders 'want to shape a world consistent with their authoritarian model'. But he did not mean to suggest that they aimed to persuade or compel other countries to adopt 'Asian values' or to encourage them to paint 'Chinese characteristics' on their own political and economic systems. They seek influence and respect, but not worldwide conversion to 'Xi JinPing Thought'. They aim, as Mattis wrote, at 'gaining veto authority over other nations' economic, diplomatic, and security decisions – to promote their own interests at the expense of their neighbors, America and our allies'.[36]

The coming clash between America and China is bound to be world-changing, but it will be about trade, resources, technology, turf and the ability to shape a global environment hospitable to the two countries' very different national interests and ideals. It will not involve a conflict between rival universal visions of the human future, in which each side attempts to recruit allies to its side by ideological conversion and revolutionary regime change. In today's international system, naked power asymmetries have already begun to replace alleged moral asymmetries. This explains why the Sino-American rivalry cannot be accurately described as 'a new Cold War'. Alliances are dissolving and re-coalescing kaleidoscopically, with countries abandoning long-term ideological partnerships for ephemeral marriages of convenience. Though the consequences are impossible to foretell, they will not produce a re-run of the forty-year conflict between the US and the USSR.

What the breathtaking rise of China suggests is that the defeat of the communist idea in 1989 was not, after all, a one-sided victory for the liberal idea. Instead, the unipolar order became a world much less hospitable to liberalism than anyone had predicted at the time. Some commentators have claimed that 1989, by eliminating the Cold War competition between rival universal ideologies, fatally damaged the Enlightenment project itself, in its liberal as well as communist incarnation. The Hungarian philosopher G. M. Tamás has gone even further, arguing that 'both the liberal and socialist utopias' were 'defeated' in 1989, signalling 'the end' of the 'Enlightenment project' itself.[37] We are not so fatalistic. After all, American and European leaders able to manage the West's decline judiciously may still emerge. A pathway to liberal recovery on foundations both familiar and novel may be identified and followed. At present, the odds favouring such a renewal seem slim. Still, the anti-liberal regimes and movements we discuss here, perhaps because they lack any broadly appealing ideological vision, may prove ephemeral and historically inconsequential. History, famously, is an invasion of the unknown. But whatever the future holds in store, we can nevertheless begin by trying to understand how we got to where we are today.

I

The Copycat Mind

There is no doubt that men like Robespierre are created by
such moments of humiliation.

Stendhal[1]

'As Gregor Samsa awoke one morning from uneasy dreams he found himself transformed in his bed into a gigantic insect.' This opening line of Kafka's *Metamorphosis* might as well be describing the astonishment felt by Western liberals when they opened their eyes, sometime around 2015, to discover that once-celebrated new democracies in Central and Eastern Europe had been transformed into conspiracy-minded majoritarian regimes where the political opposition was demonized, non-government media, civil society and independent courts were denuded of their influence, and sovereignty was defined as the leadership's determination to resist any and all pressure to conform to Western ideals of political pluralism, government transparency and tolerance for strangers, dissidents and minorities.

In the spring of 1990, John Feffer, a 26-year-old American, spent several months crisscrossing Eastern Europe in hopes of unlocking the mystery of its post-communist future and authoring a book about the historical transformation unfolding before his eyes.[2] He was no expert, so instead of testing theories, he buttonholed as many people from as many walks of life as possible and ended up both fascinated and puzzled by the contradictions he encountered at every step. East Europeans were optimistic but apprehensive. Many of those he interviewed at the time expected to be living like Viennese or Londoners within five years, ten years at the most. But these exorbitant hopes were mingled with anxiety and foreboding. As Hungarian sociologist

Elemér Hankiss observed, 'People realized suddenly that in the coming years it would be decided who would be rich, and who would be poor; who would have power and who would not; who would be marginalized, and who would be at the centre. And who would be able to found dynasties and whose children would suffer.'[3]

Feffer eventually published his book, but did not return to the countries that had briefly captured his imagination. Then, twenty-five years later, he decided to revisit the region and to seek out those with whom he had spoken in 1990. This second journey resembled the reawakening of Gregor Samsa. Eastern Europe was richer, but roiled by resentment. The capitalist future had arrived, but its benefits and burdens were unevenly, even crassly distributed. After reminding us that 'For the World War II generation in eastern Europe, communism was the "god that failed"', Feffer hits upon the thesis this chapter aims to explore: 'For the current generation in the region, liberalism is the god that failed.'[4]

THE DYING OF THE LIGHT

In the immediate aftermath of 1989, the global spread of democracy was envisioned as a version of the fairy tale of Sleeping Beauty, where the Prince of Freedom only needed to slay the Dragon of Tyranny and kiss the princess in order to awaken a previously dormant liberal majority. But the kiss proved bitter, and the revived majority turned out to be more resentful and less liberal than had been expected or hoped.

When the Cold War ended, racing to join the West, as that destination has been idealized from behind the Iron Curtain, was the shared mission of Central and East Europeans. Indeed, becoming indistinguishably Western was arguably the principal aim of the revolutions of 1989. The enthusiastic copying of Western models, accompanied as it was by the evacuation of Soviet troops from the region, was initially experienced as liberation. But after two troubled decades, the downsides of a politics of imitation had become too obvious to deny. As resentment seethed, illiberal politicians rose in popularity and, in Hungary and Poland, acceded to power.

In the first years after 1989, liberalism was generally associated with the ideals of individual opportunity, freedom to move and to travel, unpunished dissent, access to justice, and government responsiveness to public demands. By 2010 the Central and East European versions of liberalism had been indelibly tainted by two decades of rising social inequality, pervasive corruption, and the morally arbitrary redistribution of public property into the hands of a few. The economic crisis of 2008 had bred a deep distrust of business elites and the casino capitalism that, writ large, almost destroyed the world financial order. Liberalism's reputation in the region never recovered from 2008. It greatly weakened the case, pressed by a handful of Western-trained economists, for continuing to imitate American-style capitalism. Confidence that the political economy of the West was a model for the future of mankind had been linked to the belief that Western elites knew what they were doing. Suddenly it was obvious that they didn't. This is why 2008 had such a shattering ideological, not merely economic, effect both regionally and worldwide.

An additional reason why Central and East populists have got away with exaggerating the dark sides of European liberalism is that the passage of time has erased from the collective memory the even darker sides of European illiberalism. In addition, Central and East Europeans got their chance to imitate the West just as the West was losing its global dominance and prescient observers began to doubt not only the universal applicability but also the ideal superiority of the West's political model. This was not a favourable context for continuing to pursue reform-by-imitation. Being an imitator is often a psychological drama. But it becomes a shipwreck if you realize midstream that the model you have started to imitate is about to capsize and sink. Fear of catching the wrong train is commonly said to haunt the collective psyche of Central Europe. Thus, political and economic instability in the West has both energized and justified the revolt against liberalism in the East.

By identifying animus against the politics of imitation as one of the taproots of Central and Eastern European illiberalism, we do not mean to deny that the leaders of illiberal parties in the region are power hungry and benefiting politically from their efforts to discredit liberal principles and institutions. The illiberalism espoused by ruling groups in Budapest and Warsaw is incontestably convenient for incumbents who want nothing to do with the democratic alternation of parties in power. Their anti-liberalism is opportunistic in the sense that it helps them evade legitimate charges of corruption and abuse of power levelled by EU officials and domestic critics. Fidesz (the Hungarian Civic Alliance) and PiS (the Polish Law and Justice Party) regularly malign the checks and balances prescribed by Western constitutionalism as a foreign plot to stifle the authentic voices of the Hungarian and Polish peoples. The urgent need to defend the nation against 'foreign-hearted' inner enemies is how they justify their dismantling of an independent press and an independent judiciary as well as their scurrilous attacks on dissidents and critics.

But focusing on the corrupt practices and strategies for evading responsibility adopted by the illiberal governments in the region will not help us understand the sources of popular support for national populist parties. The origins of populism are undoubtedly complex. But they partly lie in the humiliations associated with the uphill struggle to become, at best, an inferior copy of a superior model. Discontent with the 'transition to democracy' was also inflamed by visiting foreign 'evaluators' with an anaemic grasp of local realities. These experiences have combined to produce a nativist reaction in the region, a reassertion of 'authentic' national traditions allegedly suffocated by second-hand and ill-fitting Western forms. The post-national liberalism associated especially with EU enlargement has allowed aspiring populists to claim exclusive ownership of national traditions and national identity.

This was the mainspring of the anti-liberal revolt in the region. But a subsidiary factor was also involved, namely, the unargued assumption that, after 1989, there were no alternatives to liberal political and economic models. This presumption spawned a contrarian desire to prove that there were, indeed, such alternatives. Germany's populist anti-euro party, Alternative für Deutschland (AfD), provides a parallel example. As its name suggests, it was launched in response to Angela Merkel's offhand claim that her monetary policy was '*alternativlos*' ('without alternative'). By describing the government's proposal as the only available option, she provoked an intense and implacable search for alternatives.[5] A similar backlash, provoked by the assumed normality of post-nationalism, gave birth, in formerly communist countries, to an anti-liberal, anti-globalist, anti-migrant and anti-EU revolt, exploited and manipulated by populist demagogues who knew how to demonize 'inner enemies' to mobilize public support.

STRAINS OF NORMALITY

According to George Orwell, 'All revolutions are failures but they are not all the same failure.'[6] So, what kind of failure was the revolution of 1989, given that its aim was Western-style normality? To what extent was the liberal and therefore imitative revolution of 1989 responsible for the illiberal counter-revolution unleashed two decades later?

Fortuitously coinciding with the bicentennial of the glorious but bloody French Revolution, the 'velvet revolutions' of 1989 were, by contrast, largely unmarred by the cut-throat methods and human suffering that are usually part of root-and-branch political upheaval. Never before had so many deeply entrenched regimes been simultaneously overthrown and replaced using basically peaceable means. The left praised these velvet revolutions as expressions of popular power. The right extolled them as both a triumph of the free market over the command economy and the well-deserved victory of free government over totalitarian dictatorship. American and pro-American liberals, for their part, were proud to associate liberalism, routinely ridiculed by leftist critics as an ideology geared to maintaining the status quo, with the romance of emancipating change.[7] Equally sympathetic were the West European sixty-eighters who, even when favouring a Marxist vocabulary, preferred cultural liberalism to Cultural Revolution. And of course these largely nonviolent changes of regime in the East were vested with world-historical significance since they marked the end of a great-power stand-off that had dominated the second half of the twentieth century and threatened the planet with nuclear Armageddon.

The non-violent nature of the revolutions of 1989 was not their only unique feature, however. Given the prominent public role played at the time by creative thinkers and savvy political activists such as Václav Havel and Adam Michnik, the events of 1989 are sometimes remembered as revolutions of the intellectuals. And it's true that of the

232 participants in the round table talks between the governing Polish Communist Party, pretending to represent the working class, and the anti-communist Solidarity trade union, representing actual workers, 195 would identify themselves as intellectuals.[8] But if they were bookish, they were anything but dreamers. What ensured that these revolutions would remain 'velvet' was their background hostility to utopias and political experiments. By 1989, moreover, regime insiders themselves had fully switched from utopian faith to mechanical rituals and from ideological commitment to corruption. They were thus fortuitously in sync with the dissidents who had no interest in remaking their societies to conform to some historically unprecedented ideal. Far from searching for an untested wonderland or craving anything ingeniously new, the leading figures in these revolutions aimed at overturning one system only in order to copy another.

As the great historian of the French Revolution, François Furet, pungently observed: 'Not a single new idea has come out of Eastern Europe in 1989.'[9] Germany's foremost philosopher, Jürgen Habermas, a life-long advocate of a cultural orientation towards the West and of remaking his country along Western lines, concurred. He warmly welcomed 'the lack of ideas that are either innovative or oriented towards the future' after 1989, since for him the Central and Eastern European revolutions were 'rectifying revolutions'[10] or 'catch-up revolutions'.[11] Their goal was to return Central and Eastern European societies to the mainstream of Western modernity, allowing the Central and East Europeans to gain what the West Europeans already possessed.

Nor were the Central and East Europeans themselves, in 1989, dreaming of some perfect world that had never existed. They were longing instead for a 'normal life' in a 'normal country'. In the late 1970s the great German poet Hans Magnus Enzensberger travelled around Europe in search of the old continent's soul. When he visited Hungary and spoke with some of the best-known critics of the communist regime, what they told him was: 'we are not dissidents. We represent normality.'[12] As Michnik later confessed, 'My obsession had been that we should have . . . an anti-utopian revolution, because utopias lead to the guillotine and the gulag.' His post-communist slogan was therefore 'Liberty, Fraternity, Normality'.[13] When Poles of his generation spoke of 'normality', it should also be said, they did not mean some earlier pre-communist period of Polish history to which their country could happily revert once the parenthesis of Soviet occupation was closed. What they meant by 'normality' was the West.

Václav Havel concurred. He described the essential condition of communist Eastern Europe as the 'absence of a normal political life'.[14] Under communism, nothing was rarer than 'normality'. Havel also referred to Western-style 'freedom and the rule of law' as 'the first preconditions of a normally and healthily functioning social organism'. And he depicted his country's struggle to escape communist rule as 'simply trying to do away with its own abnormality, to normalize'.[15] Havel's longing for a normal *political* condition suggests that, after decades of pretending to expect a radiant future, the main goal of the dissidents was to live in the present and to enjoy the pleasures of everyday life. To say that the canonical status of Western political and economic organization was accepted across the region is to say that the post-1989 transition to normality aimed at making possible in the East the kinds of lives taken for granted in the West.

In *The Captive Mind*, Czeslaw Milosz argues that in the post-Second World War period, for many East European intellectuals, the New Faith in communism resembled the Murti-Bing pills featured in Stanislaw Witkiewicz's 1927 novel *Insatiability*.[16] These pills were a medicinal means of inducing a 'philosophy of life', making those who took them 'impervious to any metaphysical concerns'.[17] By 1989, we might say, the idea of 'normal society' had become a Murti-Bing pill for many post-Cold War East European intellectuals. It assuaged all worries that the copycat mind might someday turn out to be just another captive mind.

Because Central European elites saw imitation of the West as a well-travelled pathway to 'normality' in this sense, their acceptance of the post-Cold War Imitation Imperative was wholly spontaneous, voluntary and sincere. They were neither voraciously *borrowing* Western technology like the Chinese nor cynically *simulating* Western democracy like the Russians. They were hopeful *converts* who wished to lure their societies into a collective *conversion experience*.

It is the very sincerity of this hope for a wholesale liberal makeover that distinguishes Central Europe's promoters of liberal democracy not only from the Russian charlatans but also from those Latin American reformers who, according to the American social scientist Albert O. Hirschman deployed a sales pitch he labelled 'pseudo-imitation'.[18] Studying the promotion of economic development in Latin America, Hirschman noted that reformers often deliberately understated the obstacles confronting their reform proposals, pretending that reform involved nothing more complex than copying fully worked-out foreign models, as if indigenous conditions and capacities were of trivial importance. They did so in order to 'sell' reform efforts to a sceptical public unwilling to approve projects that seemed unfeasible or forbiddingly complex, but that the reformers themselves deemed eminently doable. This is a fascinating observation. But the picture of wily reformists who 'billed' democratization 'as a pure replica of a successful venture in an advanced country'[19] in order to hoodwink a naïve public does not quite fit the post-communist experience in Central Europe, where the reformers *themselves*, encouraged by hopes of joining the EU, underestimated the local impediments to liberalization and democratization and overestimated the feasibility of importing fully worked-out Western models. The wave of anti-liberalism sweeping over Central Europe reflects widespread popular resentment at the perceived slights to national and personal dignity that this palpably sincere reform-by-imitation project entailed.

Another distinguishing feature of the liberal revolution in the region is that it was not, as earlier revolutions, thought to be a leap in time from a dark past to the bright future. It was rather imagined as a movement across physical space, as if all of post-communist Europe would be relocating to the House of the West, long inhabited by cultural kin but previously seen by Easterners only in photographs and films. The unification of Europe was explicitly likened to the unification of Germany. In the early 1990s, in fact, many Central and East Europeans burned with envy at the astonishingly lucky East Germans who had collectively migrated overnight to the West, waking up miraculously possessed of West German passports and with wallets packed with all-powerful Deutschmarks. If the 1989 revolution was a region-wide westward migration, then the main question was which Central and Eastern European countries would arrive first at their shared destination. The well-known American legal scholar and former chief counsel for US Citizenship and Immigration Services, Stephen Legomsky, once observed that 'countries do not immigrate, people do'.[20] In the case of post-communist Central and Eastern Europe, he was wrong.

LIFE IS ELSEWHERE

On 13 December 1981, General Wojciech Jaruzelski declared a state of emergency in Poland and tens of thousands of participants in the anti-communist Solidarity movement were arrested and interned. A year later the Polish government proposed releasing those willing to sign a loyalty oath as well as those prepared to emigrate. In response to these alluring offers, Adam Michnik penned two open letters from his prison cell. One was titled 'Why You Are Not Signing' and the other 'Why You Are Not Emigrating'.[21] His arguments for not signing were quite straightforward. Solidarity activists should not swear loyalty to the government because the government had broken its faith with Poland. They should not sign because signing to save one's skin means humiliation and loss of dignity but also because, by signing, they would be putting themselves in the company of those who betrayed their friends and ideals.

Why the jailed dissidents should not emigrate was for Michnik a question requiring a more nuanced answer. A dozen years before, as a Polish Jew and one of the leaders of March 1968 student protests in Poland, Michnik had been distressed to witness some of his best friends leave the country. He realized that the government wanted to persuade ordinary people that those who emigrated did so because they cared nothing for Poland. Only Jews emigrate – that was how, according to Michnik, the regime tried to turn Pole against Pole.

By 1982, Michnik was no longer angry at friends who had left in 1968. He also recognized the important contribution of the émigré community to the birth of Solidarity. But while admitting that emigration remained a legitimate expression of personal freedom, he strongly urged Solidarity activists not to go into exile, because 'each decision to emigrate is a gift to Jaruzelski'. Moreover, dissidents who left for freedom beyond Poland's borders would still be betraying those who stayed behind, especially those working and praying for a better Poland. A removal of the dissidents would also help pacify society, undermine the democratic movement and stabilize the regime by tainting the very act of dissent with selfishness and disloyalty to the nation. The most effective way to demonstrate solidarity with one's suffering countrymen and resist the policies of the communist authorities was to refuse the sly offer of personal freedom in the West, a rare opportunity which the vast majority of Poles would never share. By deciding not to emigrate, he argued, the imprisoned activists would also give meaning to the decision of those who had chosen to emigrate earlier and were supporting the Polish resistance from abroad. Freedom itself means that people have a right to do what they want. But, in the circumstances of 1982, 'the interned Solidarity activists who choose exile are committing an act that is both a capitulation and a desertion.' Michnik admitted that this statement sounded harsh and intolerant and that some might think it conflicted with his belief that 'the decision to emigrate is a very personal one'. But in 1982, to emigrate or not to emigrate was the ultimate loyalty-test for Solidarity activists. Only by choosing to remain in jail instead of accepting the lure of personal freedom in the West could they earn the trust of their fellow citizens upon which the future of a free Polish society depended.[22]

These reflections bring us back to Albert Hirschman, this time to his writings on emigration, democracy and the end of communism. Hirschman devoted much of his career to studying the complex relationship between leaving and resisting that preoccupied Michnik in his prison cell. In his most famous work, *Exit, Voice, and Loyalty*, published in 1970, Hirschman contrasted two strategies that people adopt when confronted with an unbearable status quo. People can 'exit', that is, they can vote with their feet, expressing their displeasure by taking their business elsewhere. Or they can decide to 'voice' their concerns by staying put, speaking up, and choosing to fight for reform from within. For economists, exit is the favoured method for improving the performance of producers and service providers. It is the strategy employed by the average consumer. Because they can inflict debilitating revenue losses on poorly performing businesses, customers who threaten to switch suppliers can induce a 'wonderful concentration of the mind' in a company's managers akin to what Samuel Johnson attributed to the prospect of being hanged. This is how exit (and the threat of exit) can help improve the performance of firms. But having experienced political tyranny first-hand in 1930s Europe, Hirschman also knew, like Michnik, that oppressive governments can reduce domestic pressure for change by granting the noisiest and most prominent activists an opportunity to exit.[23]

Voice represents an alternative way for individuals and groups to influence the behaviour of firms, organizations and states. Not only are the two mechanisms different, but the effective exercise of voice assumes that people who choose not to exit do so because they are deeply committed to the organization they hope to rescue or reform. Rather than shifting to another service provider, in the manner of a rational consumer, they work to better their organization's performance by participating, offering ideas, and assuming the risk that goes with publicly criticizing and opposing those charged with making decisions. Voice, therefore, unlike exit, is an activity based on loyalty. For loyalists like Michnik, exit in a time of crisis was bound to seem a kind of capitulation or desertion.

In 1990, Hirschman spent a year in post-communist Berlin and decided to revisit his theory of exit, voice and loyalty in an attempt to understand the demise of the German Democratic Republic.[24] He focused first on the unique possibility of defection open to East Germans alone among all members of the Warsaw Pact. They knew that, if they made their way to West Germany, they would be welcomed and could be integrated relatively easily. The exit option was seldom taken, since stealing past the border was extremely dangerous. But popular awareness that escaping would not leave escapees homeless, according to Hirschman, reduced the public incentive to agitate for reforms inside the DDR. East Germans who managed to leave or escape, unlike Poles who did the same, would become neither linguistically isolated émigrés nor branded as betrayers of the nation. The GDR, in Hirschman's view, did not have its 1956, 1968 or 1980 because most of those dissatisfied with the regime dreamed of absconding privately rather than organizing to voice their grievances collectively.

This constellation changed in 1989. In that year, exit took the form not of isolated wall jumpers but of a wholesale exodus. But contrary to expectations that the 'safety valve' of emigration would drain the energy from civic engagement, the very scale of the departures increased rather than decreased pressure on the regime. Indeed, it drove the disenchanted millions who stayed behind to take to the streets and demand change in the hope of convincing their fellow citizens to stay. The downfall of the GDR was a case where mass exodus and the fear that it might continue triggered a society-wide outburst of voice and demands for political reform at home. In this case, rather than exit repressing voice, it unintentionally pushed those who remained into an intense period of political protest and activism aimed at making their country a more attractive place to live. What eventually emerged from this initial synergy of exit and voice, however, was not a renewal of the GDR but its political collapse and annexation to the Federal Republic. Rather than some East Germans leaving and others staying, the entire country relocated to the West. The end of communism, in this case, meant that East and West Germans became, at least in popular imagination at the time, 'one people'.

In the rest of Eastern Europe, the story unfolded quite differently. There are no signs today that East and West Europeans – from Bratislava and Bucharest to Lisbon and Dublin – see themselves as *ein Volk*, a single people with a shared identity, even if they all presumably aspire to a European normality. Former German Chancellor Willy Brandt's prediction that 'What belongs together [the two halves of the German nation] is growing together',[25] interpreted like some law of gravity, proved overly optimistic even for Germany. Applying it to the whole of Europe was simply utopian. East-to-West migration has done nothing to stimulate serious efforts at political and economic reform in Central Europe. On the contrary, the aspiration, after 1989, to have 'a normal political life' (Havel) led only to a brain drain and the expatriation of the healthy, the skilled, the educated and the young. If in East Germany exit was followed by voice, in Eastern and Central Europe as a whole, voice was followed by exit. Initially, euphoria at communism's collapse created the expectation that other radical improvements were in the offing. Some thought it would suffice for communist officials to quit their posts for Central and East Europeans to wake up in different, freer, more prosperous and, above all, *more Western* countries. When rapid Westernization did not magically materialize, an alternative solution began to gain favour. Leaving with one's family for the West became the preferred option. After 1989, Michnik's association of emigration to the West with treasonous capitulation and desertion no longer made any sense. The personal choice to move to Western Europe could no longer be stigmatized as an act of disloyalty to nations that were now struggling to integrate seamlessly into the West. A revolution that defined its principal goal as Westernization could offer no persuasive objections to westward emigration. Democratic transitions in the region were basically a form of *en masse* removal to the West, and so the choice was only to emigrate early and individually or later and collectively.

Revolutions as a rule force people to cross borders – moral borders if not territorial ones. When the French Revolution broke out many of its enemies scattered abroad. When the Bolsheviks seized power in Russia, millions of white Russians left the country and lived in exile for years without unpacking their suitcases in the hopes that the Bolshevik dictatorship would eventually collapse. The implicit contrast with the end of communism could not be starker. After 1789, and again after 1917, the defeated enemies of the revolutions were the ones who left their countries. After 1989, the *winners* not the losers of the velvet revolutions were the ones who chose to decamp. Those most impatient to see their own countries changed were also the ones most eager to plunge into the life of a free citizenry and were therefore the first to go to study, work and live in the West.

It is impossible to imagine that, after the victory of the Bolshevik Revolution, Trotsky would have decided to enrol at Oxford to study. But this is what Orbán and many others did. The very analogy may seem inapposite, given the radical differences between their situations. But the contrast helps focus attention on one of the most interesting of these dissimilarities. Unlike the French and Russian revolutionaries, who were convinced that they were creating a new civilization hostile to the old order of kings, nobles and priests, and that Paris and Moscow were the new centres of the world where that future was being forged, the revolutionaries of 1989 were strongly motivated to travel to the West in order to observe up close how the kind of normal society they hoped to build at home actually worked in practice.

Travels westward after 1989 were nothing like the eastward flow of communists from Eastern Europe to the Soviet Union in the 1940s, of course. The latter were sent to Moscow in order to learn how to build communism at home. They travelled on their governments' orders and with the explicit requirement that they eventually come back. Nothing of the sort happened in the wake of 1989. After the collapse of communism, the emigration of liberal-minded people to the West was the result of uncoordinated individual choices. Many of them left not to study or accumulate some savings and then return home but with the intention of relocating permanently to the West. If Germany was the future of Poland – and every revolutionary wants to live in the future – then the most heartfelt revolutionaries might just as well pack up and move to Germany.

In order to grasp the almost-irresistible allure of emigration for Central and East Europeans after 1989, we should keep in mind not only the significant difference in standards of living between West and East and the logistical ease of the move but also one of the least discussed legacies of communism, namely the memory of how bureaucratically difficult it had been to change one's place of residence. After initially forcing people to move from the countryside into the cities, communist authorities began to impose strict limits on the freedom to change domicile within each country. Permission to relocate from rural areas to the cities was experienced as a social promotion. Being a worker was much more prestigious than being a peasant. But at the same time, moving from one town to another in search of gainful employment, particularly coming to live and work in the capital, was more problematic under a communist regime than is travelling to work abroad today. By turning relocation from the cultural and political periphery to the cultural and political centre into a rare privilege, communism played a role in making geographical mobility not only desirable but also synonymous with prized social success.

The dream of a collective return of formerly communist countries to Europe made the individual choice to abscond abroad both logical and legitimate. Why should a young Pole or Hungarian wait for his country to become one day like Germany, when he can start working and raising a family in Germany tomorrow? It is no secret that changing countries is easier than changing one's country. When borders were opened after 1989, exit was favoured over voice because political reform requires the sustained cooperation of many organized social interests, while the choice to emigrate is basically a solo or single-family operation, even though (like a bank run) it can become a cascade. The mistrust of ethno-nationalist loyalties and the prospect of a politically united Europe also helped make emigration the political choice for many liberal-minded Central and East Europeans. This, alongside the vanishing of anti-communist dissidents, is again why Michnik's moral excoriation of emigration lost all moral and emotional resonance after 1989.

The massive flow of population out of the region in the post-Cold War period, especially because so many young people were the ones voting with their feet, had profound economic, political and psychological consequences. When a doctor leaves the country, she takes with her all the resources that the state has invested in her education and deprives her country of her talent and ambition. The money that she would eventually send back to her family could not possibly compensate for the loss of her personal participation in the life of her native land. The exodus of young and well-educated people has also seriously, perhaps fatally, damaged the chances of liberal parties to do well in elections. Youth exit may also explain why, in many countries across the region, we find beautiful EU-funded playgrounds with no kids to play in them. It is telling that liberal parties perform best among voters who cast their ballots abroad. In 2014, for example, Klaus Johannis, a liberal-minded ethnic German, was elected President of Romania because the 300,000 Romanians living overseas voted massively in his favour. In a country where the majority of young people yearn to leave, the very fact that you have remained, regardless of how well you are doing, makes you feel like a loser. It also readies you to cheer anti-liberal demagogues who denounce copycat Westernization as a betrayal of the nation.

INTRUDERS AT THE GATES

The issues of emigration and population loss bring us to the refugee crisis that struck Europe in 2015–16, pouring fuel on the anti-liberal fire. On 24 August 2015, German Chancellor Angela Merkel decided to admit hundreds of thousands of Syrian refugees into Germany. Only ten days later, on 4 September, the Visegrád Group – the Czech Republic, Hungary, Poland and Slovakia – declared that the EU's quota system for distributing refugees across Europe was 'unacceptable'.[26] Central and East Europeans were not buying Merkel's humanitarian rhetoric. 'I think it is just bullshit,' commented Maria Schmidt, Viktor Orbán's intellectual-in-chief, adding that Merkel 'wanted to prove that Germans, this time, are the good people. And they can lecture everybody on humanism and morality. It doesn't matter for the Germans what they can lecture the rest of the world on; they just have to lecture someone.'[27] But this time Central Europeans were not about to curtsy submissively as their German neighbours lectured them condescendingly. National sovereignty means that every country has a right to decide about its own absorption capacity. This was the moment, in response to what they saw as Merkel's decision to roll out the red carpet to cultural diversity, when Central Europe's populists issued their declaration of independence not only from Brussels but also, more dramatically, from Western liberalism and its religion of openness to the world.

Central Europe's fear-mongering populists interpreted the refugee crisis as conclusive evidence that liberalism has weakened the capacity of nations to defend themselves in a hostile world. Overnight, they said, all Africans, Middle Easterners, and even Central Asians had decided to imitate East European-style 'revolutionaries' by moving *en masse* to the West. In the excessively interconnected but massively unequal 'world without walls', they argue, transnational migration has replaced the kind of revolutions that punctuated the twentieth century. The free movement of people across international borders now provides the most widely available opportunity for liberating oneself and one's family from an economically hopeless and politically oppressive environment. From this perspective, the twentieth-century revolt of the masses is therefore a thing of the past. Those who hope to defend the status quo now face a 21st-century upheaval caused not by an insurgent working class but by the mass migration into Europe of non-Westerners seeking a better life. Here is how Orbán has described the unfolding crisis:

We must confront a flood of people pouring out of the countries of the Middle East, and meanwhile the depth of Africa has been set in motion. Millions of people are preparing to set out. Globally the desire, the urge and the pressure for people to continue their lives in some place other than where they began them is increasing. This is one of history's largest tides of people, and it brings with it the danger of tragic consequences. It is a modern-day global mass migration, which we cannot see the end of: economic migrants hoping for a better life, refugees and drifting masses mixed up together. This is an uncontrolled and unregulated process, and . . . the most precise definition of this is 'invasion'.[28]

Blown out of proportion by Orbán, the northward population flow is not being instigated or steered by organized revolutionary parties. It faces few collective-action problems because it is largely the unplanned consequence of millions of spontaneous choices made by millions of disconnected individuals and families. And it is inspired not by ideologically painted pictures of a radiant imaginary future, but by photos of 'normal life' on the other side of the border where those who manage to arrive safely won't be a target of political persecution and won't spend the rest of their lives stuck in a slum.

The globalization of communication has made the world a village, but this village is ruled by a dictatorship of global comparisons. People outside of North America and Western Europe no longer compare their lot only with that of their neighbours. They contrast their living standards with the living standards of the most prosperous inhabitants of the planet. The great French political philosopher and sociologist Raymond Aron presciently observed five decades ago that 'with humanity on the way to unification, inequality between peoples takes on the significance that inequality between classes once had.'[29] The best that inhabitants of underdeveloped countries who seek an economically secure future for their children can do is to make sure their kids will be born in Germany, Sweden or Denmark or, as a second best, in Poland or the Czech Republic. Far from requiring a coherent ideology, a cohesive political movement or inspiring leaders, this 'uprising' of the migrants is a simple matter of crossing a border, openly or covertly, legally or not. For many of today's *damnés de la terre*, in fact, the European Union is more alluring than any utopia.

In a recent book, journalist Stephen Smith predicts a massive exodus from Africa, arguing that in thirty years 20 to 25 per cent of Europe's population will be of African origin compared with 1.5–2.0 per cent in 2015.[30] This is so much grist for the populist mill.

Orbán and Kaczyński have jointly described their shared political approach as 'counter-revolutionary'.[31] What makes their self-proclaimed counter-revolution historically unique is its simultaneous opposition to two wholly distinct 'revolutionary' processes that anti-liberal propagandists, for political purposes, have managed to fuse into one. These are the collective incorporation of Central and Eastern European countries into the liberal European Union after 1989 and the disorderly migration of Africans and Middle Easterners into a Western Europe struggling to control its external borders. The counter-revolutionary response to this imaginary two-headed revolution naturally takes aim at liberal tolerance for cultural diversity and the very idea of an open society.

The underlying weakness of political liberalism, according to these 'counter-revolutionaries', is revealed by the West's inability to take seriously the difference between members and non-members of a nation and therefore to invest aggressively in hardening the territorial borders that give the member/non-member distinction its practical significance. The facile optimism of liberals who believe that different ethnic and cultural groups can be assimilated, American-style, into European civilization is proving to be the undoing of the West, they assert. From this deeply anti-liberal perspective, a society with a post-national identity into which non-European migrants are welcomed has unilaterally disarmed and risks losing whatever remains of its cultural coherence.

MIGRATION AS SURRENDER

The demographic panic that raged in Central Europe from 2015 to 2018 is now fading to a degree, but has by no means disappeared, nor is it limited to the region.[32] We still need to ask in any case why it would find such politically combustible material in Central and Eastern Europe where virtually no immigrants arrived.

Two factors played a role.

The first, as mentioned, is emigration. Anxiety about immigration is fomented by a fear that unassimilable foreigners will enter the country, dilute national identity and weaken national cohesion. This fear, in turn, is fuelled by a largely unspoken preoccupation with demographic collapse. In the period 1989–2017, Latvia haemorrhaged 27 per cent of its population, Lithuania 22.5 per cent, Bulgaria almost 21 per cent. Two million East Germans, or almost 14 per cent of the country's pre-1989 inhabitants, went to West Germany in search of work and a better life. 3.4 million Romanians, a vast majority of them younger than forty, left the country only after the country joined the EU in 2007. The combination of an ageing population, low birth rates and an unending stream of emigration is arguably the principal source of demographic panic in Central and Eastern Europe.

This fear of nation-killing depopulation is seldom openly voiced, perhaps because publicizing high rates of expatriation will encourage imitators. But it is nonetheless real and may well be expressed indirectly in the nonsensical claim that migrants from Africa and the Middle East pose a threat to the existence of the nations of the region. According to UN projections, Bulgaria's population will shrink by 27 per cent between now and 2040. Almost one-fifth of the territory of the country is predicted to become a 'demographic desert'. Indeed, 'Bulgaria experienced the largest percentage drop in population not attributable to war or famine for a country in the modern era. Every day, the country was losing 164 people: over a thousand a week, over 50,000 a year.'[33]

More Central and East Europeans left their countries for Western Europe as a result of the 2008–9 financial crises than all the refugees that came there as the result of the war in Syria.

In a world of open borders where European cultures are in constant dialogue and where the new media environment permits citizens to live abroad without losing touch with events taking place at home, the threat that Central and East Europeans confront is similar to the one that the GDR faced before the Berlin Wall was erected. It is the danger that working-age citizens will evacuate their homelands to pursue better lives in the West. After all, businesses in countries such as Germany are desperately seeking workers while Europeans in general are increasingly reluctant to allow non-Europeans from Africa and the Middle East to settle permanently in their countries. An otherwise inexplicable panic in the face of a non-existent immigrant invasion of Central and Eastern Europe can therefore be understood as a distorted echo of a more realistic underlying fear that huge swathes of one's own population, including the most talented youth, will leave the country and remain permanently abroad. The extraordinary extent of post-1989 emigration from Eastern and Central Europe, awakening fears of national disappearance, helps explain the deeply hostile reaction across the region to the refugee crisis of 2015–16 even though almost no refugees have relocated to the countries of the region.

We might even hypothesize that anti-immigration politics in a region essentially without immigrants is an example of what psychologists call 'displacement', a defence mechanism by which, in this case, minds unconsciously blot out a wholly unacceptable threat and replace it with one still serious but conceivably easier to manage. Hysteria about non-existent immigrants about to overrun the country represents the substitution of an illusory danger (immigration) for the real danger (depopulation and demographic collapse) which cannot speak its name. Fears of high birth rates among allegedly invading non-European immigrants may reflect unspoken anxieties about a native birth rate below the replacement level compounded by continuous emigration. This is obviously just a conjecture. But it gains some plausibility from the fact that Eastern Europe is home to the fastest shrinking populations in the world. Orbán gives the game away when he says, 'Migration for us is surrender . . . we want Hungarian children.'[34] His pro-procreation policy is a better indicator of the government's real worries than anti-immigration talk in the absence of immigrants.[35] Exciting the public's fears of a non-existent migrant 'invasion' which can be successfully blocked by militarized borders may be one way the region's populist politicians exploit their electorate's fears of national extinction by a slow process of depopulation that has taken place over the last decades and against which hardened borders and discrimination against foreign-born inhabitants are obviously no defence.

Unexpressed dread of demographic collapse, the nightmare of a world where the age-old languages and cultural memories of the region have been erased like Byzantium from the book of history, is exacerbated by an automation revolution that is gradually making obsolete the jobs for which the current generation of workers is trained. Fear of diversity and fear of change, inflamed by the utopian project of remaking whole societies along Western lines, are thus important contributors to Eastern and Central European populism. The fact that the region is composed of small and ageing but ethnically homogeneous societies also helps explain the sudden radicalization of nationalistic sentiments. Today, a bare 1.6 per cent of Polish citizens were born outside of Poland, while Muslim-Polish citizens constitute less than 0.1 per cent of the population. In the feverish political imagination of the region, ethnic and cultural diversity is nevertheless seen as an existential threat.[36] And while Poles in Poland never encounter Muslims, Poles in the UK do, and these encounters are more frequent and more fraught than interactions between Muslims and the British middle classes. This is because Poles in the UK often live in the same neighbourhoods as Muslim immigrants and compete for the same jobs. Not history alone, therefore, but also the attitudes of Central Europeans working in Western Europe reported back home through social media contribute palpably to overwrought anti-Muslim attitudes in the region.

Alarm over depopulation and even 'ethnic disappearance' is naturally felt most strongly in small nations, inclining their inhabitants to resist reform proposals that seem to devalue their unique traditions in the name of ostensibly universal and therefore easily transferable or imitable values. A recent Pew survey reveals that East Europeans are more convinced than West Europeans of the superiority of their cultures, making them highly reluctant to embrace a cosmopolitan ethic.[37] A small nation, according to Milan Kundera, 'is one whose very existence may be put in question at any moment; a small nation can disappear and it knows it'.[38] We should keep this in mind when analysing Orbán's overheated claims that young African and Middle Eastern men, organized like armies, are kicking down the doors to Europe and threatening to wipe Hungary off the map. The trauma of people pouring *out* of the region explains what might otherwise seem mysterious, the strong sense of loss even in countries that have benefited handsomely from post-communist political and economic change. Across Europe, analogously, the areas that have suffered the greatest haemorrhaging of population in the last decades are the ones most inclined to vote for far-right anti-liberal parties. Orbán's pronatalist policies, too, strongly suggest that the illiberal turn in Central Europe is deeply rooted in the outflow of people, especially young people, from the region and the demographic anxieties that this 'expatriation of the future' has left behind.

While there has been no 'invasion' of African and Middle Eastern immigrants into the region, Central and East Europeans are constantly exposed, through sensationalized television reporting, to the immigration problems plaguing Western Europe. The consequence has been a reinterpretation of the essential divide between the two halves of the continent. While the East is still homogeneous and mono-ethnic, the West has become, as a result of what anti-liberal politicians consider a thoughtless and suicidal immigration policy, heterogeneous and multiethnic. The radical revaluation of values here is remarkable. Rather than West Europeans being far ahead and Central and East Europeans far behind, West Europeans are now described, in the rhetoric of the xenophobic populists, as having lost their cultural identities. In the populist imagination, West Europe has become the periphery of a Greater Africa and Greater Middle East. This portrayal of the West as in the throes of an identity crisis provoked by swarms of refugees seems to confirm Nietzsche's thesis that 'resentment' is usually expressed 'in imaginary acts of vengeance'.[39]

In populist propaganda, Western Europe no longer represents the model of a culturally superior West that East and Central Europeans once admired and aspired to imitate. The West's putative undoing is announced by the populists of the region with a tone of self-satisfied retribution against their previous tormentors. The implied superiority of the model over its mimics has finally come to an end.

Unable to defend their borders against foreign (and especially Muslim) 'invaders', the open societies of Western Europe now provide a basically negative model, a living picture of the social order that Central and East Europeans are most eager to avoid. This is the context in which Orbán and Kaczyński repeatedly decry Merkel's decision to admit close to a million refugees into Germany, since it was a decision made undemocratically, without heeding German public opinion. Fidesz and PiS claim that Merkel's 'liberal paternalism' bolsters their claims to be, unlike the German Chancellor, truly faithful representatives of the popular will.

Since heroic resistance to communist tyranny is a thing of the past and entire nations across the region are now undergoing Westernization, East European governments, haunted by the fear of demographic collapse, are looking for good reasons why their discontented citizens, especially their youth, should hesitate to pick up and move to Western Europe. Orbán sometimes sounds as if he would like to implement a Closed Country policy with a ruthlessly enforced veto on emigration as well as immigration. But since he has no way of doing anything of the sort, he is reduced to pleading with young Hungarians not to move away. An undercurrent of panic is clearly audible in the way Orbán addresses the threat posed by young Hungarians wishing to leave the country and to live abroad:

> Dear Youngsters, perhaps you feel like the world is yours for the taking . . . But in your life there will come a moment when you realize that you will need a place, a language, a home where one can be with his own, safely, surrounded by love, [a place where one] can live out his life. A place where you can return, a place where you can feel life is not without meaning and even at the end will not fall into nothingness. [You] will add and build on the thousand-year-old creation which we simply call 'homeland', the Hungarian homeland. Respected Hungarian youngsters, your homeland now needs you. The homeland needs you. Come and fight with us so when the time comes when you will need the homeland, you will still have it.[40]

But how to convince young Hungarians that they will not find a better 'homeland' in the West, especially when Orbán's own policies are destroying most chances for living rewarding and creative lives inside the country?

A notorious shortcoming of communism was that the ideal society, which it was promising to bring about, had never existed. Nor did anyone really believe that it ever would exist. The Westernizing revolutions suffered from the opposite problem: the longed-for social order they aimed to create genuinely existed and therefore could be visited and observed up close, bringing previously unnoticed defects into disheartening focus. The socialist utopia may have been unachievable. But being forever beyond reach meant that it never had a chance to disappoint its visionary admirers. It also possessed a reassuringly unchanging quality. Western liberal democracy, by contrast, like all this-worldly things, proved shape-shifting, constantly morphing before the eyes of its would-be emulators. What's worse, the ordinary pace of social evolution has today been greatly accelerated by technological innovation. And every resulting change in Western society yields a new image of what is normal for those who identify normality with life in the West. A revolution in the name of existing Western normality, therefore, faces a problem absent from revolutions in the name of some imagined utopia. It becomes impossible to fix or pin down the vision of society one is trying to recreate.

This dilemma is especially acute for post-communist societies. That is because the West that the dissidents urged their fellow citizens to imitate in 1989 no longer exists today, three decades later. Their model society was the globally dominant and adamantly anti-communist West of the Cold War. But the very process that allowed the countries of Central and Eastern Europe to join the anti-communist West ensured that anti-communism would no longer be the West's defining ideology. We might consider this a grand version of bait-and-switch, although it was obviously in no way intentional or planned. Those who were most eager to imitate and join the West in 1989, in any case, were bound to think differently about Westernization a few decades later when Atlanticism was on its death bed and both Western Europe and the United States were in the throes of simultaneous economic and political crises.

The populists of the region have now found an alternative strategy to resurrect the moral disapproval that dissidents such as Michnik once attached to emigration. It is vital for them to reject the claim that Hungary, Poland and the other countries of the region can succeed politically and economically only if they faithfully imitate the West. Seen from this perspective, the rise of anti-immigrant rhetoric looks suspiciously like a desperate attempt to build a loyalty wall that will staunch the demographic haemorrhaging and stop Central and

East Europeans from wanting to leave their countries. Formulated differently, populists in Warsaw and Budapest seem to have turned the refugee crisis in the West into a branding opportunity for the East. Citizens will stop leaving for the West only if the West loses its allure. Dispraising the West and declaring its institutions 'not worth imitating' can be explained as imaginary revenge born of resentment. But it has the collateral benefit of serving the region's number one policy priority by helping discourage emigration. Denying that the West is a land of opportunity and that Western liberalism is the gold standard of advanced social and economic order helps reduce its magnetic appeal to a restive population. Imitating the West cannot possibly be a pathway to prosperity since it would inevitably involve copying the West's allegedly suicidal immigration policy. Populists rail publicly against the way Western Europe has welcomed Africans and Middle Easterners. But their genuine complaint is that Western members of the EU have opened their doors invitingly to Central and East Europeans themselves, potentially draining the region of its most productive citizens.

This entire discussion brings us to a core idea of contemporary illiberalism. Contrary to many contemporary theorists,[41] populist rage is directed less at multiculturalism than at post-national individualism and cosmopolitanism. This is an important point politically because, if accepted, it implies that populism cannot be combatted by abandoning identity politics in the name of liberal individualism. For the illiberal democrats of Eastern and Central Europe, the gravest threat to the survival of the white Christian majority in Europe is the incapacity of Western societies to defend themselves. They cannot defend themselves because liberalism's bias against communitarianism allegedly blinds its adherents to the threats they face.

Illiberal democracy promises to open citizens' eyes. If the liberal consensus of the 1990s was about individual legal and constitutional rights – including freedom of the press, the right to choose one's profession, the right to vote for one's rulers in periodic elections, and freedom of travel – the anti-liberal consensus today is that the rights of the threatened white Christian majority are in mortal danger. To protect this besieged majority's fragile dominance from the insidious alliance of Brussels and Africa, Europeans need to replace the watery post-nationalism foisted on them by cosmopolitan liberals with a muscular identity politics or group particularism of their own. This is the logic with which Orbán and Kaczyński have tried to inflame the inner xenophobic nationalism of their countrymen, creating an anti-liberal R2P (Right to Protect) targeting exclusively white Christian populations allegedly at risk of extinction.

Threatened majorities are playing havoc with European politics today. Members of previously dominant national majorities look with dismay at the growing scale of global migration. They are aware that the people likely to relocate to their countries are imbued with different cultural traditions and that, in Europe today, as the British political theorist David Miller observed, 'People are both less sure of what it means to be French or Swedish, and less sure about how far it is morally acceptable to acknowledge and act upon such identities.'[42]

In a Europe populated by threatened majorities who can no longer take the survival of their inherited way of life for granted, populist leaders insist, against the multiculturalism they believe liberals naively promote, that indigenous majorities have a right to decide how many immigrants will come to their country, and from where. They stridently assert that unequivocal adoption of the majoritarian culture should be made a pre-condition for gaining citizenship precisely because they think such an onerous standard will choke off immigration at its source.

There are two spectres haunting Europe today. Anti-liberals fear the spectre of Exemplary Normality. To praise the European way of life as a norm for all the world is, unintentionally, to invite the whole world to come and partake of its benefits by immigration. Liberals, by contrast, fear the spectre of Reverse Imitation, namely the suggestion that, in some respects, the players in the post-1989 imitation game are changing places. In a few cases, at least, the mimics have become the models and vice versa. The ultimate revenge of the Central and Eastern European populists against Western liberalism is not merely to reject the initially welcomed Imitation Imperative but to invert it. We are the real Europeans, Orbán and Kaczyński repeatedly claim, and if the West will save itself, it will have to imitate the East. As Orbán explained in a speech in July 2017, 'Twenty-seven years ago here in Central Europe we believed that Europe was our future; today we feel that we are the future of

Europe.'[43] Stealing the thunder of liberals in 1989, he claims that History with a capital 'H' has shifted to the anti-liberal side.

In the heyday of de-colonization, spokesmen for former Western colonies argued that refusing to imitate the West was a key to achieving or retrieving national dignity. Hostility to the imitation of colonial masters was part of the armed liberation struggle aimed at driving the foreigners out of their lands. In *The Wretched of the Earth*, French-Caribbean philosopher and revolutionary Frantz Fanon wrote of Africa's 'nauseating mimicry' of the West and said that an African imitator of Europe was bound to become 'an obscene caricature'. 'We today can do everything,' he went on to say, 'so long as we do not imitate Europe'; adding, 'let us decide not to imitate Europe and let us tense our muscles in a new direction.'[44]

No counterpart to Frantz Fanon appeared in post-communist Central and Eastern Europe in the first two decades after the fall of the Wall. On the contrary, political elites in the region were almost universally enthusiastic about the imitation of West European and American 'normality'. They were well-meaning converts trying to guide their countries through a collective conversion experience. At the end of the first decade of the twenty-first century, however, hostility to imitating the West became a key theme of the populist revolt. Despite sharing the resentment at Western impositions typical of anti-colonial movements, the anti-liberals of the region never quite speak like Fanon. For them, Western proselytizing in the East was similar to, but also different from, Western proselytizing in the South. This is because Central and East Europeans *already* felt themselves completely European before Brussels began a project to 'Europeanize' them, a project that was therefore experienced as gratuitously insulting.[45] This is what makes Orbán-style populism distinct from non-European anti-colonial movements fuelled by a desire for national self-determination. While the velvet revolutions of 1989 represented anti-colonial repudiations of Soviet domination, they were simultaneously pro-colonial with regard to the West. This is why their organizers and leaders could be classified as aspiring 'converts' as opposed to cynical 'simulators' like the Russians. At the beginning, as a result, no important voices in the region were crying out against the heinous crime of copying Western forms and norms.

And when Orbán and Kaczyński attacked Western liberalism, they did so while claiming the mantle of Europeanness for themselves, describing Central Europe not only as the true Europe but as Europe's last line of defence. Fanon would have never said anything of the kind about France's former colonies in Africa. The PiS government frequently cites the heroic role of the Polish-Lithuanian Commonwealth under Jan III Sobieski in lifting the Muslim siege of Vienna in 1683 and thus helping roll back the last great Muslim invasion of Europe. Both Orbán and Kaczyński, in fact, present themselves to their publics as what Carl Schmitt called 'forestallers': heroic resisters against a looming Islamic takeover of Europe.[46] The illiberal democrats of Central and Eastern Europe are now prepared, they say, to take up the historic anti-Muslim mission so recklessly abandoned by Western Europeans. 'We were the ones who stopped the migrant invasion launched against Europe at the southern borders of Hungary,' Orbán said, referring to the fence he built along the Hungarian–Serbian border in 2015.[47] This is why Central and East Europeans, to the perplexity of some, declare themselves adamantly pro-European even as they also claim to be violently anti-EU.

The clock cannot be turned back. Ethnic and cultural homogeneity cannot be restored. Europe's former periphery is therefore styling itself as Europe's new core. West European opponents of eastward enlargement have occasionally denigrated the chances for democratization in Central and Eastern Europe by recycling the shop-worn slogan 'geography is destiny'. The caustic populist response today is: No, not geography, but *demography* is destiny.

Whether or not the historical core is beginning to imitate the erstwhile periphery, the prospects of such a Great Reversal looms large in the minds and speeches of Central Europe's populists. Instead of the West spreading its influence eastward, the East brags of spreading its influence westward. This is what they believe, and not without some justification. Illiberal populism everywhere, including in the United States, seems to be taking a page from Orbán's illiberal playbook. Those who interpret the simultaneous outbreak of reactionary nativism in parts of the United States and Western Europe as a re-emergence of illiberal currents in both places have a point. But they also have to answer the question: 'Why today?' One possible answer is 'contagious imitation'. The Westerners have become the aspiring plagiarists now.

It is one thing for Kaczyński to say that migrants are bringing diseases into his country, however. It is another thing for Trump to say the same. It is one thing for Kaczyński to say to Orbán that 'You have given an example and we are learning from your example.'[48] It is much more significant and ominous for Steve Bannon to describe Orbán as a 'hero', an inspiration and 'the most significant guy on the scene right now'.[49] A non-negligible degree of sympathy with Orbán's anti-EU politics can be found in almost every country of Western Europe. This is why critics of Brussels subsidies to Hungary and Poland blame the EU, to paraphrase Lenin, for giving Orbán and Kaczyński the rope with which to hang the West.[50]

The fact that politicians in the West are now adopting the xenophobic nationalism of the East contains a final vengeful twist. The West's openness to non-European immigrants guarantees that its attempt to imitative the East will fail. The Central Europeans are sending the same double message to Western Europe that the West sent to them three decades ago: 'We are inviting you in, but (to tell the truth) we won't let you in.'

THE UNBEARABLE AMBIVALENCE
OF NORMALITY

The populist revolt against the utopia of Western-style normality has proved so successful in Central and Eastern Europe not only due to demographic panic but also because, over the past three decades, post-communist societies have come to see some of normality's unexpected defects and downsides.

For starters, there is something paradoxical about a thrilling revolution in the name of an unremarkable 'normality'. This problem first emerged in the personal lives of the dissidents. In 2007, when celebrating the anniversary of the founding of Charter 77, Václav Havel publicly lamented that 'all the solidarity, the *esprit de corps* and spirit of combat that tied us together thirty years ago' had been utterly lost 'in the climate of "normal" democracy in which we live today and for which we fought together'.[51] To this confession of nostalgia for the glory days leading up to 1989, when the dissidents were persecuted and ostracized, Havel adds his subsequent disappointment with the humdrum normality of life after communism. Having initially cheered the 'return' to normality, some of the leading dissidents ended up disillusioned by the monotony of post-heroic times. The psychological strain of readjusting from life under communism to life under capitalism affected everyone. But dissidents who had seen themselves as daring protagonists in a great historical drama were a case apart because they felt, in Michnik's words, 'contempt for normalcy, for a life without conspiracy'.[52]

This made their participation in a revolution for the sake of normality all the more incongruous and all the more likely to end in disillusion. Such personal maladjustments don't tell us much about the failures of 'a revolution for the sake of normality', however. To look deeper, we need to see how citizens living in the region after 1989 fell victim to the multi-layered meaning of the 'normality' they aimed to imitate.

For starters, we need to recall the primary meaning of the word 'normalization' (*normalizace* in Czech) in the two decades prior to 1989. It referred to the political purges, censorship, police brutality and ideological conformity imposed in Havel's homeland after the crushing of the Prague Spring in 1968. This was 'normalization' in the sense of a restoration of the *status quo ante*, a return to the situation in Czechoslovakia prior to the Dubček reforms. There would be no more attempts at giving communism a human face. Soviet-style communism was *alternativlos*. It needed to be imitated without deviations. As Michnik wrote in 1985, normalization under Kádár and Husák 'in essence, meant total destruction of all independent institutions. Forty months after the Soviet invasion, Hungary resembled a political cemetery; forty months of normalization in Czechoslovakia transformed it, in Aragon's apt phrase, into the cultural Biafra of Europe.'[53]

What we have here is a self-conscious clash between two distinct and opposing pictures of normality. A plausible way to understand why the dissidents embraced a non-violent revolution to install an anti-Soviet and pro-Western normality, is as an act of defiance, a deliberate inversion of the Soviet Union's violent imposition of a cruelly repressive normality.

Moreover, the dissidents' elevation of Western-style normality as the principal goal of political revolution provides a rare opportunity to see not only how Central and East Europeans imagined their future but also how they viewed the communist societies from which they wished to escape. A standard narrative, commonly reprised in both East and West, portrays the communist system as a prison-house. But the Central and Eastern European fixation on normality suggests something different. For dissidents, in particular, the late communist system resembled not a penitentiary but a madhouse. Under communism, inmates were not only incarcerated, but everything in their lives was turned on its head. According to official propaganda, people were expected to work for the benefit of society and care nothing about their individual interests and hopes. Equality was the overriding principle, at least officially, but neither the efforts nor the rewards of individual members were equal. And communist authorities, following the perverse logic of their upside-down societies, treated dissidents not as criminals but as mentally unstable persons with 'reformist delusions' to be confined in mental clinics under debilitating sedation.

After 1989, this communist-era contrast between two images of normality, one Soviet and the other Western, became a thing of the past. But the warfare between conflicting ideas of normality was immediately rekindled in another form. And this second conflict is still with us today. It involves a pathological disconnect between what is considered normal in the West and what is considered normal in the region.

In *The Normal and the Pathological* (1966), the French philosopher and physician Georges Canguilhem explains that the concept of 'normality' has a double meaning, one descriptive and the other normative. 'Normal' can refer to practices that are factually widespread or to practices that are morally ideal. This is not precisely the ambivalence we have in mind here but, given the widespread belief that the moral ideals of the West became canonical after the collapse of communism, it is close enough. After 1989, the gap between the presumptively normative and the actually descriptive meaning of normality became the source of multiple miscues and misunderstandings between Westerners, on the one hand, and Central and East Europeans, on the other.[54]

For instance, when a visitor from the IMF explained in Sofia or Bucharest that giving and taking bribes was 'not normal', their Bulgarian and Romanian interlocutors could be excused for not understanding what in the world was meant. Celebrated Romanian film director Cristian Mungiu's 2016 film *Graduation* powerfully captures the tragic divide between being 'normal' in the sense of adapting to the shabbiness of one's local environment and being 'normal' in the sense of embracing expectations taken for granted in the West.[55]

The protagonist of the story, Romeo Aldea, is a middle-aged doctor employed at a local hospital. He lives with his wife and daughter in a tatty apartment on a grisly Ceausescu-era estate in the city of Cluj-Napoca in northwest Romania. In the universe of his small provincial town, he is a successful man, but it is clear that he wishes he had lived his life somewhere else. Aldea and his wife are intensely, almost desperately proud of their daughter, who has been offered a scholarship from a British university to study psychology conditional on her receiving top marks in her final high-school exams. If all goes well, their daughter Eliza will have the first-rate education and the normal life her parents have always wished for her. The day before she is scheduled to take her exams, however, Eliza is attacked and almost raped. Although her physical injuries are minor, she is in no state psychologically to ace her exams as she was expected to do. Desperate to rescue the situation, Aldea agrees to a corrupt bargain, illegally exploiting his medical contacts in exchange for the needed 'upward adjustment' of Eliza's grades. He arranges for a local politician to get a liver transplant that, according to the rules, should go to somebody else. For the illicit scheme to work, though, his daughter's conscious participation is required. The key scenes in the film involve Aldea trying to convince his daughter that she has to wise up. Romania isn't like the West, where no such morally despicable underhandedness is required. If she wants to live her life in a normal country, she first has to lower herself to the humiliatingly unethical normality that reigns in the country of her birth.

Once communist authority was overthrown, a vocabulary lesson was in order. Bribery, for example, must henceforth be labelled 'abnormal', just as law was declared, by definition, 'impartial and fair'. But the fact that such Western assumptions could be easily parroted on command did not make them any more congruous with Eastern realities.

If we examine the gap between Western expectations and Eastern realities after communism, we can discover an important source of the mental stress created in Central and Eastern Europe by a revolution that aimed at importing or imitating a foreign version of normality. To clarify what is at stake it will help to distinguish between horizontal *coordination* and vertical *synchronization*. Ordinary norms that govern social interaction, such as traffic regulations, are best understood as conventions enabling everyday coordination among members of the community. Adapting to such local expectations and patterns of behaviour is a necessary condition for successful action and interaction in every society. In order to govern, therefore, post-communist elites in Central and Eastern Europe had no choice but to adjust, at least at first, to the habitual practices commonplace in their countries. Romanians operating inside Romania, for example, had to adapt their behaviour to the routine conduct of fellow citizens. Just so, a businessman in Bulgaria who wants to keep his integrity by stubbornly refusing to give bribes, soon becomes an ex-businessman. At the same time, such national elites are seeking global legitimacy under Western eyes. This depends on their doing what is perceived as normal in the West – refusing to give or accept bribes, for example. To synchronize their behaviour with the lofty expectations of their Western colleagues, in other words, Central and Eastern European elites were pressured to turn their backs on the expectations that prevailed in their own societies. The opposite was also true. To coordinate their behaviour with that of their proximate neighbours and kin, they had to defy the expectations of their Western mentors and colleagues. Thus, in order to be effective, post-communist elites had to accept bribery locally and, simultaneously, campaign against corruption globally. Straddling two identities, parochial and cosmopolitan, they were unlikely to feel at home in either. Trying in vain to combine two contradictory ideas of what is normal, they began to feel chronically phoney, if not schizophrenic, and often ended up mistrusted both at home and abroad.

As it turns out, a revolution in the name of normality generated not only psychological disquiet but also its share of political trauma.

Rapid changes afflicting the Western model itself have exacerbated the gnawing sense of self-betrayal among its would-be Eastern imitators. Studying these trends requires commentators to shift their emphasis from political institutions, such as multi-party elections and an independent judiciary, to social customs. In the eyes of conservative Poles in the days of the Cold War, for instance, Western societies were normal because, unlike communist systems, they cherished tradition and believed in God. But today, suddenly, Poles have discovered that Western 'normality' means secularism, multiculturalism and gay marriage. Should we be surprised that some Central and East Europeans felt 'cheated' when they found out that the conservative society they wanted to imitate had disappeared, washed away by the swift currents of modernization? From the West's perspective, it should be said, illiberal efforts to refashion the political order in post-communist countries on the model of a now-surpassed sexist, racist and intolerant version of the West not only represent a futile attempt to turn back the clock. They also come across as attacks on the West's hard-earned 'moral progress', and are thus roundly condemned as expressions of anti-Western animus.

There is a second way in which many Central and East Europeans associate Westernization with betrayal: an important dimension of the ongoing culture war between the two halves of Europe concerns the troubled relationship between generations after communism. One consequence of the unipolar Age of Imitation is that school children began to be taught to look westward and only westward for role models. The resulting reforms in public education meant that they found the prospect of imitating their parents less and less attractive. For those born after 1989, in particular, it was as easy to 'synchronize' their attitudes and behaviour with Western standards as it was uncool to 'coordinate' their expectations with those of earlier generations at home. In post-communist societies, as a result, parents lost their ability to transfer their values and attitudes to their offspring. How the parents lived and what they achieved or suffered under communism ceased to matter in either material or moral terms. The young were not really revolting against their parents, as happened in the West in 1968. Instead, they started feeling sorry for them and otherwise ignoring them. The emergence of social media also meant that communication took place predominantly within distinct generational cohorts. Hooking up across state borders became more straightforward than talking across generational lines. Faced with their inability to program their children with their own values, parents in the region began, somewhat hysterically, to demand that the state should do it for them. Government rescue squads must be dispatched to liberate the children from their insidious Western kidnappers. This *cri de coeur* may sound pathetic. But it is another important source of the popular appeal of the region's illiberal populists. Children must be compelled to hear in school what they refuse to listen to at home. The collapse of parental influence, even though it is actually a characteristic feature of every revolution, is here blamed squarely on the West. Operating through the EU, the West has taken over national education and thereby corrupted the children. Nowhere does the cultural war in Central and Eastern Europe rage more fiercely, in fact, than it does around sex education in schools.[56]

The dogmatic-sounding assertion that Western-style political and economic arrangements cannot be challenged because no other options are on the table has led several prominent Czech critics of Westernization to describe the period after 1989 as one of 'neonormalization', a term meant to be harshly derogatory, given its deliberate echo of 'normalization', used to describe one of the most repressive periods of Czech history.[57] Rule by the local agents of Brussels after 1989 was certainly less coercive than rule by the local agents of Moscow after 1968. But its justification, according to populists, differed in only one respect. The latter was based on the pretence that the dictatorship of the Communist Party provided a pathway to a 'normality' superior to anything offered by the West. The former, by contrast, was based on the post-competitive claim that the European Commission's directives provided the sole pathway to the only legitimate 'normality', defined exclusively along liberal lines.

Former dissidents such as Orbán and Kaczyński can describe themselves as counter-revolutionaries because the normalizing revolution of 1989, in their view, produced a social order in which the national heritage and traditions of post-communist societies risked being wiped out. The request to imitate Western-style morality was an invitation to cultural suicide and not only because of the incentive it created for emigration to the West. To reclaim 'the spirit of combat' that Havel himself described as having gone missing in post-communist societies, illiberal populists fulminate against what they consider the absurd 'belief in the "normalcy" of liberal democracy'.[58] Strange as it may seem, this is how dissidence and counter-revolution can indistinguishably merge. And this is how a Westernizing revolution can trigger an anti-Western counter-revolution, much to the shock and consternation of the West.

A final perverse effect of the double meaning of normality should be briefly mentioned here. In order to reconcile the idea of 'normal' (meaning what is widespread and habitual) with what is normatively obligatory in the West, cultural conservatives in Central and East Europe sometimes seek to 'normalize' Western countries by arguing that what is widespread in the East is also ubiquitous in the West, even though, according to them, Westerners hypocritically pretend that their societies are different. Populist leaders help their followers relieve the normative dissonance between giving bribes to survive in the East and fighting corruption to be accepted in the West by alleging, in a classic expression of resentment, that the West is just as corrupt as the East but that Westerners are in denial or simply hiding the ugly truth.

Hungarian and Polish governments defend the constitutional shell games and political cronyism for which they are regularly criticized in Brussels along the same lines. They try to show that what they are doing is common practice in the West, too, but that Westerners are not ready to confess it. Here we find another paradox of the Age of Imitation. Central and Eastern European populists justify their own provocative illiberalism by pretending that they are, in fact, perfectly faithful disciples of Western ways, which this time means that they are just as bad as their counterparts in the West.

THE NEW GERMAN IDEOLOGY

It has been three decades since the foreign policy world was turned on its head by the claim that Western-style liberal democracy had become the ultimate norm and form of human existence. Today Thomas Bagger, one of Germany's most respected policy intellectuals, looks back, like the owl of Minerva, on an intellectual framework that is now universally regarded as dead and buried and argues that Europeans rather than Americans were the true believers in the definitive triumph of liberalism over all alternative ideologies. For the same reason, Europeans and particularly the Germans have turned out to be those most vulnerable to the ongoing collapse of the liberal order.

What fascinated Europeans and especially Germans about the end-of-history paradigm, Bagger claims, was that it liberated them from both the burdens of the past and the uncertainties of the future: 'Toward the end of a century marked by having been on the wrong side of history twice, Germany finally found itself on the right side. What had looked impossible, even unthinkable, for decades suddenly seemed to be not just real, but indeed inevitable.'[59] The observable transformation of Central and Eastern European countries into parliamentary democracies and market economies was taken as empirical proof of the validity of the bold claim that humanity, in its pursuit of freedom, need look no further than Western-style liberal democracy.

Even better from a German point of view: personal agency and charisma in politics were no longer decisive. History was bending towards liberal democracy. For a country so badly burnt by a catastrophic 'Führer' that the word 'leadership' could no longer be innocently translated into German, it was deeply reassuring that greater but abstract forces would take care of history's general direction. Individuals would only matter at the margins – their task was limited to administering the advent of the inevitable.[60]

In a world governed by the moral imperative to imitate the insuperable model of Western-style liberal democracy, no country need be trapped by its past or compelled to take responsibility for its future. Reducing political life to the more or less successful imitation of this fully worked-out political and ideological 'supermodel' gave humanity in general, and Germans in particular, both past and future for the price of one.

To this reassuring German dream we can add that the Imitation Imperative, as it was experienced or imagined in Central and Eastern Europe, tacitly implied that Germany was the real model being held up for admiring emulation. Because Germany was the champion 'convert' to liberal democracy, it was Germany that would show post-communist nations how imitation was expected to work.[61] The historically and geographically proximate model for the newly liberated states of the East was not America, then, but Germany, the country that had imitated America most successfully in the past. By 1965, only twenty years after the end of the Second World War, West Germany was not only a consolidated democracy but also the wealthiest and most productive country in Europe. The West German miracle was therefore front and centre in the minds of East and Central Europeans after 1989.

Germany's role as the implicit model for post-communist political reform is important because the East's backlash against the imitation of the West is rooted not only in the politically manipulated feeling of abandoning one's (selectively remembered) cultural identity for an allegedly superior post-ethnic identity imported from abroad but also in the fact that, when it came to facing up to their troubled history, Central and East Europeans were asked to follow the path taken by Germany, a country whose *Sonderweg* (special path) was obvious for all to see. There was a radical misfit between the democratization process in post-Second World War West Germany, a militarily occupied country where aggressive authoritarianism had wrought national catastrophe, and democratization in post-1989 Central and Eastern Europe. The abortive attempt to encourage the latter to emulate the former is yet another factor fuelling the disheartening rise of ethnic nationalism across the post-communist world.

The Bulgarian artist Luchezar Boyadjiev has come up with the perfect visualization of the official Brussels view of the 'final stage' of European history. Titled *On Holiday*, his work is based on the famous statue, located on Berlin's Unter den Linden, of the Prussian King Frederick the Great on horseback – only this time without the king mounted on the horse's back. By unhorsing the imposing leader of men, the artist has transformed the monument to a national hero into a statue of a riderless horse. All the complexities attached to an important but morally controversial figure of the past are suddenly eliminated. The idea of Europe that Boyadjiev aimed to convey is a Europe 'on holiday from history', without hopes of domination or fears of oppression. For some, at least, being truly European in the early twenty-first century means being unapologetically anti-heroic as well as anti-nationalistic. And the Germans today are the foremost exemplars of how to be both. After all, they navigated the transition from authoritarianism to liberal democracy with unparalleled success and their country, from the perspective of envious outsiders, has become 'exceptionally normal' in the Western sense.[62]

The identity politics that is roiling Eastern Europe today represents a delayed backlash against the several decades of identity-denial politics, otherwise known as Westernization, which began in 1989. Overheated particularism is a natural reaction to an overselling of the innocence of universalism. One consequence is that populists everywhere love to disparage universalism as the particularism of the rich.

The initial eagerness of the formerly captive nations to join the liberal West in 1989 stemmed at least as much from nationalist resentment at Moscow's forty-year hegemony as from a deep-seated commitment to liberal values and institutions. The slogan of Poland's anti-communist movement before 1989 had been *wolność i niezależność* (freedom and independence), the latter referring to independence from Moscow. But in the intellectual climate of the 1990s, the moral unacceptability of ethnic nationalism was woven into the ideal of a sought-after 'normality'. Ethno-nationalism was also associated with the bloody Yugoslav wars. In addition, post-national talking points were eagerly exported eastward by the European Union. These factors militated against total candour about the role of national feeling in the rush of formerly communist nations to join the West.

Attempts by the relatively small number of liberal reformers in Central Europe to give 'German lessons' to their fellow citizens backfired. While the liberal elites continued talking the language of universal rights, their nationalist counterparts eventually took control of the national symbols and national narratives. Faced with a mounting threat from the nationalist right, liberals would have been wise to heed the Romanian novelist Mihail Sebastian's warnings about the psychological power of symbols and signs.[63]

Imitating Germany's transition to liberal democracy required a radical disavowing of ethno-nationalism because of the unspeakable violence into which its Nazi incarnation had plunged the world. Reactionary nativists would have none of this. They focused instead on national victimhood and undeserved suffering. What distinguishes the national populists is that they never apologize for anything their nation has ever done in its entire history. To behave like a villain while presenting oneself as a victim is the nationalistic populist's signature conceit.

In the framework of democratic transitions, it was commonplace to view fascism and communism as two sides of the same totalitarian coin. When it comes to the potentially murderous consequences of the two ideologies and their associated regimes, this is a completely legitimate comparison. But viewing communism and fascism as twins misleadingly suggests that, in the democratic age, nationalism itself (of which fascism is an extreme version and distortion) will eventually fade away just as communism disappeared in 1989–91. This was never realistic. The reason is that communism was a radical political experiment based on abolishing inheritable private property, while democracy presupposes the existence of a bounded political community and is therefore inherently national. Nationalism cannot disappear, like communism, with the rise of liberal democracy, because loyalty to the nation is a necessary precondition for any stable liberal democracy. It was commonly believed, in the 1990s, that Russia was failing at democracy-building, while Poland and Hungary were succeeding, because Russia lacked the national cohesion forged in Poland and Hungary by resistance to Soviet occupation. Unlike liberalism, in any case, democracy is an exclusively national project. This is why, in the end, de Gaulle's 'Europe of fatherlands' has resisted all pressures to dissolve separate member-country identities into a common post-national identity.[64] Because of its inherent affinity with the universalism of human rights, liberalism is more hospitable to trans-national globalization than is democracy. But liberalism, too, works best within the context of politically bounded communities. After all, the most effective human rights organization in the world is the liberal nation-state.

Imitating the way post-1945 Germany dealt with history turned out to be problematic for Central and East Europeans in at least four respects.

First, post-Second World War German democracy was to some extent built on the worry that nationalism, given unlimited room to grow, may gradually lead to a rebirth of Nazism (*Nationalismus führt zum*

Faschismus). The EU originated in a plan to block a potentially dangerous reassertion of German sovereignty by integrating that country economically into the rest of Europe and by giving the Federal Republic a 'post-national' identity. As a result, not only the mystical idea of a Germanic *Rassenseele* (race-soul) but also ethno-nationalism in general was disavowed by most (not all) of the political establishment in post-Second World War West Germany.[65] Central and Eastern European countries, by contrast, find it difficult to share such a comprehensively negative view of nationalism because, first of all, these states were children of the age of nationalism following the break-up of multinational empires after the First World War and, second, because anti-Russian nationalism played an essential role in the basically non-violent anti-communist revolutions of 1989.

In Eastern Europe, for historical reasons, nationalism and liberalism are more likely to be viewed as mutually supportive than as mutually exclusive. Most Poles would find it absurd to cease honouring the nationalistic leaders who lost their lives in defending Poland against Hitler or Stalin. The fact that communist propaganda was intensely doctrinaire about denouncing nationalism is another reason why Central and East Europeans are wary of the German liberal elite's desire to detach citizenship in the state from hereditary membership of an ethno-national community. During the 1990s the Yugoslav wars led political leaders in Europe as a whole, including in Central and Eastern Europe, to dissociate ethnic homogeneity and xenophobic nativism from the justified right of national self-determination.[66] In the long run, however, the implicit association of liberalism with anti-nationalism has fatally eroded national support for liberal parties throughout the region.[67] Post-national liberals tend to view ethno-nationalism, or the belief that current citizens have some mystical moral connection to their biological forefathers, as atavistic and irrational. Anti-nationalist universalism of this sort is a perfectly humane and humanitarian stance to take. But it does not necessarily make good politics. From the viewpoint of those voters with intense nationalist emotions and attachments, post-national 'constitutional patriotism' seems to be a new 'German ideology' designed to belittle the eastern periphery of Europe and govern the whole of Europe in the interests of Berlin.[68]

Secondly, postwar German democracy was organized in response to the way the Nazis came to power through competitive elections. This is why non-majoritarian institutions like the Federal Constitutional Court and the Bundesbank are not only powerful but also among the most trusted institutions in Germany. In the immediate aftermath of 1989, although they were thrilled to be regaining their long-lost sovereignty, Central and East Europeans did not initially view constraints on their elected governments as attempts to limit the right of the people to govern themselves. At one point, Hungary's Constitutional Court was considered 'the most powerful high court in the world'.[69] Initially, the Polish Constitutional Court, too, was relatively effective and independent. But eventually populist incumbents invoked the sovereign will of the people to justify dismantling these and other 'counter-majoritarian' limits to their power.

After the First World War, the newborn Central and Eastern European states were organized around a fusion of the traditional German idea of the *Kulturnation*, the nation as a cultural community, with the French idea of the interventionist centralized state.[70] This distant legacy has faded with time, of course, but it has not entirely disappeared from the political sensibilities of the region. That helps explain the slowly developing domestic resistance, two decades after 1989, to reorganizing these states in line with two alternative foreign models: the new German idea of a decentralized state and American multiculturalism. Allergic reactions to both represented the first stirrings of the coming anti-liberal counter-revolution whose supporters associate working democracy with neither constitutional checks nor the assimilation of immigrants but with cultural homogeneity and executive power.

Thirdly, when sharing their postwar transformation experience of incorporation into the West with the post-communist countries, the Germans fell into a trap. They were proud of the success of their transition from a totalitarian society into a model democracy but at the same time, in many cases, they counselled the Central and East Europeans not to do what they did in the 1950s and 1960s but to do what they believed they themselves should have done back then. German democracy, as it developed in the aftermath of the Second World War, had a complicated relationship with the country's Nazi past. While Nazism was officially denounced after the war, it was not a subject that Germans were eager to discuss in any detail. For one thing, there were many ex-Nazis among the postwar West German elite. But when time came for the incorporation of East Germany into a unified liberal-democratic Germany, the approach was the opposite. The silent treatment became a gabfest. In Germany, a wholesale purge of ex-communists became the order of the day, and many of the East Germans who today willingly vote for the far-right Alternative for Germany interpreted the post-1989 'purification' process not as a sincere search for historical justice but as a way for the West to dominate the East, opening up employment opportunities for Westerners by unceremoniously ousting 'Ossi' elites from their jobs.

And fourthly, Germany was and is very proud of both its welfare state and its system of co-determination, by which labour unions were given a pivotal role in corporate governance. But these were aspects of their political system that the West Germans never pressed the EU to export to the East. The official reason they gave was that Central and East Europeans could not afford them, but perhaps they also expected that weakened state protections for Central and Eastern European workers and citizens would create favourable investment opportunities for German industry. Of course, various other factors were also involved, especially the evolution of the globally dominant form of American liberalism from Roosevelt's kinder and gentler New Deal, promising freedom from fear, to Reagan's deregulated market, meant to rattle people, to make them feel insecure at work, to take away their pensions, and so forth. The general refusal to invest heavily in the political stability of the new entrant states by supporting the economic importance of labour unions, while totally in line with the Thatcherite zeitgeist, deviated radically from the Allies' basically pro-labour union policy in West Germany after the Second World War. The most important reason for this change was presumably the disappearance of a communist threat and the corollary that no special efforts needed to be made to maintain the loyalty of workers to the system as a whole.

The old German question revolved around the idea that Germany was too small for the world and too big for Europe. The new German question is different. In the post-Cold War world, it turns out that Germany's transition to liberal democracy was too unique and path-dependent to be imitated by countries inhospitable, given their own recent histories, to the very idea of a post-ethnic society. The formerly communist countries of Central and Eastern Europe refused to build a new national identity around half-repressed feelings of contrition for the past. This goes at least some way towards explaining their revolt against the New German Ideology of de-historicized post-nationalism and culturally bland constitutional patriotism.

THE ILLIBERALISM OF EX-LIBERALS

Co nie jest biografią – nie jest w ogóle. (*What is not biography is nothing at all.*)
Stanisław Brzozowski, diary entry, 1911

In late 1949 *The God that Failed* – a book that collected the personal reminiscences of six prominent intellectuals about how and why they became communists and how and why they eventually broke from the Communist Party – became a turning point in the intellectual history of the Cold War. As one of the authors, Arthur Koestler, wrote: 'when all is said we ex-communists are the only people . . . who know what it is all about.'[71] Erstwhile insiders and former true believers alone held the key to the inner workings of an oppressive and hateful system. The plausibility of this claim helps explain why ex-communists played such a pivotal role in de-legitimizing the Soviet system. One-time adherents who have lost their former faith know the enemy well and have strong personal motives for discrediting and defeating the ideology they once so ardently espoused.

Lapsed liberals in Central and Eastern Europe today have played a similar role in de-legitimizing the region's post-1989 liberal order. Seeing post-communist development through the eyes of these ex-liberals is critical for understanding why and how so many Central and East Europeans have become deeply alienated from the post-Cold War world.

We are never going to unravel the enigma of Central and Eastern European illiberalism if we cannot grasp why, in the words of journalist and historian Anne Applebaum, some of the most feverish conservative intellectuals in the region turned out to be liberal mothers of gay sons or why, in Eastern Europe, anti-capitalist sentiments often take the form of violent anti-communism. In today's Hungary, if we are to trust the opinion polls,[72] many supporters of the militantly anti-communist Fidesz party tend to have a favourable view of János Kádár, the communist leader of the country from 1956 until 1988. The most heinous crime of communism, they seem to believe, was the role the ex-communists played in the transition period. Communists are often blamed not so much for what they did in the 1970s and 1980s but for the offhandedness with which they remade themselves into heartless capitalists in the 1990s.[73]

The political biography of Viktor Orbán presents us with the best opportunity for reflecting on the making of an ex-liberal. Here we have an energetic, ruthless and talented newcomer who fell in love with freedom but ended up enthralled with his own absolute power. He was born in 1963, in the wretched village of Alcsútdoboz, about 50 kilometres west of Budapest. His childhood was defined by poverty and lacked any revolutionary romanticism. At some point Orbán's father became a member of the Communist Party but, as Orbán's biographer Paul Lendvai observes, Orbán *père* was a typical '*Homo Kádáricus*' – a hard-working pragmatist trying to organize a better life for himself and his family.[74] Neither dreams of revolution nor political passions played much of a role in Orbán's family home. Nobody there was reading newspapers, and the real passion was not for politics but for football.

His time in the army politicized young Orbán and made him into an enemy of the communist regime. There he demonstrated his strength of character by refusing to collaborate with the Hungarian secret police. His years at university solidified these contrarian instincts and views. But it was his speech on 16 June 1989 at the ceremonial reburial of Imre Nagy – the murdered leader of the 1956 uprising – that first brought him to the attention of the public. Some anti-communist radicals felt too disgusted to attend the event. For them, it was a state affair masquerading as a revolution. But Orbán knew that his six- or seven-minute speech would be broadcast live and that the entire nation would be watching. And he was right. It was during Nagy's reburial that the young student leader demonstrated for the first time the defining characteristic of his political persona — his talent for catching the public's mood and his determination to seize the moment. Prior to the reburial, the scheduled opposition speakers all met and agreed that, to avoid provoking Moscow, nobody would demand the withdrawal of Soviet troops from the country. But when he mounted the stage, that is exactly what Orbán proceeded to do. This was the moment when the Hungarian public first saw and remembered him.[75] He was courageous, young and liberal. He went on to found Fidesz, the party of the young generation. The first Constitution of the party stipulated that nobody older than thirty-five would be allowed to join.

Orbán's break with liberalism is often explained as either pure opportunism (he moved to the right because that was where the votes were) or as a result of his growing contempt for the liberal Budapest intellectuals whom he had initially admired, but who looked down on him with a transparent sense of superiority. The moment that best captures Orbán's tense relationship with Hungarian liberals who, unlike him, came from Hungary's urban intelligentsia, is the widely reported story of how, during a reception, the well-known Free Democrat MP Miklos Haraszti went up to Orbán, who was dressed like the other guests, and adjusted his tie with a supercilious gesture. Everyone present remembers that Orbán blushed and was visibly flustered. The young and aspiring political leader was mortified at being treated as an uncouth relative from the countryside. Stendhal would have known how to describe what the young provincial felt at that moment.

It is tempting, then, to reduce Orbán's disappointment with liberalism to either political expediency or personal resentment at his condescending treatment by Budapest's liberal intellectuals. But it cuts much deeper than this. Indeed, it goes to the heart of the liberal understanding of politics, including liberalism's systematic ambivalence about the exercise of power. While Hungary's liberals were preoccupied with human rights, checks and balances, a free press and judicial independence (all valued because of the constraints they place on power), Orbán was interested in using power to upend the political order. While Budapest liberals wanted to win arguments, he wanted to win elections. His passion for football taught him that what matters in any contest, be it politics or sports, are killer instincts and unwavering loyalty. What matters especially is that your followers stick with you even when you occasionally lose. The exemplary leader is not the one who is judiciously fair to everybody but the one who inspires and mobilizes his own team or tribe.

To rally his supporters, Orbán harps single-mindedly on the standard list of liberalism's sins perpetrated, he claims, by the servile imitators of liberal democracy who misgoverned Hungary for two decades after 1989. First, the liberal picture of society as a spiritually empty network of producers and consumers cannot capture the moral depth and emotional solidarity of the Hungarian nation. Liberals are basically indifferent to the history and fate of the nation. In Orbán's boilerplate anti-liberal rhetoric, liberalism's language of human rights, civil society and legal procedures is described as cold, generic and ahistorical. Liberals are so blasé about immigration because they divorce citizenship from ethnic descent and replace the ideals of substantive justice and the public good with bland and abstract notions of procedural justice, the rule of law and individual utility. From the populist perspective, cosmopolitan distrust of ethnic bonds makes members of the vast ethnic majority in Hungary feel like foreigners in their own country. This is how universalism destroys solidarity. If everybody is your brother, then you are an only child. That is why Hungary's reactionary nativists claim that no principled liberal can take a genuine interest in the fate of Hungarians living outside the country.

This is how all anti-liberals talk. But Orbán's recitation of the anti-liberal catechism also reflects some region-specific concerns. For example, liberalism's focus on individual rights obscures the principal kind of political abuse in post-communist Hungary, namely the privatization of the *public* patrimony by former regime insiders, a kind of industrial-scale corruption that violated no individual rights and was indeed consolidated by the creation of individual rights to own private property.[76] This is what Orbán means when he says that 'in Hungary liberal democracy was incapable of protecting the *public* property that is essential in sustaining a nation.'[77] Liberalism, he also claims, ignores the social question and withdraws the state's paternalistic protection from the citizenry, arguing that 'free' individuals should shift for themselves. This is why, in the two decades after 1989,

We constantly felt that the weaker were stepped upon . . . It was always the stronger party, the bank, which dictated how much interest you pay on your mortgage, changing it as they liked over time. I could enumerate the examples that were the continuous life experience of vulnerable, weak families that had smaller economic protection than others during the last twenty years.[78]

One effect of the perceived Imitation Imperative in Hungary was the widespread tendency of low-income families to borrow money denominated in Swiss francs. They did so, it seems, in order to *imitate* the consumption patterns they observed in the West. Household debt soared in a heedless and futile attempt to catch up with and replicate Western living standards. Unfortunately, after a radical devaluation of Hungary's currency, the incautious borrowers had to make skyrocketing monthly payments in depreciated Forints. According to government statistics almost a million people took out loans in a foreign currency and 90 per cent of the foreign currency loans were in Swiss francs. This is what Orbán has in mind when he remarks that 'the liberal Hungarian state did not protect the country from indebtedness.' Liberal democracy, he concludes, 'failed to protect families from bonded labour'.[79] Such crushing burdens reinforced the sense that integration into the global economic system was degradation and impoverishment, not freedom and prosperity, as had originally been promised by its liberal cheerleaders.

Liberalism's justification of economic inequality by prettying up the myth of meritocracy, moreover, masks the central role of luck in the arbitrary distribution of wealth in society, a masking which is humiliating for the losers of the economic lottery because it encourages the winners to attribute their success to superior talent and greater personal effort. The myth of meritocracy is additionally offensive in the region's historical context because of the privileged access to economic success provided, *after* 1989, to those who occupied important political positions in the previous oppressive system. What distinguished 1989 from all previous revolutions was the ease with which the ostensibly 'dethroned' elites managed to preserve their power and influence. The reasons are very simple. The old elites participated in dismantling the previous system and contributed importantly to the peaceful nature of transition. As a result, they were the ones best positioned to transform their symbolic capital into financial and political capital. They were better educated and better connected, and they knew the West much better than any of their fellow citizens – even those opposition leaders who swore their undying love for it.

On his visit to Hungary in the late 1970s, Hans Magnus Enzensberger had a long talk with a member of the country's communist management class who later, in the 1990s, would join Hungary's new business elite. The man was in his fifties, dressed in an Armani jacket and extremely flexible in his ideological convictions. 'The Party is our social escalator,' he told his West German visitor, calling it 'better than the Harvard Business School. In this respect the Party has no competition – there are no alternatives . . . The day the Americans send their GIs to Budapest, I'll be the first to say to hell with Leninism.'[80] This is exactly what happened. As a result, in Central and Eastern Europe, defending private property and capitalism came to mean defending the privileges illicitly acquired by the old communist elites.

On acceding to power, the region's populists have not declared war on private property. What they dislike about liberty, instead, is the right of electoral losers to criticize the winners between elections, to try to win voters over to their perspective, and to survive to compete in the next contest. Political opponents don't have to flee, go into exile, or hide underground while their possessions are seized by the victors. By preserving the opposition's chance to oust the incumbents in the subsequent round of voting, liberal democracy subsidizes patience with regime failures and defends the system from unpredictable revolutionary violence.

This all sounds perfectly admirable. But there is a little-remarked downside to such an arrangement. Liberal democracy offers provisional victories only. It denies the electoral winners the chance for a full and final victory. It reinforces discontent with the 'legal impossibilism' (*imposybilizmu prawnego*) that Kaczyński is fighting against in Poland. Liberal democracy's renunciation of definitive and decisive victories, as opposed to temporary and indecisive ones, is what makes the allegedly full and final victory of liberal democracy itself in 1989 seem so anomalous and problematic. How could a political ideology that glorifies ongoing competition, ideological alternatives and merely provisional victories, the populists ask, claim to have done away with all three? According to Andrzej Nowak, one of the intellectual allies of PiS's leader, 'Kaczyński perceived that the lack of revolutionary change after 1989 was something for which Poland paid very dearly.'[81]

One paradox of Orbán's crusade against the hated liberal Left is that his political strategy was very much shaped by the Left. Young Orbán was an admirer of the Italian Marxist philosopher and activist Antonio Gramsci, and Fidesz's return to power in 2010, after eight years in opposition, was rooted in a Gramsci-inspired civil-society strategy, including the building of civic clubs as a springboard. But while liberals and leftists were talking about the rights of minorities, Orbán was talking about history and the rights of the majority.

Orbán's anti-liberalism is mostly fuelled by nationalist resentment against the post-national European Union which cares nothing for Hungarian identity. The calculated rage percolating through Orbán's attacks on the EU's quota system for distributing refugees throughout the member states suggests that the Hungarian PM sees a bounteous source of political support in popular dreams of payback for the Treaty of Trianon, the peace agreement of 1920 whereby the European powers punished Hungary by amputating two-thirds of its territory:

> The situation, Dear Friends, is that there are those who want to take our country from us. Not with the stroke of a pen, as happened one hundred years ago at Trianon; now they want us to voluntarily hand our country over to others, over a period of a few decades. They want us to hand it over to foreigners coming from other continents, who do not speak our language, and who do not respect our culture, our laws or our way of life: people who want to replace what is ours with what is theirs.[82]

The Treaty's centennial is coming up in 2020. So what better way to celebrate than savouring sweet revenge as the EU crumbles helplessly into pieces.

Reading Orbán's historic speech of 26 July 2014, in which he re-affirmed his militant commitment to building an illiberal state in Hungary, one feels his palpable contempt for those who try to blur the border between victory and defeat.[83] He would agree completely with Robert Frost's scoffing definition of a liberal as 'a man who cannot take his own side in an argument'. Orbán was not only disappointed with liberalism and its spirit of compromise; he wanted to defeat it decisively. There would be no compromises and no good-faith negotiations. The victory he sought would not be provisional, moreover, but final. This was his copycat reply to the alleged *definitive victory* of liberalism in 1989. He was also going to re-enact his youthful debut as a slayer of Soviet hegemony by bringing down the liberal-democratic empire administered from Brussels with American backing. Seen in this framework, Fidesz's electoral success is not just the momentary victory of one political party over others, but a sign that 'the era of liberal democracy is over'.[84] What interests Orbán is the kind of victory that entails his rivals' utter humiliation and defeat. This is the type of victory that forges and consolidates partisan political identity. Perhaps Orbán is using the intensity of his rejection of liberalism to compensate for the ideological emptiness and banality of his born-again illiberalism.

Whatever its long-term political consequences, the lack of intellectual originality in Central Europe's current strain of illiberalism has its roots in the intellectual poverty of the 1989 revolutions undertaken in the name of normality.

SING

Hungarian director Kristóf Deák's movie *Sing* won the 2017 Oscar for best live-action short film. The movie successfully captured the mixture of desire and humiliation that is characteristic of post-1989 democratic transitions in Central Europe. The events dramatized in the film take place in Budapest in the early 1990s. Having recently enrolled in a new school, young Zsófi is thrilled at the possibility of singing in its award-winning choir. The music teacher, Erika, permits Zsófi to join, but restricts her to mouthing the lyrics silently so that her amateurish voice will not blemish the choir's overall performance.

A disheartened Zsófi reluctantly acquiesces. But her best friend, Lisa, on discovering the vow of silence, confronts the teacher who replies that the choir is competing for a trip to Sweden so that all participants should want only the most talented vocalists to be heard. Those who merely mime the words should be grateful for the chance they've been given to play even a walk-on part. As it turns out, Zsófi is not the only disappointed child whom Erika had turned into an unheard member of the chorus. Indeed, permitting the best alone to sing aloud is the teacher's secret winning strategy. But collective sympathy for the muzzled children excites the whole choir into open revolt against their teacher's obsession with winning. After mounting the stage on the day of competition, the entire choir lip-syncs voicelessly, in solidarity with Zsófi. Only after a mortified Erika flees in desperation from the stage, do they all burst freely into song. Central European populists, such as Orbán and Kaczyński, like to portray their revolt against the once-embraced, now-detested Imitation Imperative as analogous to the students' revolt against their manipulative teacher. They claim to have restored Central Europe's voice.

It is a self-serving interpretation, to be sure. But it is also true that while Brussels tended to view enlargement, in a self-flattering light, as an act of open-handed generosity towards previously subjugated nations,[85] many in Central and Eastern Europe came to see it as a form of soft colonization.[86] Having escaped from Moscow's imperial grip and been promised that they could join the liberal world as politically equal partners, the formerly communist countries of the region felt that they were being treated with casual condescension as if they belonged to the non-Western 'rest', as if they were not really 'Europeans' after all, but should be grouped alongside the peoples of Africa, Asia and the Middle East.[87] To understand the psychological downsides of being regarded in this light, it helps to recall the outrage with which colonized peoples outside Europe viewed the colonial-era Imitation Imperative. We have already cited Frantz Fanon on this subject, but he is just the best-known example of non-Western resentment towards mandatory imitation of Western forms and norms. Writing of nineteenth-century Egyptian imitators of Europe, the Lebanese-born French scholar Amin Maalouf explained the trauma of imitation in the following way:

> They have had to admit that their ways were out of date, that everything they produced was worthless compared with what was produced by the West, that their attachment to traditional medicine was superstitious, their military glory just a memory, the great men they had been brought up to revere – the poets, scholars, soldiers, saints and

travelers – disregarded by the rest of the world, their religion suspected
of barbarism, their language now studied only by a handful of specialists, while they had to learn other people's languages if they wanted to
survive and work and remain in contact with the rest of mankind.[88]

As discussed in the Introduction, and as Fanon's references to the
'nauseating mimicry' of the West confirm, the imitator's life inescap-
ably mixes feelings of inadequacy, inferiority, dependency, lost
identity and involuntary insincerity. Anti-colonial resistance to the
Western European powers has assumed such different contours in the
North African and Central European cases as to make comparisons
seem hopelessly superficial. But we can at least say that a specific
irritant comes into play in the latter case because the imitators
believed they belong to the same cultural space as the imitated and
also thought they were being invited to join 'the free world' on an
equal footing with their fellow Europeans. It is this conjunction of
factors that has led us to stress, among the multiple causes of the
wave of authoritarian xenophobia washing across Central and Eastern Europe today, the feelings of self-betrayal incubated, during the
first post-communist decade, by a drawn-out process of what Gabriel
Tarde would have called 'contagious imitation' of the West.

Focusing on the backlash against a historically specific and socially
wrenching experience of imitative politics, we believe, is a more fruitful way to approach the populist counter-revolution in Central and
Eastern Europe than overstating the causal force of the region's allegedly 'indelible' traditions of anti-democratic and intolerant nativism.
But why can't we explain the populist turn in the region in a simpler
way, as an expression of disappointment in liberalism itself? Citizens
had initially embraced the democratic-capitalist model on the assumption that it would bring prosperity, for example, and when that didn't
happen, they turned against it. This explanation works well in theory,
but it does not fit the facts. The Polish case suggests that Central
Europe's rightward metamorphosis cannot be blamed on 'the economy, stupid'. Poland's relative economic success did nothing to
immunize that country's electorate from the populist appeal. As Polish sociologist Maciej Gdula has shown, pro-liberal and anti-liberal
political attitudes in Poland cannot be explained by who won and

who lost from the country's post-communist economic transform-ation.[89] Jarosław Kaczyński's partisan base includes many who seem completely satisfied with their private lives and have shared boun-teously in their country's prosperity. Their objection to the liberal order is that, for conservative Catholics zealously opposed to legalizing abortion and gay marriage, accepting liberalism feels like self-betrayal. 'Identity', moreover, is essentially a compact with one's dead ances-tors. And this compact is threatened by forces that seem bent on forcing Hungarians and Poles to abandon their 'own way of life'.[90] The most hated of these forces are the bureaucrats from Brussels who, according to many Hungarians and Poles, are brewing some dark conspiracy with immigrants from Africa and the Middle East.

In March 2018, speaking in southwestern Poland at an event mark-ing 100 years of Polish independence, the country's President, Andrzej Duda, compared membership in the European Union to the country's previous periods of foreign occupation under Prussia, Austria and Russia: 'between 1795 and 1918,' he said, 'Poles answered to occupying powers in faraway capitals' who 'made decisions for us'. Post-communist Poland is experiencing a similar form of foreign domination and exploitation today, he went on to say. Poland's national sovereignty and Catholic heritage are being erased by the EU's project of incorp-orating the country in its post-national anti-religious confederation. Seen from this preposterous perspective, there is no real difference between communist authoritarianism and liberal democracy. Both 'impose', with or without tanks, the will of a godless foreign minority on 'ordinary Poles'.[91]

If we accept the testimony of the movement's leaders, therefore, the rise of Central European illiberalism was due in good measure to pent-up rancour engendered by the centrality of mimesis in the reform processes launched in the East after 1989. When the Cold War division between communists and democrats was replaced by the post-1989 division between imitators and imitated, a moral hierarchy was established that would prove profoundly destabiliz-ing. Commenting on the Western media's coverage of Orbán's Hungary, Maria Schmidt remarked that they 'talk down from above to those below like it used to be with colonies'.[92] It would be wrong to equate the history of colonial domination and exploitation in the non-Western world with Central Europe's originally voluntary decision to accept the burdens of harmonization into a post-national EU. In both cases, however, voluntary importation of Western norms and institutions entailed not only an explicit acceptance of sometimes onerous duties and obligations but also a tacit acceptance of subordination and even subjugation. Anti-liberal movements in the region are a reaction to a humiliating subordination that is arguably all the more galling for those who expected to be welcomed as fellow Europeans into the West.

To upend the hierarchy implicit in the relationship of imitators to the imitated, Central European leaders now say that the main difference between East and West has once again changed. It is neither the communists versus the democrats nor imitators versus the imitated. It has become, instead, the difference between ethnically homogeneous and ethnically pluralistic societies, between countries where traditional majorities rule and countries where a 'mishmash' of minorities thwart majority will. This imagined contrast between the pure and the mongrel is obviously meant to turn the tables and establish Central Europe as the true Europe fighting a last-ditch battle to preserve a struggling white Christian identity.

What makes imitation on a national and regional scale so irksome is not only the implication that the mimic is somehow morally, culturally and humanly inferior to the model. Because copycat nations are legally authorized plagiarists, they must, on a regular basis, seek the blessings and approval of those who hold the copyright to the political and economic recipes being borrowed and applied second-hand. They must also unprotestingly accept the right of Westerners to evaluate their success or failure at living up to Western standards. The surprising passivity of Brussels in the face of outrageous violations of judicial and press independence in both Poland and Hungary means that this is not a practical issue but a symbolic one. That does not make such Western judgementalism any less consequential psychologically. Even without coercion or enforcement, being regularly evaluated by foreign judges bereft of serious knowledge of one's country can fuel a politics of rage.

Although the post-communist imitation of the West was a free choice of the East, it was encouraged and supervised by the West. Our point is not that the region would have flourished politically if the

West had sat on its hands and done nothing. What we have been trying to explain is why an adaptation to foreign standards that was initially desired ended up being experienced as non-consensual and imposed. What matters most to the region's new breed of anti-liberal is less the violation of national sovereignty than the affront to national dignity.

The rise of authoritarian chauvinism and xenophobia in Central and Eastern Europe has its origins in political psychology not political theory. Where populism rules, it does not do so intellectually. Whatever popularity it has stems from a deep-seated disgust at a perceived post-1989 Imitation Imperative with all of its demeaning and humiliating implications. And it is fuelled by the rejection of the minorities-centred cultural transformation that followed the 1968 protest movements in the West. The origins of Central and Eastern European illiberalism are therefore emotional and pre-ideological, rooted in rebellion against the 'humiliation by a thousand cuts' that accompanied a decades-long project requiring acknowledgement that foreign cultures were vastly superior to one's own. Illiberalism in a philosophical sense is a cover-story meant to lend a patina of intellectual respectability to a widely shared visceral desire to shake off the 'colonial' dependency; an inferiority implicit in the very project of Westernization. When Kaczyński accuses 'liberalism' of being 'against the very notion of the nation'[93] and when Maria Schmidt says, 'We are Hungarians, and we want to preserve our culture',[94] their overheated nativism embodies a refusal to be judged by foreigners according to foreign standards. The same can be said of Viktor Orbán's expressions of anti-immigrant nostalgia: 'we do not want to be diverse and do not want to be mixed . . . We want to be how we became eleven hundred years ago here in the Carpathian Basin.'[95] This is a good example of how populists select one of their country's many pasts and claim that it is *the* authentic past of the nation which must be rescued from contamination by Western modernity. (It is, of course, remarkable that the Hungarian prime minister remembers so vividly what it was like to be Hungarian eleven centuries ago.) And while he is informing Westerners that 'we' are not trying to copy 'you', and that it therefore makes no sense for foreigners to consider Hungarians low-quality or half-baked copies of themselves, he is also pretending that the imitation of one's remote ancestors, of whom few traces remain, requires no more effort than being oneself.

Illiberal politicians owe their political success to popular resentment at having spent two decades genuflecting before putatively canonical foreign models. This explains why, in the populists' over-the-top speeches, the European Union and the Soviet Union are discussed interchangeably.[96] Both Moscow in the late 1940s and Brussels in the late 1990s 'created a set of geographically contiguous replica regimes in Eastern Europe'.[97] That this analogy is strained needs no emphasis, since the imitation of Soviet communism was imposed and the imitation of European liberalism was invited. But populists nevertheless treat them as morally equivalent since, as they see it, both Moscow and Brussels demanded a style of obedience from their 'vassals' that aimed at extirpating national traditions.

Nationalist resistance to a generally acknowledged Imitation Imperative has a perverse unintended consequence, however. By passionately invoking tradition as the antidote to imitation, East Europe populists are forced into regularly rewriting their national histories. In the days of the Cold War, when resisting Moscow's demand that they copy the Soviet model, Central Europeans described their tradition as fundamentally liberal and European. It was just another current in the broad stream of Western civilization. Today, by contrast, they invoke 'their tradition' to justify their opposition to being incorporated against their will into the liberal West. This startling volte-face makes it clear that there really is no such thing as 'their tradition'.[98] Every country, as suggested, has many pasts and many traditions, which are often at odds with one another. The rhetorical gambit of populists involves singling out the least benign and most intolerant strand in the past of, say, Hungary or Poland, and arbitrarily elevating it into 'the' authentic past that must be preserved from the corrosive influence of the West.

This brings us back, in conclusion, to Mary Shelley's *Frankenstein*. Without pushing the analogy too far, the American sociologist Kim Scheppele describes today's Hungary (presided over by another Viktor) as a 'Frankenstate', that is, an illiberal mutant composed of ingeniously stitched-together elements of Western liberal democracies.[99] What she shows, remarkably enough, is that Orbán has succeeded in parrying threats to his power by implementing a clever policy of piecemeal imitation. When attacked by Brussels for the illiberal character of his reforms, the Hungarian government is always quick to point out that every controversial legal procedure, rule and institution has been faithfully copied from the legal system of one of the member states. Instead of suffering imitation passively, the Prime Minister employs it strategically. Selective imitation has allowed Orbán to stymie EU attempts to penalize Hungary for the regime's attacks on freedom of the press and judicial independence. By assembling an illiberal whole out of liberal parts, Orbán has managed to turn the very idea of a Western Imitation Imperative into an in-your-face joke at Brussels' expense.

Rather than censoring the press, in the old communist manner, Orbán has forced the closure of hostile newspapers on trumped-up economic grounds. And he has subsequently arranged for his wealthy friends and allies to buy much of the national and local media and to turn TV channels and newspapers alike into organs of state power. This is how he has shielded from public scrutiny both his electoral manipulation and epic levels of insider corruption. By packing the courts with loyalist judges, he can also claim to have legality and constitutionality squarely on his side. The legitimacy of such a system depends less on electoral victories, therefore, than on the rulers' claim to be defending an arbitrarily delineated 'genuine nation' against its inner as well as outer enemies. The Orbán-style illiberal regimes that are on the rise in Eastern Europe thus combine Carl Schmitt's understanding of politics as a melodramatic showdown between friends and enemies and the institutional façade of liberal democracy. This game of hide-and-seek has allowed Orbán not only to survive inside an EU that defines itself as a union of values but also to become a leader of an increasingly powerful pan-European 'Frankenstein coalition' that aims to transform Europe into a Confederation of Illiberal Democracies. There is scant reason for confidence that he is destined to fail.

2

Imitation as Retaliation

*The only good copies are those which show up the absurdity
of bad originals.*

La Rochefoucauld[1]

On 1 January 1992 the world awoke to discover that the Soviet Union
had vanished from the map. Without military defeat or foreign invasion, one of the world's two superpowers had crumbled into dust. How
can such an extraordinary turn of events be explained? The break-up
happened contrary to all expectations that the Soviet empire was too
big to fail, too rock-solid to disintegrate, and too nuked-up to be bul-
lied by the West. The USSR had survived many decades of turbulence
substantially intact. How could it implode essentially without warning at a moment when the majority of the people 'didn't even have the
feeling that the country was falling apart'?[2] As historian Stephen Kotkin asks: 'why did the immense Soviet elite, armed to the teeth with
loyal internal forces and weapons, fail to defend either socialism or
the Union with all its might?'[3]

For the West, the bombshell abruptness with which the 'Main
Enemy' – and the principal embodiment of an alternative to the
liberal-democratic model of political and economic organization –
ceased to exist seemed to prove that the great age of ideological
conflict was over. The collapse of communism was unexpected and it
was precisely its unexpected nature that was cited as proof that not
simply America or the West but History itself had declared communism dead. Now that liberal democracy's only viable competitor had
passed from the scene, there would be no more surprises about the
ideal form of government for most of the world. The Western way of

life was on a roll. 'There is something deeply ironic,' as Thomas Bagger observed, about the fact 'that from the life-changing experience of an entirely unexpected, non-linear event like the end of the Cold War', the West 'has derived a thoroughly linear expectation of the future'.[4] Ironic or not, the belief that Russia, too, was on a gradual pathway towards liberal democracy was shared at the time by many Western Russia watchers.

After the end of the Cold War, a few optimists even assumed that Russia would follow in the footsteps of post-Second World War Germany, embracing multi-party politics and enjoying the benefits of a legally regulated market economy. It would adopt Western institutions and political practices and, instead of resisting re-education by the Cold War winners and defining itself in opposition to the spirit of liberal democracy, it would cooperate in upholding the Western-dominated world order. Why this did not happen is the story this chapter aims to tell.

In fact, Russia's behaviour over the past decade *does* resemble that of post-war Germany, but of Germany after the First World War, rather than after the Second World War when the German 'economic miracle' consolidated public support for democratization. Like post-First World War Germany, Putin's Russia has become an angry revisionist power, seemingly focused on destroying the European order. And while Russians continue to mimic Americans, their goal is not conversion or assimilation but revenge and vindication, pursued even when it does little or nothing to help Moscow recover its lost status and power. A characteristic example of the Kremlin's anti-Western (as opposed to pseudo-Westernizing) resort to mimicry is the way Russian trolls, in the American presidential campaign of 2016, pretended to be Americans online in order to sow confusion, boost Trump's chances and divide the country against itself.

Imitation of Western forms and norms has been central to Russia's post-Cold War experience. Although the style of imitation has evolved over time, in no case was *conversion* a realistic option. Russia's only previous attempt to import a political model from the West (as opposed to borrowing Western technology and methods of industrial production) was in the brief Kerensky period that ended in the Bolshevik Revolution. There, as the latest generation of Russian anti-Westernizers see it, lies a cautionary tale.

The politics of imitation in post-communist Russia has unfolded in three distinct phases. Already in the 1990s, the electoral accountability of politicians to citizens was stage-managed and illusory. If the Yeltsin regime had been accountable, it would not have shelled the Supreme Soviet in 1993, stolen the 1996 election, carefully avoided putting the Gaidar economic reform programme to a popular vote, or allowed Russia's national wealth to be 'looted by a narrow group of future oligarchs with the complete consent of Boris Yeltsin and his team of "reformers"'.[5]

Nevertheless, *simulating* democracy proved useful as a way for the Kremlin to reduce pressure from Western governments and NGOs while the leadership engaged in root-and-branch economic reforms that had little or no public support. According to Putin confidant Vladislav Surkov,

> The multilayered political institutions which Russia had adopted from the West are sometimes seen as partly ritualistic and established for the sake of looking 'like everyone else,' so that the peculiarities of our political culture wouldn't draw too much attention from our neighbors, didn't irritate or frighten them. They are like a Sunday suit, put on when visiting others, while at home we dress as we do at home.[6]

This fakery helped regime insiders survive a turbulent and stressful decade. The second phase, which segued smoothly from the first, began around the turn of the millennium, when Putin acceded to the presidency. He continued to organize elections, but did so primarily to persuade Russian citizens that there were no viable alternatives to the current wielders of state power. The third phase, which represents a more radical break, can be traced to 2011–12. At around that time, for reasons to be discussed, the Kremlin shifted to a strategy of selective *mirroring* or violent parody of Western foreign policy behaviour meant to expose the West's relative weakness in the face of Kremlin aggression and to erode the normative foundations of the American-led liberal world order.

We are still in this third phase today.

Life after the end of history has stopped being a 'sad time' characterized by 'bourgeois ennui' and has begun to resemble the iconic

Hall of Mirrors scene in Orson Welles' 1947 classic *The Lady from Shanghai*, a world of shared paranoia and escalating aggression.

THE SOURCES OF RUSSIAN REVISIONISM

The Munich Security Conference is an annual gathering of defence ministers, parliamentarians and national-security experts from around the world. It was launched in the early 1960s, not long after the shocking overnight construction of the Berlin Wall. When Vladimir Putin delivered his speech to the Conference on 10 February 2007, the audience in the hushed auditorium was almost as stunned as the Berliners had been when they awoke back on that fateful Sunday morning in August 1961 to find their city split cruelly in two. Putin's caustic words were meant to signal the end of Russia's post-communist deference towards the Western powers. He was informing his unjustifiably complacent listeners that a new barricade between East and West, bristling with unfriendly intentions, was being constructed as he spoke.[7]

Sitting side-by-side at their front-row table, too close to the lectern for comfort, German Chancellor Angela Merkel looked dismayed, CIA Director Robert Gates embarrassed, and Senator John McCain enraged. Western political leaders and media commentators had of course assumed that the Russian President would express some passing displeasure at the unipolar, US-dominated international order. But they were totally unprepared to find themselves at the epicentre of a geopolitical firestorm. Putin's belligerent speech was like a declaration of war. It was a scathing assault on the global security architecture crafted by the Western powers. It was seeded with pungently sarcastic asides meant to violate informal norms about how non-Western supplicants seeking favours from Western governments were expected to behave in polite company. He denounced NATO expansion as an act of betrayal, citing verbatim one long-forgotten official promise that such eastward encroachment would never be allowed to happen. But his list of grievances against the West cut much deeper. He accused the United States of 'global destabilization' and blatant 'disdain for international law'. America's bid to be the world's 'one centre of authority, one centre of force, one centre of decision-making', dictating permissible behaviour to other countries, had scandalously backfired. Washington's 'almost uncontained hyper use of force – military force – in international relations,' he elaborated, 'is plunging the world into an abyss of permanent conflicts'.

Putin's rhetoric became especially truculent when he touched on the conceit that all countries outside the West were morally obliged to adopt the 'international human rights norms' of the West. The duty of all mankind to strive for liberal democracy was an offensive Western conceit. The Americans justified 'interfering in the internal affairs of other countries' by invoking the worldwide desirability and imitability of their own political and economic system. While lecturing the world about human rights, democracy and other lofty values, Western leaders were all the while pursuing their own countries' selfish geopolitical interests. Such a shameless resort to double standards had, by this time, become one of Putin's gnawing obsessions, matched only by his resentment at the lack of 'respect' with which he believed Russia was routinely treated by the West. In his view, the post-Cold War's Age of Imitation was actually an Age of Western Hypocrisy. The so-called 'liberal international order', Putin implied, was nothing nobler than a projection of America's will to dominate the world. Universalism was the particularism of the West. The US disguised the enlargement of its sphere of influence as an expansion of the frontiers of freedom. What the West celebrated as popular democratic revolutions were simply Western-sponsored *coups d'état*.

The most striking thing about Putin's speech was not his recycling of standard Kremlin complaints about how shabbily Russia had been treated after the end of the Cold War. Nor were his listeners shocked by the verbal intensity of Putin's anti-Western diatribe. What took them by surprise was the way the Russian President wrapped himself in the mantle of an all-seeing prophet. During the Cold War, the Soviets had spoken as if they knew exactly what the future would be like. In Munich, Putin adopted a superficially similar pose. But unlike his Soviet predecessors, he was not speaking on behalf of an ideology that assumed its future preponderance in global affairs. His new assertiveness derived, on the contrary, from an unspoken conviction that not the victorious but the defeated have a superior grasp of what dangers the future holds in store. His claim was that Moscow's defeat in 1989–91 was a blessing in disguise. This tragic event had steeled his country for the cruelly competitive and utterly amoral world to come.

The idea that the vanquished have a clearer picture of the future than their vanquishers is not a new one. According to one renowned German intellectual historian, winners of international conflicts, drunk on victory, usually see their success as the triumph of justice and the predestined culmination of deep historical trends. The defeated, with a more accurate grasp of the decisive role played by contingency in history, 'search for middle-or-long term factors to account for and perhaps explain the accident of the unexpected outcome'.[8]

This is why Putin's 2007 Munich speech represented such a decisive turning point in international politics. It was in Munich that the Kremlin forced the vainglorious winners to listen, at long last, to the Cold War's sadder-but-wiser losers. It was in Munich that Russia stopped pretending to accept the celebratory storyline that the end of the Cold War represented a joint victory of the Russian people and the Western democracies over communism. And it was also in Munich that Putin announced that Russia was not about to behave like West Germany after 1945, repenting its sins and begging to be allowed into the Western club where it could be schooled in proper behaviour. In 1985, Germany's President Richard von Weizsäcker famously described Hitler's defeat as *'ein Tag der Befreiung'* ('a day of liberation') not only for Germany's neighbours but for the German people too.[9] Putin was not about to echo those words. Stationed at the KGB's Dresden outpost in East Germany at the time, he experienced the fall of the Wall in 1989 as a national humiliation, not a national liberation.[10] In Munich, therefore, the Russian President portrayed his country as a power that, having been accidentally defeated in the Cold War, was looking for ways to strike back. He brazenly echoed an older Germany's legendary resentment at the punitive Versailles Treaty imposed by the victorious powers after the First World War. And he did so before a historically conscious audience gathered in the heartland of Europe's bloodiest twentieth-century tragedies. The provocation coded in Putin's choice of venue for delivering his message of defiance magnified its galvanic effect on his audience. 'Munich', evoking the West's appeasement of Hitler in 1938, is one of the most overused tropes in Western foreign policy discourse after the fall of the Berlin Wall. NATO cited its commitment not to allow another 'Munich' to justify its military intervention in the former Yugoslavia. And this was also how the United States rationalized its war in Iraq. The salience of this historical analogy increased the impact of Putin's Munich speech. It was in this city that Putin informed his Western counterparts that Russia was determined to destroy the post-Cold War liberal order. The shock was palpable. The West was wholly unprepared for the Kremlin's anti-Western turn because, for two decades, it had got post-communist Russia wrong.

It is not difficult to explain why, after some initial moments of hopefulness, Russian society was unable and unwilling to accept the idea that the end of the Cold War was a 'bloodless change' from which Russians and Westerners alike emerged victorious. What was initially celebrated in Eastern Europe as liberation and independence, made visible by the withdrawal of Soviet forces, was mourned in Russia as a loss of territory, population and global stature. Inside Russia, the 'independence' of the Russian Federation from the Soviet Union was a bitter joke. This is one reason for the deep unpopularity of the 'democratic reformers', already registered in the parliamentary elections of 1993 and 1995, elections which otherwise revealed little about how Russians wished to be governed.

Though we are used to thinking of the Cold War as an economic and political contest without direct military confrontation, the fall of the Berlin Wall revealed that when economic systems and expectations collapse people die just as inexorably as they do in a shooting war. Russia's social and economic indicators from the final decade of the last century resemble those of a country that had just lost a war. In the early 1990s, in the immediate aftermath of the communist collapse, life expectancy in the former Soviet Union and Eastern Europe fell precipitously. It is estimated that in Russia alone, between 1989 and 1995, there were 1.3 to 1.7 million premature deaths. Average life expectancy plummeted from 70 in 1989 to 64 in 1995. The proximate causes included a significant increase in suicides and drug and alcohol abuse, which led to an epidemic of cardiovascular and liver diseases. The primary victims were middle-aged men and women. In-depth studies found that neither direct deprivation nor the deterioration of the health system accounted for these deaths.[11] They could be traced, rather, to the psychological stress likely produced by the shock of severe economic dislocation. After the disintegration of the Soviet Union, 25 million Russians found themselves suddenly living in a foreign country. They were a stranded diaspora, involuntarily expatriated as the borders of their country retreated. Professional careers and personal networks were destroyed, and families were both financially ruined and morally broken. For almost a decade, the country was flooded with chaos and criminality. 'Traumatology' not 'transitology' was the most appropriate science for researching the lived experience of those years. The Russian world had been upended. Life plans and expectations were irreparably shattered. As Vladimir Yakunin, friend and ally of Putin, former KGB officer and head of Russian Railways from 2005 to 2015, wrote in his memoirs: 'This sense of loss and hurt, which left many people looking back fondly on the Communist era, has never been truly appreciated by other nations.' While disavowing nostalgia for the Soviet Union, he goes on to claim that 'someone who does not make an attempt to comprehend Russia as it was then, in the hard years after 1991, will, I think, struggle to understand much about Russia as it is now.'[12] Similarly, no one who, today, describes the end of the Cold War as a triumph of the highest moral aspirations of mankind will be able to make sense of Russia's vindictive, rather than strategic, swerve towards anti-Western belligerence today.

It is common in the West to recount the death of communism and the end of the Soviet Union as if they were a single event. For Russians generally, however, and not only for Putin loyalists, these are two very different stories. Most Russians were happy that Soviet communism and the Party dictatorship were dead and gone. But they were heartbroken by the unwished-for and unexpected disintegration of the Soviet Union because it had been their country, their birthplace, and their fatherland. Pent-up anger at national dispossession explains why so many ex-Soviets basically agreed with Putin's remark that the end of the USSR was 'the greatest geopolitical catastrophe' of the twentieth century.[13]

According to Russia's leading dissident and anti-Putin activist, Alexei Navalny, 'the Russian people have been sold the idea of giving up a normal life for the sake of a completely idiotic and useless confrontation with the West.'[14] He is right, but with a twist. Many Russians have indeed been persuaded by the Kremlin that the idiotic and useless collapse of the USSR was somehow orchestrated by the perfidious West in the name of an elusive 'normality'.

The wholly peaceful nature of the political collapse of 1989–91 made it additionally traumatic. This paradox is seldom appreciated in the West. The Soviet Union had been destroyed without suffering an attack or putting up a fight. A military superpower capable of obliterating life on earth disappeared like an illusionist's mirage. The nuclear missiles that had threatened humanity with Armageddon proved useless for staving off the system's downfall from within. Why this 'collapse without defeat' had such a convulsive effect on the population becomes clear once we recall that Soviet identity had been a heroic one. It was centred not on chimerical aspirations for the future but on past sacrifice and the defence of the fatherland. Memories of the epic struggle of Soviet people in the Great Patriotic war of 1941–5 were at the heart of this identity. The hare-brained planning and execution of the failed August 1991 coup, allegedly staged to save this fatherland, added insult to injury. No serious effort was made to defend this system for which so many had sacrificed so much. There were almost no suicides,[15] since apparently few felt dishonoured by the elite's unwillingness to fight for the survival of the USSR, perhaps because the communist dogma on which it was ostensibly based had by that time become a hollow ritual in which almost no one any longer believed. In any case, not a single official resigned in protest when Gorbachev acquiesced in Yeltsin's push for the Union to dissolve.

In the late 1920s, while visiting Soviet Russia, the Italian writer Curzio Malaparte observed, 'The torment that oppresses the masses in a revolution is their obsession with betrayal. The revolutionary masses are like soldiers who are always afraid of their leaders' betrayal ... They don't feel so much vanquished by the enemy as betrayed by their leaders ... They feel betrayal as soon as it arrives.'[16] More than six decades later, in 1991, a few Russians may have felt aggrieved by the end of communism, but many more felt betrayed by their leaders who, without being defeated militarily, let the Soviet Union fall apart.

The Soviets lost the Cold War without putting up a fight. That humiliation could not be papered over by Westernizing talk of a shared victory for humanity. The need to explain the unfathomable mystery of a collapse without defeat made conspiracy theories all the rage in post-communist Russia, including among political and intellectual elites.[17] The historical failure of the communist system, obviously a major cause of the Soviet collapse, has been obscured by endlessly recycled stories of domestic betrayal and foreign meddling in Russian affairs. The rise of communist China as a great power after the end of communism allegedly proved that the implosion of the Soviet Union, far from being historically inevitable, was the unintended consequence of a series of inept political choices. It was not communism but the weakness and naïveté of Gorbachev and other key Soviet leaders that supposedly brought it about. In today's Russia, 'being naïve' is probably the most damning accusation one can level at a politician. It is much worse than being corrupt or ruthless. And 'being naïve' includes believing that innocent political action, without ulterior motives, is possible, or that your former enemies could somehow become intimate friends.

Blaming Moscow's loss of its hard-won superpower status on political naïveté is tantamount to embracing unprincipled cynicism and ruthlessness as pathways to Russia's geopolitical revival. That is not a particularly promising way to forge a better future. In December 2011, at the peak of anti-Kremlin protests on the streets of Moscow and after accusing Hillary Clinton of encouraging the protesters to overthrow the government, Putin told his supporters: 'We are all grown-ups here. We all understand the organizers are acting according to a well-known scenario and in their own mercenary political interests.'[18] Russia's domestic discontent is really an American plot. The most memorable lesson of the unexpected end of the Soviet Union for most Russians may be that history is a series of covert operations. Not the revolutionary masses, apparently, but the cloak-and-dagger intelligence agencies, in both East and West, are the real locomotives of history.

Unlike East Europeans, Russians could not reconcile themselves to their system's collapse by portraying communist authority as a foreign occupation. For them, communism was not rule from abroad. Adding to the strangeness of the USSR's break-up was the fact that it involved the victory of one group of ex-communists over another. The leader of the Revolution, Boris Yeltsin, had been, until quite recently, a member of the Politburo of the Communist Party. Although almost everything else began to change in Russia after 1991, the ruling class remained more or less the same. Not the anti-communists but the ex-communists were the ones who profited most conspicuously from the end of the communist system.

Under certain circumstances, Russians might have been willing to view the defeat of communism as a victory for themselves, even though they had not, like the Poles and others, been liberated from foreign rule. But this would have depended either on a miraculous improvement in their standard of living or on their vast empire being preserved. The latter is what happened in the 1920s when the Bolsheviks, while talking the language of communism and constructing their Party State, succeeded in holding onto a great deal (not all) of the Romanovs' empire. But this miracle of replacing the political system while preserving much of the state's territorial extent was not repeated in the 1990s. For most Russians, a significant improvement in living standards was also postponed for later times. An important reason why regime change did not prove especially popular was that it was accompanied by a harrowing loss of territory and population. Russians were shocked to see their once mighty state turned into a geographically and demographically diminished international beggar, depending for its survival on the goodwill of the West. As a result, Russians refused to endorse the West's self-serving story of 1989–91 as a shared victory without losers. What distinguished an old-regime monarch such as Louis XIV from a modern populist tyrant such as Napoleon was that the former oppressed the people while the latter oppressed them while forcing them to say that they were free.[19] The Russians had a similar experience after 1991. In their view, the West asked them, just as their country was collapsing around them, to celebrate Russia's miraculous 'liberation' from the chains of Soviet rule. This liberal pantomime continued to be performed, with a straight face, for a few years. But the economic crisis of 1998 and NATO's bombing of Yugoslavia, fiercely opposed by Russia, exploded the Western pretence that the end of the Cold War was really a joint victory, shared by the Russian people too. These keenly resented disappointments, and not merely the gravitational pull of the country's allegedly authoritarian DNA, explain why 'Putin came to office determined not to force-feed democracy to Russia.'[20]

UPENDING THE WESTERN NARRATIVE

Putin's Munich 2007 speech was his Declaration of Independence from the self-flattering historical storyline written by the Cold War victors. The dissolution of the Soviet Union, on 25 December 1991, was not experienced as a deliverance by the Russian people. It was not a shared triumph, but a humiliating debacle celebrated only by mortal foes. By acknowledging without euphemism that liberalism's victory over communism represented Moscow's definitive loss of the Cold War, Putin was publicly rejecting the official Western interpretation of 1989–91. The gesture may seem trivial, but it was enormously consequential. By openly speaking of Russia's tragic *defeat*, Putin escaped the clutches of those members of the Yeltsin clan who had engineered his accession to power and who were commonly seen as morally compromised collaborators with the West. By speaking this way, he was soon acclaimed to be the liberator of his people. What he liberated them from was liberal hypocrisy. He allowed his countrymen to stop pretending that 'the transition' was taking Russians to a better place. By the early 2000s, he successfully freed them from a demeaning post-1991 'made in America' hierarchy of values.[21] By the time of the 2014 Crimean annexation, his bare-chested bravado was widely celebrated as having firmly established Russia's independence from the moralistic parochialism of the American-led unipolar world.

In the minds of Western democracy-promoters, Russia, like all countries exiting from communism, wished to imitate the West because it wanted to be like the West. Russians allegedly longed for free and fair elections, the separation of powers and a market economy because they, too, hoped to be free and prosperous like their counterparts in the West. But while overly optimistic Westerners were right that Russia, after 1991, was predestined to imitate the West, they were wrong to assume that the mimic's desire to become like the model is the sole reason for imitation. Russia was undoubtedly weak, but its elites, except for a handful of socially isolated and unrepresentative liberals, were not prepared to accept the kind of moral subordination required from willing imitators of an acknowledged superior.[22] Many members of Russia's political elite, in fact, were dreaming secretly of revenge without regard to strategic gains. As German cultural historian Wolfgang Schivelbusch wrote in his elegant and insightful book *The Culture of Defeat*: 'Losers imitate winners almost by reflex.' But such imitation is not necessarily deferential: 'The borrower is not interested in the soul, the spirit, or the cultural identity of the creditor nation,' he argued.[23] On the contrary, imitative politics can be essentially competitive and conflictual. The defeated may borrow the strategies, procedures, institutions and norms of the enemy, not to mention stealing their breakthroughs in nuclear weapons technology, with the long-term aim of acquiring the arts of victory and turning the tables on their erstwhile vanquishers.

After the controversial elections of 2011–12, the Kremlin stopped seeing the simulation of Western democracy as a makeshift strategy for fending off Western pressure to engage in serious institutional reform or for shoring up domestic support by sidelining political rivals and testing the reliability of local officials. Two decades after the collapse of the Soviet Union, Russia did not abandon the politics of imitation, however. It merely shifted from simulating the West's domestic order to parodying America's international adventurism. With this move, the Kremlin repurposed imitation of the West into a declaration of war against the West. This was a natural switch of venue because war, as a distinguished military theorist has explained, is 'the most imitative of all human activities'.[24]

The most common objects of wartime imitation are the means, modes and aims of conflict. A consequential example, which also provides essential background to our story, is America's self-conscious imitation, in the late 1970s and early 1980s, of Moscow's clandestine support, in the late 1960s and early 1970s, for third-world insurgencies. By lending military aid to the Afghan mujahedeen, the Americans deliberately set out to give Moscow 'its Vietnam'.[25] Since Moscow had helped engineer America's Vietnam, which was its most demoralizing post-First World War military defeat, this operation was explicitly conceived as a tit-for-tat response that the Kremlin would not soon forget. That Moscow would contrive to perpetuate the revenge cycle was presumably understood at the time and unwisely ignored.[26]

One version of wartime imitation involves replicating the strategies of the enemy. A second version, which is our focus here, involves holding up a mirror in which the enemy can observe the immorality and hypocrisy of its own behaviour. Such *mirroring* is an ironic and aggressive way of imitating a rival's objectives and modes of conduct. The aim is to rip off the West's liberal mask and show that the United States, too, contrary to its carefully crafted image, plays in the international arena according to the rules of the jungle.

From Moscow's perspective, the West desired and conspired to break the Soviet Union (and the Warsaw Pact) into bits. In Munich, by way of response, Putin vowed to return the favour. Under his leadership, in fact, the Kremlin has been conspiring to break the Western Alliance and NATO into bits. Information operations are essential to this end. That Putin's anti-NATO and anti-Western talking points are now being echoed verbatim by the White House, whether or not blackmail and side-payments are involved, strongly suggests that *mirroring* is an effective geopolitical tactic. The American President now publicly echoes Moscow's cynically anti-American view that the United States operates internationally with zero regard for the good of mankind.

The Kremlin first experimented with holding up a mirror to the West several years before the 2011–12 elections. In February 2008, one year after his contentious Munich speech, Putin referred to the West's recognition of Kosovo as a 'terrifying precedent' that 'is breaking open the entire system of international relations that have prevailed not just for decades but for centuries. And it without a doubt will bring on itself an entire chain of unforeseen consequences.' The Western powers that recognized Kosovo 'are miscalculating what they are doing,' he said, adding, 'In the end, this is a stick with two ends, and that other end will come back to knock them on the head someday.'[27] The other end of the stick smacked the West in the head a few months thereafter when Russia occupied South Ossetia and Abkhazia after the Russo-Georgian war of August 2008. Savouring the irony, Moscow justified its intervention by adopting America's bright and shiny liberal rhetoric and invoking human rights. This sneering parody of US rationales for foreign intervention was repeated after the annexation of Crimea.[28] As one journalist correctly observed:

> In justifying Russian policies toward Syria and Ukraine, Putin and his supporters have explicitly relied on arguments the Clinton administration used in Kosovo. If NATO can stumble into Yugoslavia's civil war, why can't Russia do the same in Syria? Indeed, Russia is Syria's ally, sworn by treaty to protect its government. And if Saddam Hussein's genocide against Kurds was a reason to violently unseat him from power, then why shouldn't Russia protect persecuted ethnic Russians, as it has claimed to do in Georgia and Ukraine?'[29]

Russia had built Potemkin replicas of Western institutions, such as a constitutional court, in the 1990s because pretending to share liberal-democratic aspirations was a way of appearing agreeable to, and ingratiating its leaders with, the dominant powers of the time. Indeed, this was probably the only available posture for surviving in a world dominated by the West. As Putin consolidated power, Russia shifted to imitating the West in a much more combative style. The Kremlin's new retaliatory form of imitation was meant to discredit the West's over-praised model and make Western societies doubt the superiority of their own norms and institutions. The promise of liberal hegemony was that the world organized around imitation of the West would be a liberal world amenable to American interests. Putin set out to radically rewrite this narrative, transforming imitation of the West into a tool for unpicking the international order that post-Second World War America had so laboriously struggled to create.

SIMULATING DEMOCRACY TO CONSOLIDATE POWER

In the last days of the communist regime, millions of Russians demanded change. Many were open to the promise of democratization but most ordinary people, seven decades after the Russian Revolution, were apprehensive about what regime change and historical rupture would bring. One reasonable fear was that the privileged Soviet elites would fight back, making the general population's exit from history a bloody one. Happily, this did not happen. One reason is that Marx's final gift to the Soviet elites was persuading them not only that capitalism was designed for the predatory self-enrichment of a few but also that Western democracy was a shrewdly constructed system for maintaining class domination. Democracy, viewed in this cynical light, had nothing to do with the accountability of politicians to citizens. On the contrary, the democratic illusion of accountability helped mask and preserve the autonomy of a political ruling class that was never, as a whole, chosen in a fairly contested multi-candidate election.

In the 1990s, of course, the old communist nomenklatura still made up the bulk of the ruling class. Their vague memories of school-book Marxism provided an instruction manual for building capitalism and democracy in post-communist Russia. Instead of fearing the kabuki theatre of sham democracy, the country's survivalist elites cheerfully embraced it. They disliked people protesting on the streets, admittedly, but they championed electoral masquerades as a clever way to rule without a costly resort to repression and with an un-spoken promise that they would be allowed to bequeath all their power and privileges to their children. Fig-leaf democracy also helped post-Soviet elites socialize hypocritically with forgiving global elites and park their families and money safely outside Russia. Foreign visitors to Russia in the 1990s were surprised to encounter people on the street who felt nostalgia for the old regime, especially for the security it provided, while the old elite, having discovered a world of opportunity, spoke enthusiastically about 'democracy' as well as 'capitalism'. This raised the question: Would simulating democracy help democratize Russia or, instead, help perpetuate Russian authoritarianism and Russian oligarchy?

Writing in the context of a disintegrating country and a frightening power vacuum, Moscow political scientist Dmitry Furman was convinced that, while the only democracy Russians could expect in the short run was 'imitation democracy', in the long run, faking democracy would inculcate democratic habits regardless of the will of governing elites. As Perry Anderson observed, Furman 'viewed democracy simply as a normal attribute of a given age of humanity, as literacy, firearms or railways had been of other ages'. In his view, 'There was no way of knowing how Russians would dress, eat, live, work or fear in the future, but it could be predicted with some confidence that they would choose their rulers at the ballot box, take decisions by a majority and guarantee the rights of the minority.'[30] But while Furman was an optimist about the long run, he harboured deep-seated fears when it came to the immediate future of the democratic transition.

Unlike Western and Westernizing optimists, he viewed the disintegration of the USSR less as a golden opportunity than as a serious obstacle to the gradual democratization process on the territory formerly controlled by the Soviet Union. It was in this context that he developed his signature concept of 'imitation democracy'. For him, societies engage in a politics of imitation when they cannot implement in practice the norms they extol in theory. This definition implies that 'imitation democracy' will emerge in countries where the social and cultural conditions for democracy are lacking but where no ideological alternative to democracy exists. This halfway house is not a necessary stage in all processes of democratization, but rather a distinctive type of regime having its place in history next to Tsarism and communism, although certainly more ephemeral. In imitation democracies, politics is a constant struggle between democratic forms and non-democratic substance. At the end of the day, he believed, the democratic façade, because of the psychological expectations it creates, would foster the emergence and stabilization of electorally accountable government. In Furman's theory, therefore, the series of 'colour revolutions' (especially the Rose Revolution in Georgia and the Orange Revolution in Ukraine)[31] that shattered post-Soviet space at the beginning of the twenty-first century were a logical sequel to imitation democracy. It may take decades, but people will eventually take to the streets to protest against regimes that brazenly violate the norms which they publicly endorse.

Gleb Pavlovsky was no theorist of imitation democracy. Instead, he was one of its most prominent practitioners. His life story reads like a Dostoevsky novel. Pavlovsky was born in Odessa on the same date that Stalin was to die two years later. He was a nonconformist who in the 1970s joined the dissident movement. He served his term in prison and struck his not-always-admirable compromises with Soviet power. For him political technology, conceptualized as the art of turning apparitions into realities, was the only way to overcome the governability crisis caused by the unbearable weakness of the post-communist Russian state. He saw his role not as serving power but as conjuring up the illusion that power exists. For this spinmeister, imitating democracy was a strategy for helping the inchoate post-communist Russian state and those charged with running it survive the absence of a well-funded and professionally staffed bureaucratic apparatus adequate to the times and capable of enforcing its decisions.

In 1994, Pavlovsky founded his Foundation for Effective Politics (FEP), a think tank that played a pivotal role in Yeltsin's 1996 Presidential campaign and subsequently in the elections of Vladimir Putin in 2000 and 2004, and finally in Medvedev's election in 2008. After the electoral fiascos of 2011 and 2012, political technology lost its pre-eminent role in Russian statecraft. The Kremlin today seems to have little interest in creating the illusion of a political contest that Putin can triumphantly 'win'. But revisiting the heyday of political technologists like Pavlovsky can nevertheless help us explore the causes and consequences of the faux Westernization that characterized Putin's first decade in power.

In his scandalous political thriller, *The Politologist*, published in 2005 and written in the best tradition of conspiratorial realism, Alexander Prokhanov, then a leader of Russia's patriotic opposition and now a Putin loyalist, gives us the most sinister and at the same time most profound psychological portrait of the kind of Russian political technologist represented by Pavlovsky.[32] He is a creature from hell: talented, cynical, disloyal, ambitious and greedy. He is highly creative and deceptive at the same time. He is hostage to his love of manipulating others. He is the consummate social engineer, but also a tool of Kremlin politics. He is as well a tragic figure – confused, fearful and insecure. The political technologist sees himself as the saviour of Russian democracy. Others see him as its gravedigger.

What distinguishes political consultants in the West from Russian political technologists is that the former work closely with independent media: their tradecraft involves influencing news organizations that they cannot directly control. Political technologists ply a different trade. They are experts in manipulating politically dependent media. Political consultants in the West are experts at winning votes for their candidates. Russian-style political technologists, too, are specialists at winning votes. They take an additional step, however. They also specialize in the 'creative counting' of votes. A political consultant works for one of the parties in an election and does his best to help that party win. The Russian political technologist is not so much interested in the victory of his party as in the victory of 'the system'. His goal is not simply to maximize the vote count for his client, but to obtain an election result as close as possible to the electoral percentage that the Kremlin has planned in advance for a given candidate or party list.

At the height of their influence, political technologists were tasked with maintaining the illusion of competitiveness in Russian politics. As Andrew Wilson puts it, 'Post-Soviet political technologists' would see 'themselves as political meta-programmers, system designers, decision-makers and controllers all in one, applying whatever technology they can to the construction of politics as a whole'.[33] Their role in Russian politics recalled that of Gosplan apparatchiks in the Soviet economy: they were the ideologues and icons of Russia's managed democracy. They operated in

> a world of 'clones' and 'doubles'; of 'administrative resources,' 'active measures,' and 'kompromat' (compromising information); of parties that stand in elections but have no staff or membership or office . . . of well-paid insiders that stand as the regime's most vociferous opponents; and of scarecrow nationalists and fake coups.[34]

Political technologists were, and to a limited extent still are, uncompromising enemies of electoral surprises, genuine party pluralism, political transparency and the freedom of well-informed citizens to participate in the choice of their rulers.

They also play a variety of institutional roles at one and the same time. Wearing his 'grey cardinal' hat, Pavlovsky urged the Kremlin to adopt new legislation that would create a body known as the Public Chamber in order to monitor Russia's NGOs and to marginalize and displace any NGOs that dared display autonomy from the state.

Serving as a policy expert, he supported this move, and then, in his role as an independent political commentator, he explained to the public what a wise policy the Kremlin had initiated. In the end, he became a member of the Public Chamber. The circle was closed.

In Pavlovsky's view, democracy in post-communist Russia was primarily a technology for loosely governing a basically ungovernable society without resorting to excessive physical violence. He saw himself as an emulator of Western ways, admittedly. But he had no interest in the idealized model of democracy that, he believed, Westerners and especially Americans righteously preached. He wanted to do what Westerners were doing and therefore paid no attention to the instructions they were giving. He boasted of peering through the hype and the mirage for the real thing – eating the candy and tossing away the wrapper, to paraphrase Putin's advisor and Pavlovsky's boss, Vladislav Surkov. Pavlovsky took his cues from 'really existing' democracy (as he understood it) not from the schoolbook idealization celebrated by political children. He assumed that he had more to learn from a cynical spin-doctor such as Paul Manafort than from quixotic theories of accountable government.

Understanding the political technologists' interactions with Western political consultants who came to help 'build democracy' in Russia is also critical for understanding the complex nature of post-communist imitation games. In the aftermath of the Kremlin's meddling in the 2016 Presidential elections in the US, American political commentator Anne Applebaum blamed Paul Manafort for importing Russian political technologies, hatched in KGB laboratories, into American politics. But the true story is not quite so one-sided. Russians learned at least some of their dirty tricks from the American consultants who came to teach them political marketing. Stalin and other Soviet leaders were accomplished liars, of course, but they seldom bothered to focus their mendacity on electoral politics. Before becoming an American import *from* Russia, therefore, a sophisticated form of post-truth democracy was arguably America's export *to* Russia.

Russian political technologists immediately grasped the central role being played in contemporary democracies by the application of commercial advertising techniques to electoral campaigns. Subliminal appeals are crafted to put the critical faculties of voters to sleep – to smear rivals, magnify fears, and wildly over-promise – and thereby to increase the number of votes for the candidate or party being puffed. Candidates are not screened by peers who have worked with them for decades but instead are selected freely by poorly informed and easily manipulated voters who saw them for the first time a few months earlier on television. This exposes the entire 'democratic' process to behind-the-scenes manipulation, which is exactly what political technologists understood and appreciated. Rachel Boynton's 2005 documentary, *Our Brand is Crisis*, shows very clearly how American political consultants promote democracy in post-authoritarian regimes by exporting 'the vicious arts by which elections are too often carried'.[35] Although the film concerns Bolivia, its lessons are easily applicable to post-communist Russia.

The anti-American turn taken by the Russian authorities who freely borrowed campaign gimmicks and ruses from US political consultants is a grim example of what Hannah Arendt labelled the 'boomerang effect'.[36] American political consultants helped Russia's political technologists learn the vicious arts by which elections are often carried, thereby increasing the popular legitimacy of the Kremlin's power that is now being wielded with evident success against American democracy itself. Having learned the Jedi mind-games pioneered by American political marketers, the Russians who continue to orchestrate covert operations to influence US elections are presumably unimpressed by claims that they are violating the sacred integrity of American democracy.

It is tempting to view 'imitation democracy' – or what the Kremlin used to call 'managed democracy' – simply as a cynical ploy of post-communist elites to deprive people of political representation. But talking to Pavlovsky gives one a much more complicated view of its origins.[37] The collapse of communism was simultaneously the collapse of the Soviet state. This left Russian society decapitated, thrown back onto informal networks alone and, compared to the past half century, essentially shapeless. Even if Russian elites had believed in political representation, they would not have been able to identify which social groupings should be represented. Representative government assumed a society less pulverized by decades of communist rule and more clearly configured than Russia was in the wake of 1991.

In Pavlovsky's view, imitation democracy was a response to the unprecedented challenge of recreating popular trust in political authority in a demoralized, disorganized and distrustful society where elites were accumulating fabulous wealth in mysterious ways. Gazprom (a massive, government-controlled natural-gas company) and Channel One of the Russian State Television service were the only organized forces keeping the country together. Imitation democracy was not simply the brainchild of cynics, therefore. It was, instead, a last-ditch strategy born of desperation.

When reading opinion polls in preparation for Yeltsin's 1996 re-election campaign, Pavlovsky was struck by the discovery that the polarity of democracy-versus-authoritarianism that Western observers tried to impose on Russian politics did not exist in the minds of Russian voters. What people wanted was a combination of democracy and authoritarianism. They wanted a very strong government that could keep Russia territorially united and restore its great-power status but at the same time a state that would respect its citizens and not interfere in their private lives. Pavlovsky decided to dedicate himself to building such a state. It would not have to be spectacularly competent in the art of governance since most Russians don't think of politics as a way of improving their lives.[38] But it would have to project an imposing public image. His project was not simply to help Yeltsin's chosen successor accede to power. For him, the 2000 Presidential election was a God-sent opportunity to reinvent the Russian state. The goal was to create a political regime where the legitimacy of those in power came less from the rulers' ability to represent the people and deliver palpable results than from the impossibility of imagining any alternative to the current political leadership, even though the policies adopted under a long-serving leader would shift unpredictably from time to time.

In explaining the inspiration for his strategy, Pavlovsky likes to tell a story about an ordinary voter he interviewed during the run-up to the 1996 election. The voter reported that she supported Gennady Zyuganov, the Communist Party candidate, but was going to vote for Yeltsin. When he asked her why she wasn't going to vote for Zyuganov, she replied, 'When Zyuganov is president, I will vote for him.'[39]

It turns out that people often support, or at least accept, rulers not for what they do but simply because of the offices they inhabit or titles they hold. 'Popularity' in Russia is a consequence not a cause of the power one wields. Instead of representing people's interests, elections register the willingness of voters to submit to incumbents who are able to sideline any and all challengers to their power.

The manufactured absence of plausible alternatives makes Putin's 'popularity' impossible to measure in an absolute sense, although its ups and downs can be tracked over time. Admittedly, public acceptance of Putin's rule during his first decade in power depended as much on the prosperity and stability that he delivered after a decade of misery and turmoil as on the 'no alternative' impression inculcated by political technologists.[40] People appreciated it – just like any nation would – and still today are distrustful of political 'trouble-makers', convinced as they are that a declining status quo is preferable to experimental change.[41] This seems to be the mentality that reconciles Putin's supporters to his no-alternative legitimacy formula.

HOW RIGGED ELECTIONS WORK

In an attempt to explain the Russian Revolution to Lady Ottoline Morrell, British philosopher Bertrand Russell once remarked that Bolshevik despotism, appalling though it was, seemed the right sort of government for Russia. 'If you ask yourself how Fyodor Dostoevsky characters should be governed, you will understand', was his not-so-subtle point. In explaining the recent resurgence of authoritarianism in Russia, many commentators invoke Russia's authoritarian political culture, allegedly inhospitable to liberal democracy.[42] But whatever the merit of cultural determinism, it fails to make sense of the central role played by rigged elections in Putin's political system. That is no minor defect since it is simply impossible to make sense of Putin's Russia without taking electoral manipulation into account.

Comparing rigged elections in post-communist Russia to show trials in Stalin's Soviet Union may at first seem far-fetched, but it turns out to be quite revealing. Why revolutionary heroes were willing to confess to crimes they had not committed and how this legal charade contributed to Stalin's power are central mysteries of the 1930s, captured best in Arthur Koestler's *Darkness at Noon*.[43] The 'show trials' were intended to demonstrate universal loyalty and love of the tortured for the torturer. In today's relatively soft regime, those under prosecution for political infractions are defiant and can hire good lawyers. As a result, their trials do not provide an inspiring spectacle for the general public. In compensation, the Kremlin resorts to show elections. To understand these, we should ask: Why did Putin need elections if only a minority of Russians believed that Russia was becoming a democracy and almost no one outside Moscow believed that Russia was already one?[44] Why did Putin regularly rig presidential and legislative elections when he was well positioned to win them even if competition had been free and fair? And why did the Kremlin rig elections in a manner so flagrant that nobody could doubt that they were being rigged (by barring potentially appealing candidates, for example) and that the Kremlin was doing the rigging? What makes this democratic masquerade so fascinating is that it did not really aim to deceive.

In the period 2000–2012, Putin fashioned a political regime in which elections were both meaningless and indispensable. That elections are 'engineered', as Julia Ioffe has remarked, is 'something everyone in Russia, no matter what their rhetoric or political persuasion, knows and accepts'.[45] The dubious invalidation of signatures and disqualification of candidates, the stuffing of ballot boxes, the miscounting of votes, a monopoly on media, smear campaigns – these have been staples of all Russian elections during the three postcommunist decades.

At the outset of the twenty-first century, then, most Russians knew that, when it came to elections, the fix was in. The Kremlin had a monopoly on television coverage of politics. It also decided which political forces Russian businessmen could finance. But most people sensed that, had the electoral process been free and fair, Putin would have come out on top anyway, due to the prosperity and stability he was delivering. This was enough to reconcile most voters to a swirl of corruption, inequality, injustice and elections with pre-ordained results. By making all these seem 'normal', moreover, the Kremlin was able to paint would-be reformers as dangerously utopian dreamers. Even when labelling Putin 'the most sinister figure in contemporary Russian history', a leading spokesman for the Russian human rights movement reluctantly admitted some years ago that 'Putin would have won the campaigns of 2000 and 2004 – though perhaps without such large, unseemly margins – even if they had been free of vote tampering and the illegal use of the government's so-called 'administrative resources', and if the candidates had actually had equal access to the voters through television and the press.[46]

Yet Putin could not have gained and maintained his power without resorting to periodically rigged elections. This paradox may be post-communist Russia's most closely guarded secret. No historian treats periodic elections as consequential or even conspicuous events in the history of the Soviet Union. No Russian remembers anything about electoral results under communism. By contrast, the story of post-communist Russia is, in some fundamental sense, the story of its elections and the deep political shifts they registered and wrought. Yet Putin-era elections have been anti-democratic in a basic sense. Rather than giving active citizens a voice in the exercise of power, they were meant to increase the sway of the Kremlin over essentially passive citizens.

In the Kremlin's approach to exercising and maintaining power from 2000 to 2010, engineered elections performed several critical functions which fair elections, even if Putin had won them, would not have so successfully achieved. Russia's rigged elections were transparently inadequate imitations of Western democracy. But they were not just a decorative façade. Nor were they simply meant to persuade clueless Western monitors that Russia was slowly making the transition to democracy or to provide arguments with which the West could convince itself that Russia was already a democracy of sorts. Instead, rigged elections were functioning gears in the machinery by which Putin exercised and maintained his power.

First of all, as Pavlovsky foresaw, periodic elections helped construct and drive home, on a regular basis, the 'no alternative' rationale for Putin's rule. A 2007 Levada-Center poll reported that 35 per cent of respondents said that they 'trusted' Putin because they did 'not see anybody else to rely on'.[47] Sceptics at the time were right to question how much electoral results told us about Putin's vote-getting power, given that no serious alternatives were ever allowed to appear on the ballot. Indeed, polling in 2011 confirmed the thesis that Putin's 'popularity' reflected public 'inertia' and 'a lack of other alternatives'.[48] But this is exactly the point. If voters could be convinced that no feasible alternative to the current leadership existed, they would adapt fatalistically to the status quo. That explains why the political technologists in the Kremlin spent so much time disqualifying and side-lining even vaguely plausible alternatives to Putin, and making sure he ran against palpably unattractive sham opponents such as Vladimir Zhirinovsky and Gennady Zyuganov. Their exaggerated fear of relatively weak challengers with no independent political base reflected the insecurity they felt about Putin's grip on popular favour. They wanted to make sure that no counter-elite of any kind was ever allowed to form or build an electoral base. Public disappointment and frustration with the system could not simply be crushed by intimidation and force. Instead, disappointment with the government had to be artfully managed by increasing the collective-action problems hobbling opponents of the regime. Fraudulent elections provided the 'site' or context in which this dicey management – including the periodic splintering of politically hostile voting blocs, the cyclical building up and tearing down of rival coalitions, and the regular purging of potentially credible competitors before they gained momentum – occurred.

Rigged elections also provided periodic opportunities for the ostensible party of power to rebrand itself. By coining new slogans and even introducing new faces, Putin's United Russia Party was able to present itself as a force for both stability and change.[49] Political marketing is premised on the insight that sellers can keep the attention of buyers only if the former occasionally offer products that are new – or at least repackaged to look new. 'People vote for the spectacle, not for the routine,' remarked French marketing guru Jacques Séguéla: 'All elections are dramaturgical.'[50] In the Russian case, this has been spectacularly true.

Rigged elections were also at the heart of Putin's constantly re-negotiated contract not with the people but with regional elites. In the absence of either a serious party of power (like China's Communists) or a well-organized and efficient bureaucracy, elections served as the principal instrument for controlling the country's political elite and recruiting new cadres while minimizing the risk of dangerous splits in its ranks. Russia's *vybori bez vybora* (elections without a choice) functioned like full-dress military manoeuvres or rehearsals for actual 'combat', including shooting at simulated targets and the certainty that the government's side would emerge victorious. Rigged elections helped gauge the readiness of crack troops, and tested which regional leaders were competent and dependable and which were not. Local officials were required not simply to profess their loyalty but also to demonstrate their capacity to exercise control by delivering desirable electoral results. Their ability to stuff ballots or falsify tabulations could be field-tested, as could their capacity to force-march students or public-sector workers to the polls. What the regime gathered from a rigged election was information about which lower-level officials and party members were playing or bungling their assigned roles.

During the first decade of the twenty-first century, periodic elections also served to demonstrate (that is, to exaggerate) Russia's national unity and to dramatize the imagined coherence and solidarity of Putin country. Russia is an orderly federal state according to its constitution, a highly centralized state according to Kremlin rhetoric, and a chaotically fractured, disunited and feudalized entity in the way power is actually exercised in much of the country. Russia's fraudulent elections were critical not simply for disciplining the local cadres of United Russia and constructing a political space in which Putin and his ruling circle could appear to be the only plausible choice. They also gave a psychological boost to the otherwise dubious political unity of the nation at a moment when many Russians viewed the current borders of the country as temporary, when a majority could not identify Russia's national day or say what happened on that date, and when the only collective experience that people could recall with pride was the Soviet victory over Nazism. On periodically scheduled election days, unlike every other day of the year, Russian citizens were called to act in unison, to do something together. Even when elections were rigged and the outcome was known in advance, voters across the country's far-flung regions traipsed to the polls. They did so, arguably, to demonstrate their loyalty not only to the leader but also to the unity of this exceptionally diverse political space. The geographer's map of Russia is a vast, discontinuous landmass stitched loosely together out of multicoloured patches. The electoral map of Russia turns these swatches, symbolically if briefly, into a coherent political whole. For ordinary Russians, haunted by the sudden demolition of the Soviet house where they were born, rigged elections, in which Chechnya voted 95 per cent (and higher!) for Putin and the government's United Russia Party, provided psychological reassurance that the country retained its territorial integrity, however fraught and frayed.

Another function of Russia's rigged elections during the first Putin decade was to draw a line between the 'loyal opposition' and what the Kremlin saw as a fifth column of enemies and traitors. In this context, the essential political struggle in Russia involved and still involves not power-wielders vying for the approval of the people but a few wealthy citizens and many low-level officials vying for the approval of the powerful. Registration of parties or independent candidates by the Central Election Commission equalled permission to undertake political activity. Elections, in this sense, presuppose a calculated political decision about where to draw the line between the harmless opposition (which is legalized) and the dangerous opposition (which is outlawed). The refusal by the Commission to register a political coalition functions as a clear warning: funding or supporting a banished faction is tantamount to sabotaging the system. The biggest challenge for Putin's adversaries has not been winning an election but simply being registered to contest one.[51] Seen from the Kremlin's perspective, the elections held in the first decade of the twenty-first century provided ideal occasions for purging and refreshing the list of licensed opposition candidates and parties.

Finally (and flipping the popular cliché on its head), Putin's rigged elections served not to mimic democracy, but rather to imitate authoritarianism. This suggests that Putin-era show elections had a demonstration effect once again vaguely analogous to, though certainly far less murderous than, that of the Stalin-era show trials. Sham elections allowed Putin to display his ability to manipulate the accreditation, nomination and voting process in an orderly and predictable way and thereby, paradoxically, to demonstrate his authoritarian credentials as a man who can get things done. Rigged elections, known to be rigged, were not only an act of defiance in the face of Western pretentions to 'supervise' Russia's political makeover after 1991. They were also the cheapest and easiest way for the regime to show that it was not afraid of 'colour revolutions' of the sort that broke out in Georgia in 2003 and Ukraine in 2004, since blatant rigging dared dissatisfied citizens to stick their heads above the parapet and openly challenge the regime. If no one protested in the face of such flagrant doctoring of electoral results, the implication was that society obediently accepted the regime in place.

Rigging an election also allowed the government to mimic the authoritarian power that it did not actually possess and thus to bolster its faltering grip on the country, or at least give itself a bit more breathing room. Keen to avoid any appearance of weakness and aware that public support can be artificially inflated by the illusion of power, Putin's team was attracted to theatrical displays that required little capacity to stage but gave spectators an outsized sense of what the government could achieve. What 'managed democracy' simulated, in other words, was not democracy but management. It took only modest administrative capacity to rig an election; it was certainly easier to engineer elections than to provide a high-quality education to Chechen youth. But rigged voting, in a country where Soviet-era 'elections' lingered in memory as a symbol of irresistible power, allowed a corrupt regime incapable of addressing the country's problems or making and implementing policies in the public interest to imitate a degree of autocratic authority and to present itself as omnipresent and all-seeing. In Putin's first decade in power, organizing a pseudo-election was like wearing sheep's clothing to prove that you are a wolf.

Fixed elections were the instrument that allowed Putin and his clique to rule without having to confront the enormous challenges of governing a country beset by so many seemingly unmanageable problems. Such elections were well adapted to the nature of a regime that was neither exploiting the people (as in China's export industry today) nor trying to 'remake' the people (as in the Soviet Union of old) but rather was placating them with relative prosperity and stability and afterwards ignoring them while amassing astronomical riches from the sale of Russia's natural resources abroad. Incapacity-hiding, not capacity-building, was (and remains) at the heart of Putin's statecraft. It has allowed him to exercise uncontrolled power with minimal resort to force. As Furman asserted, 'no tsar or general secretary had ever enjoyed such power in society based so little on fear.'[52] Functioning in 'democratic' framework, Putin could not put 100,000 people in prison in order to secure his unchecked power. But he could arrest a few and make sure that other potential challengers got the message.

In 1953, appalled by the way the communist government of East Germany had reacted to a workers' protest, Berthold Brecht wrote a poem called 'Solution' ('*Die Lösung*') suggesting that if the government was so disappointed with the people, the government should simply dissolve the existing people and elect a new one. For all practical purposes, this is what Russian authorities have been doing. Every few years, they use administrative measures to shape and select a voting public to the government's liking. Rather than representing the voters, these rigged elections were meant to exaggerate the effectiveness of power to a public both intimidated and reassured.

THE IMITATION TRAP

Yet imitation democracy, according to Furman, is more exposed to self-subversion than its architects in Moscow initially understood. When a government promotes the illusion that citizens are choosing their rulers, he believed, it is laying the groundwork for future colour revolutions.

Alexei Slapovsky's 2010 novel, *March on the Kremlin*, opens with a young poet accidentally killed by a policeman. Not knowing whom to blame and what to do, the poet's mother picks up the body, cradles her dead son in her arms, and walks almost unconsciously towards the Kremlin. Her son's friends and several strangers trail close behind. Alerted via social media that something is happening, other people start to arrive. Most of them are not really sure why they have come out onto the streets. They do not have a common platform, a common dream or a common leader; yet they are held together by a conviction that 'enough is enough'. They are excited by the fact that, at long last, something is happening. The Special Forces fail to stop them. The march suddenly reaches the Kremlin. And then . . . the people go back home.[53]

The real-world version of these events unfolded in Russia in December 2011. In that year, Moscow witnessed its largest protests since 1993. Manipulated legislative elections, not a poet's death, provided the spark that ignited the crowd's anger. But the protesters shared one important characteristic with the disaffected marchers in Slapovsky's novel: they seemed to emerge out of nowhere, taking almost everyone – including perhaps themselves – by surprise. The protesters were composed of an almost unimaginable congregation of liberals, nationalists, and leftists who had likely never spoken to each other and who for a few dizzying weeks dared to begin imagining life without Putin.

Asked if the Kremlin was surprised by the unfolding of events, a senior United Russia functionary, Yuri Kotler, responded: 'Well, imagine if your cat came to you and started talking. First of all, it's a cat, and it's talking. Second, all these years, the government fed it, gave it water, petted it, and now it's talking and demanding something. It's a shock.'[54] Political technology, based on the conviction that 'democracy' was simply a non-violent strategy for sustaining elite rule, was being put to the test by a public that, inexplicably, believed democracy gave the people the right to talk back.

The explosion of protest in Russia seems in retrospect to have been simultaneously inevitable and impossible. It was born out of a sense of injured pride, not deteriorating standards of living.[55] Protesters were irate at the brazenly shameless way in which Medvedev and Putin privately decided to swap positions in 2008. True, when Putin chose to return to the Kremlin in 2012, afraid that the constraints of Western-style constitutionalism were starting to threaten Russia's interests (as he understood them), no one was especially surprised. Everyone knew that Russia only pretended to be a democracy. What fuelled the demonstrations, therefore, was not a sudden realization that electoral results were engineered by the Kremlin. What drove the protesters onto the streets of Moscow was the cavalier breaking of a political understanding that had previously been in place. Since the collapse of the Soviet Union, voters in the Russian Federation had pretended to choose their rulers and in exchange the rulers pretended to rule by popular consent. By deciding to reclaim the Presidency as if it were his personal property, Putin dropped the pretences. The casualness of the act was less a violation of the popular will than an affront to popular self-respect. Public opinion obviously mattered not a bit. The winter protests of 2011–12 seemed to confirm Furman's claim about the internal instability of fake democracy. They provided tantalizing evidence for his prediction that ephemeral regimes of this sort would end when the democratic 'word' became 'flesh' and an awakened electorate poured onto the streets to defeat the outdated authoritarian machinery.

But Furman's hoped-for democratic awakening never materialized. In the next few years, Russia's simulation of democracy did not morph into a triumph of the democratic façade over the authoritarian apparatus operating behind the scenes, but the other way around. As in Slapovsky's novel, the demonstrators just went home.

From 1991 to 2011, roughly speaking, simulating Western democratic forms had been the Kremlin's low-cost and minimum-effort strategy for exaggerating a chronically weak state's reputation for power as well as shielding the wealth of regime insiders. In the first post-communist decade, *trompe l'oeil* democracy was a defensive weapon, pacifying low-information proselytizers from the West and making Russia look respectable as it bargained fitfully with Europeans and Americans. The official line, also spun for Western consumption, was that the country was trying to be a democracy but it was simply taking more time than expected. This was the message contained in Putin's First Inaugural Address of 2000:

> Today is really an historic day, I want one more time to focus on this. In fact, for the first time in the history of our country, in the history of Russia, for the first time the supreme power in the country was transferred in the most democratic and simplest way, by the will of people, legally and peacefully. The change of power – a check of the constitutional system, a test of its strength. Yes, it is not the first test, and obviously not the last, but it is a test. It is a milestone in our lives of which we have proved worthy. We have proved that Russia is becoming

a modern democratic state. A peaceful succession of power – an essential element of political stability, which we dreamed of with you, to which we aspired, which we sought.[56]

It's true that Putin's accession to the presidency was peaceful. But the assertion that power was transferred by the will of the people is a bedtime story. He was selected by the Yeltsin team after he had helped repress an anti-Yeltsin insurgency engineered by then Prime Minister Evgeny Primakov and supported by independently elected governors as well as by Yuri Skuratov, the Procurator General who was investigating corruption in Yeltsin's family and entourage. Having established his bona fides by capably shielding regime insiders from an anti-corruption campaign launched by political rivals, Putin was handed the presidency on a silver platter. Because this was perfectly obvious at the time, Putin's genuflection to 'the will of the people' showed only how comfortable the Kremlin had become with democratic hypocrisy.

In the context of multilateral summits, façade democracy gave Russia the vague aura of being a modern power. But, terrified by the global wave of colour revolutions (beginning with the 2003 Rose Revolution in Georgia and the 2004–5 Orange Revolution in Ukraine), Russian leaders slowly realized that simulating democracy might eventually destabilize a regime that engaged in it too flagrantly and wantonly.

The first decade of Putin's presidency coincided with the second phase of post-communist Russia's imitation of the West. In this period, the legitimacy of the ruling coterie was based on the fact that demonstrably rigged elections were followed by the public's tacit acquiescence. This kind of wink-and-nod legitimacy became unsustainable during the protests of the 2011 legislative election. The absolute number of protesters was not high, but they had substantial support in opinion polls, and the Kremlin was feeling under pressure at the time from an economic slowdown that threatened its ability to manage public discontent. The frantic search for a new legitimacy formula to replace 'rigged-elections-without-protest' began immediately after Putin returned to the presidency in the spring of 2012. This search led directly to the Crimea annexation, which filled the streets of Moscow with cheers, not protests, and subsequently to the bloody proxy war in eastern Ukraine. Russia's annexation of Crimea was the most momentous (though not the last) act in the post-protest transformation of Putin's regime. What started as the anti-Putin protests of 'Occupy Abay' in 2012[57] turned into the pro-Putin celebrations of 'Re-occupy Crimea' in 2014.

What motivated Putin's improvised Ukraine gambit was not so much fear of NATO warships in the Black Sea as fear that disenchanted Muscovites might imitate what he imagined to be remote-controlled street protests in Kiev. As United States ambassador to the Russian Federation Michael McFaul recalls in his memoirs, Putin seems never to have doubted that the 2011–12 anti-government street demonstrations in Moscow, like those that took place in Ukraine first in 2004 and then in 2013–14, were sponsored and orchestrated by the West. He also believed that their goal was, if not thoroughgoing regime change, at least his personal removal from power. As McFaul wrote, 'in Putin's world the masses never acted on their own. Rather, they were tools, instruments, or levers to be manipulated.' Indeed, Putin 'saw the US as a promoter of regime change around the world, including in Russia. Putin blamed the United Sates for everything bad in the world and in Russia.'[58] He was also bothered by the unseemly readiness of his own elite, some of them Kremlin insiders, to collaborate openly with the 2011–12 protesters. Putin concluded not only, like Furman, that his fake democratic regime was vulnerable but also that the West was malevolently plotting to exploit that vulnerability. Coincidentally, his pronouncements tend to echo the twentieth-century Russian publicist Ivan Ilyin's idea that the West's objective has always been to 'dismember Russia in order to force it under Western control, to dismantle it and finally to make it disappear'.[59] Containment was not a new Western strategy developed towards Soviet communism after the Second World War. It was instead, according to Ilyin, part of the West's traditional policy towards Russia, which included promoting a culturally and geographically inappropriate democratic form of government in Russia that could result only in weakening the country. After the politically embarrassing and stressful 2011 and 2012 elections, mimicking the West's domestic institutions and slogans stopped being the regime's preferred method for sheltering itself from Western influence. The Russian regime needed to go on the offensive not in order to reclaim its position as a global super-power but simply in order to survive. To that end, it even dreamed of destroying the American-created post-1989 liberal order. American support for the 2010–12 Arab Spring and especially the NATO-led military intervention in Libya confirmed the Kremlin's darkest fears that the United States is a revolutionary power with which Putin's Russia could not peaceably coexist. The path it chose was surpris-ing, however. To subvert Western hegemony, Russia did not abandon but refashioned, redirected and weaponized its strategy of imitating the West.

AN ANGRY MAN ON CRUTCHES

In a speech made on 8 January 1962 that remained secret for more than forty years, Soviet leader Nikita Khrushchev announced to his Kremlin colleagues that the Soviets were so thoroughly outmatched in the superpower struggle that Moscow's only option was to seize the initiative in international affairs. Some decades from now, future archivists may unearth a similar speech delivered by President Vladimir Putin to his inner circle in February 2014. This is when he decided to shock the West by annexing Crimea and proving he could get away with it. This lightning move also allowed him to obscure the humiliating fact that Russia had just lost Ukraine. Most strikingly, it successfully staunched the haemorrhaging of popular support for his regime. Some of his public rhetoric at the time might lead one to con-clude that ethnic Russian nationalism played an important role in the decision to annex Crimea. And it is true that Kremlin ironists must have enjoyed the poetic reversal of Moscow coming to the rescue of a 'captive nation'. But one must remember that Putin is to some extent a Soviet man and that, however much he blames the West, he also realizes that ethno-nationalism played a central role in ripping the Soviet Union apart.

Studies of imitative behaviour in the animal world describe anti-predatory camouflage whereby hunted animals modify their appearance to blend invisibly into the background, hoping to avoid detection by predators. This is a very helpful concept for understanding the first phase of imitation democracy in Russia in the 1990s and early 2000s. By feigning a desire to conform to a Western *political* model, the Russian government was able to preserve its power to restructure the economy (often for corrupt purposes) at a time of great weakness and vulnerability. But this strategy of survival did not convey a sense of victory. Passing for a democracy in the eyes of near-sighted observers can help you survive, but not to effectively stand up to the West or invoke national exceptionalism as a source of political legitimacy.

The Crimean annexation was, fundamentally, a bid to re-legitimize a system that was losing its credibility. It did this by demonstrating that Moscow could defy the West with impunity. The spectacle of an unopposed violation of international norms replaced the spectacle of an unopposed violation of democratic norms. Small successful wars fought in symbolically important places like Crimea turned out to have a bigger political pay-off than winning rigged elections. Putin's brazen defiance of Western norms and expectations gave his regime a greater boost than ethno-nationalism or any strategic gains achieved by 'returning' Crimea to the motherland. Against those who 'pursue only one goal – to destroy Russia as a nation', as Putin said in his election victory speech of 2012, 'we have demonstrated that nobody can impose anything on us. Nobody can impose anything.'[60] The Crimea annexation proved the point. Putin had staged a sovereignty drama. It was a one-man performance and the public's applause was thunderous. Restoring Russia's strength and sovereignty, meaning its de facto independence from Western influence, remains today the fundamental theme of Putin's public discourse. 'Efforts to contain Russia have failed, face it,' he repeated in 2018. 'Nobody listened to us. Listen now.'[61]

Such hypersensitivity and pushiness suggest that Russia's geopolitical adventures post-2012 were (and are) driven largely by its leadership's deep anxiety about the country's weakness vis-à-vis the West. Russia is bereft of soft power, its economy is uncompetitive, its petrodollar-subsidized living standards are stagnant and plummeting, and its population is ageing and dwindling. The socially untethered elite is deeply distrusted by ordinary men and women. So finding some way to anchor state power in popular sentiments remains the leadership's central dilemma. The Kremlin became aware that combustible emotions are just as important for its legitimacy as combustible hydrocarbons. It helps to remember that Putin's first interview after he assumed the presidency included the following claim: 'there is harsh competition taking place not only on the market place, but also between governments, on the international arena. I am very sorry to say – for it is very worrying – but we are not listed in the top ranks of leaders in this competition.'[62] Putin's self-assigned task from the beginning, therefore, was to revive Russia's role as a serious player in the Great Game from which Moscow had been unceremoniously ejected in 1991. The 2008 Russo-Georgian War was a dress rehearsal. But pursuing this goal by foreign-policy adventurism began in earnest only after 2012.

Moscow's relative weakness as a global power does not mean that Russia should not be taken seriously, or that its success in restoring part of its global relevance – as Assad's supplier of security and Germany's supplier of gas – should be underestimated. But, unlike China, Russia cannot be defined as a classic rising power. Its global weight is minimal compared to the influence once exerted by the Soviet Union, and while it has succeeded in improving its position in the short term, its long-term prospects as a global heavyweight are questionable. The Crimea annexation enhanced Putin's legitimacy, but the intervention in Syria has left most Russians indifferent, and Russia's still small but growing (and costly) involvement in Africa and Latin America is not known or appreciated by the broader public. What cannot be doubted, though, is the Kremlin's capacity to play a spoiler's role on the global stage.

Admittedly, today relative power is frustratingly hard to measure, due to what columnist David Brooks has called 'the revolt of the weak'.[63] America's overwhelming military superiority has driven its challengers not into docile submission but into adopting forms of asymmetrical warfare that effectively shift the battle to terrain where the US's war-fighting pre-eminence is inconsequential. According to a remarkable Harvard study, the weaker side in asymmetric wars waged between 1800 and 1849 achieved their strategic goals only 12 per cent of the time. (Researchers measure 'strength' by number of soldiers and magnitude of firepower.) In the wars that erupted between 1950 and 1998, by contrast, the weaker side prevailed a start-ling 55 per cent of the time.[64] The explanation most commonly given for this ascendancy of the weak is that, especially in the second half of the twentieth century, the less powerful side need not defeat or destroy its enemy but only hold out, usually on home turf. It need merely sabotage the gears of the enemy machine and wait for a nom-inally superior adversary to lose its appetite for the conflict. Not the conqueror, therefore, but the thwarter seems to be, for the moment, the signature figure of modern war.

In its confrontation with the West, Russia is undoubtedly the weaker party. But it has effectively used spoiler tactics to take the initiative and thereby define and shape the conflict in accord with its own interests and world-view. It has succeeded by taking advantage of the West's relative passivity and disengagement, postures which predate the Trump presidency. The Kremlin's dizzying game of escal-ation and de-escalation in eastern Ukraine and its military intervention in Syria have shown that Putin has made obstructionism and unpredictability his weapons of choice.

Until the Crimean annexation, Russia's politics of imitation cen-tred on the mimicry of the West's domestic institutions, most notably periodic elections. This strategy had the unintended and unwelcome side effect of planting in the public mind hopes of government trans-parency and accountability that could be used to criticize and attack a government that sustained itself by rigged elections. It opened the government, on the domestic front, to rumblings about hypocrisy, about the insulting gap between the pretence of respecting voters and the non-existence of a genuinely political society where citizens would be treated with 'dignity'. This is what led to the massive demonstra-tions against electoral rigging in 2011–12, where the slogan 'Civic dignity' ('*Dostoinstvo*') was used by the protesters to discredit the legitimation formula on which the regime had previously relied.

After 2012, the Kremlin jettisoned its attempts to shore up its domestic legitimacy by imitating Western-style democracy. Rigged elections continue to take place, but they no longer serve as weight-bearing pillars of the regime's popularity and authority. The displacement of the politics of imitation to the international arena meant that the Kremlin would henceforth be spared public discontent and accusations of hypocrisy for failing to live up to its democratic pretences. The new purpose was to discredit the Western-dominated international order by exposing its fundamental hypocrisy. The tone of the new approach was sarcastic: Americans give lip-service to international law, we are told, but act according to 'the rule of the gun'. Responding to Western criticisms of the Crimea annexation, Putin quipped: 'They say we are violating norms of international law. Firstly, it's a good thing that they at least remember that there exists such a thing as international law – better late than never.'[65] Instead of Moscow's rebellious crowds teaching Putin a lesson, Putin, with the crowd at his back, was going to teach the West a lesson. By insisting on Russia's cultural and political exceptionalism, this new approach also provided a moral basis for rejecting out of hand all the condescending lectures that the West had been giving Russians since 1991. As a retired Russian military officer, proud that Putin had restored Russia's prestige by annexing Crimea and fighting for the Donetsk separatists against the Ukrainian government, told a visiting journalist: 'I want a Russian idea for the Russian people; *I don't want the Americans to teach us how to live.* I want a strong country, one you can be proud of. I want life to have some meaning again.'[66] Thanks to Putin, Russia had stopped taking lessons from the United States, meaning it had stopped being 'an imitation democracy with an inferiority complex'.[67] Its inferiority complex had by no means vanished, but the Kremlin was no longer going to cope with it by simulating democracy. Instead, it was going to use 'daring aggression to mask weakness, to avenge deep resentments, and, at all costs, to survive'.[68]

A half-decade earlier, in 2007 (the same year that Putin delivered his jaw-dropping Munich speech), Nikita Mikhalkov, the celebrated Russian film director and well-known Putin ally, released a fascinating film. A remake of Stanley Lumet's 1957 classic *Twelve Angry Men*, Mikhalkov's *12* represents an overture to the next, more aggressive phase of Russia's imitation of the West, a phase which was to begin in earnest only years later after the protest winter of 2011–12 which, as we have been arguing, led by a circuitous route to the annexation of Crimea.

In Lumet's *Twelve Angry Men*, an eighteen-year-old Puerto Rican boy is on trial for stabbing his father to death. If found guilty, he will be executed. Impatient to finish their deliberations quickly, eleven jurors agree that the boy's guilt is self-evident, while the twelfth juror (played by Henry Fonda) stands up to the stampede and, claiming that he has 'a reasonable doubt', begins a process of picking apart the state's evidence until, after much back-and-forth, the boy is acquitted.

Appearing regularly on lists of the greatest Hollywood movies of all time, *Twelve Angry Men* is a classic expression of American liberalism. It is a symphony of praise for the power of free individuals to fight for truth and against class and ethnic prejudice. It is a cinematic tribute to rational argument, attention to evidence and disinterested justice. Produced in the wake of McCarthyism, it remains a powerful if highly stylized defence of American liberal values.

Also successful with its intended domestic audience, *12* is an artistic expression of post-communist Russia's struggle to use imitations of the West to declare independence from the West. The film revolves around a Chechen youth charged with killing his adoptive father who, as a Special Forces officer, had brought the boy back to Moscow after his parents were killed in the Chechen wars. As in Lumet's original, the film begins with the all-male jury assembled and basically agreed on the guilt of the accused. Once again, a single hold-out raises doubts, the jurors disclose personal information about themselves, and ask to re-examine the evidence.[69] Not abstract argument but concrete experience slowly modifies the jurors' views. Not truth but compassion helps them find justice. But the denouement of the Russian remake is very different from that of the American original. What matters in Mikhalkov's version is not justice in the abstract but the individual fate of the boy. It becomes clear that freeing the boy from prison means that the real murderers will seek him out and kill him. So the character who represents Mikhalkov's alter ego – an ex-KGB officer who tries to look and speak like Putin – frames the choice before the jury. They should either keep the innocent boy in prison in order to save his life, or they, the jurors, should be prepared to commit themselves to protecting the boy if he is declared innocent and released. The only person willing to dedicate himself to this thankless task, unsurprisingly, is the ex-KGB officer.

The Chechen boy in Mikhalkov's movie is an abandoned post-imperial orphan doomed to be destroyed in the dog-eat-dog globalized world unless a heroic protector arrives in the nick of time. After watching Mikhalkov's remake of Lumet's film at the Russian President's suburban residence in Novo-Ogarevo, together with Chechnya's strongman president, Ramzan Kadyrov, Putin allegedly said that the film 'brought a tear to the eye'.[70] Explaining Putin's tears may be the last refuge of the underemployed Kremlinologist.[71] But from Putin's perspective, if we may be allowed to speculate freely, Mikhalkov's ironic Russian adaptation of a classic American paean to liberalism captured the dramatic choice facing his country: Russia will either put an end to American-led globalization or American-led globalization will put an end to Russia.

But to challenge American-led globalization effectively, Russia needed a different strategy than the one it had adopted prior to 2012. In the immediate aftermath of 1991, imitating the West was a way of surviving the crisis by cosying up to the global hegemon. Mimesis was a natural response to the chaotic uncertainty of the time, including uncertainty about the strategic goals the Kremlin would eventually want to pursue. Copying the organizational forms of the Western powers on whom the government would depend for its survival in the short term made perfect sense. But conformism to a foreign model did not allow Russia to recover its lost status as a protagonist in world history. True sovereignty was not a seat on the UN Security Council. Nor could it be reacquired by a generous invitation to join the World Trade Organization. Respect on the international stage is worthless if it reflects nothing more than the kindness of strangers. It has to be earned by political capacity, economic dynamism, military strength and cultural identity. Moscow's nuclear arsenal, however formidable and frightening, is not sufficient to regain the kind of international respect that Putin obviously craves: 'I would not like my country, Russia, to lose its originality and identity. I would like the cultural root, the spiritual roots of Russia . . . to be preserved' was Putin's official line after 2012.[72] Russia's new strategy had two elements: a conservative turn away from fake Westernization at home and new initiatives of aggressive imitation abroad. 'Sovereign democracy' now meant the right and the power to slam the door rudely in the face of the West.

The Kremlin's putative return to traditional conservative values, signalling and sealing its repudiation of Western liberalism, was not totally unexpected. Fukuyama's *The End of History and the Last Man* was never a bestseller in Russia, but Samuel Huntington's *The Clash of Civilizations* was. Russia's nationalist-minded intellectuals enthusiastically endorsed the late Harvard professor's claim that 'the fundamental source of conflict in this new world will not be primarily ideological or primarily economic. The great divisions among humankind and the dominating source of conflict will be cultural.'[73] Along similar lines, a hard-shelled state that can be integrated safely into the global economy only if its national traditions, domestic politics and civil society are sealed off to some extent from external influences has been a principal goal of Putin's state-building project ever since he acceded to power.

From Putin's perspective, an important source of his regime's vulnerability is the Russian elite's cultural and financial dependence on the West. Putin controls everything in Russia except the things that really matter: the price of hydrocarbons, public sentiments (his popularity dropped significantly in 2018-2019),[74] and to some extent the loyalty of the rich. His sway over an economic elite that does so much of its business offshore is substantial but nevertheless limited. This explains why, early in his presidency, the renationalization of the country's globe-trotting business classes became one of his major objectives. His long-term imprisonment of the now-exiled Russian oligarch Mikhail Khodorkovsky, the 2008 war in Georgia, and the egregious strut and rudeness with which he regularly flouts unspoken norms about how world leaders are supposed to behave in polite company were all meant to scandalize the West in order to bolster, against strong countervailing forces such as the digitalization of communications,[75] Russia's economic, political and cultural detachment from the world. Putin's war on gays, meant to recruit Russian conservatives outraged at decadent Westernizers into a pro-Putin majority, and his annexation of Crimea, meant to thrill Russian nationalists while appalling the liberal West, may seem unrelated when viewed from a distance. But they come from the pages of the same aggressive isolationist playbook.

Much has been written about the conservative turn in Russian politics, but this observably rightward shift is difficult to understand without taking Russia's aggressive isolationism into account. The most common interpretation is that Russia decided to become the champion of the conservative revolution because of the authoritarian preferences of its leaders. In these theories, Putin's version of Russian conservatism is attributed to the ideological influence of such thinkers as Ivan Ilyin or Aleksandr Dugin. But Putin, despite his occasional references to Ilyin, does not easily fit the image of a classical ideological dictator. Unlike Stalin, for instance, he is not known to be an avid reader. Almost all of his biographers agree that he is 'fundamentally Soviet'. His rhetorical postures derive less from a resuscitated Slavophile tradition than from an *ironic imitation* of the talking points of the Soviet Union's enemies. Indeed, when the Kremlin blames the West today, it uses the same terms that the West used when pouring scorn on the Soviets in the 1920s: the West has lost its faith in God; it tries to destroy family by promoting free love and all-corrosive relativism. By turning the tables in this way, Russia positions itself as the defender and saviour of an Old Europe that has been betrayed by the decadent West. But the 'Slavophile conservatism' echoed here is skin deep.

This is because, even as Russian leaders preach arch-conservatism, Russian society is anything but conservative. Marriages in today's Russia, for example, are less stable than marriages in the Soviet era, when the country's divorce rates were already notoriously high. Russia has 56 divorces for every 100 marriages, an imperfect but telling indicator of waning matrimonial traditionalism and fidelity.

Not only are divorce rates just as elevated as in the putatively decadent West; abortions, too, are more frequent, though not as shockingly frequent as they were in the Soviet Union of the 1970s and 1980s. Church attendance is lower. So how can we explain Russia's putative conservative turn?

We can do so only if we understand that Russian leaders are haunted not only by the nightmare of territorial disintegration, but also (exactly like their counterparts in Eastern Europe) by the spectre of demographic decline.

From 1993 to 2010, the Russian population shrank from 148.6 million to 141.9 million. By various measures, Russia's demographic indicators resemble those of many of the world's poorest and least developed societies. In 2009, overall life expectancy at age 15 was estimated to be lower in Russia than in Bangladesh, East Timor, Eritrea, Madagascar, Niger, and Yemen. Russia's adult male life expectancy was estimated to be lower than Sudan's, Rwanda's, and even AIDS-ravaged Botswana's. Although Russian women fare relatively better than Russian men, the mortality rate for Russian women of working age in 2009 was slightly higher than for working-age women in Bolivia, South America's poorest country. Twenty years earlier, Russia's death rate for working-age women was 45 percent lower than Bolivia's.[76]

Not the Slavophile classics in the Kremlin library, but Russia's unique combination of African mortality rates and European birth rates is what best explains the conservative turn in Kremlin political rhetoric.[77]

Conservative rhetoric was also needed to give some ideological shape to Putin's majority and to help the Kremlin draw a line between patriotic Russians and liberal traitors who, in their picture of the world, are controlled by foreign embassies. But it is useful sloganeering not moral conviction, and its grip on behaviour is negligible and evanescent. Paranoia about foreign plots, by contrast, has far-reaching effects.

In the Kremlin's fevered political imagination, demographic decline is not only Russia's unwelcome fate. It is also a malign Western conspiracy. In 1994, at the Wright Laboratory in Ohio (predecessor to today's US Air Force Research Laboratory), an over-imaginative employee came up with the idea of developing a 'gay bomb'.[78] The concept behind this hypothetical psycho-chemical device was that spraying female sex pheromones over enemy forces would make combatants feel sexually attracted to one other, leading moonstruck enemy fighters to make love not war.

Needless to say, the ridiculous proposal of a gay bomb never got beyond the 'bright idea' stage. But Russian leaders nevertheless behave as if a gay bomb had been tossed at them in 1991. 'My relations to gay parades and sexual minorities in general is simple,' Putin explained, concluding 'it is connected with my official duties and the fact that one of the country's main problems is demographic.'[79] In Putin's mental world, Russia's demographic crisis reflects a global moral crisis. Following the West today means 'to recognize everyone's right to ... freedom of consciousness, political views and privacy, but also to accept without question the equality of good and evil'.[80]

It is impossible to understand the series of repressive laws being adopted in Russia recently, including legislation against 'gay propaganda',[81] if we do not realize that what is at stake is the dramatic impact that the Westernization of Russian society had on the fraught relations between generations, particularly within the Russian elite. One of the principal forces that corroded the legitimacy of communism was the limited extent to which Soviet elites could transmit their privileges to their own children. To be sure, nomenklatura children were *zolotaya molodyozh* (gilded youth), and everyone knew just how privileged they were. But they could not legally inherit their parents' status. This residual infringement on a hard-wired proclivity of human nature to favour biological offspring was a fundamental weakness of a regime founded on the egalitarian idea that opportunities in life should never be distributed according to the social status of one's birth family.

Having finally escaped these constraints in 1991, Russia's post-communist elites threw themselves enthusiastically into giving their own children a leg-up in the social competition for power, wealth and prestige. They often did so by sending them to study abroad. The problem was, many of these lucky kids decided never to return. And those who did came back with very different, non-Russian habits and beliefs.

Understanding the psychology of national elites in formerly communist countries means understanding this paradox: at the very moment when these elites regained the chance to favour their children, these children began to shake off their parents' influence. Having *synchronized* themselves with the normative framework of the West, the elite's foreign-educated offspring were no longer *coordinated* with the normative expectations of the homeland where previous generations had lived. Thus, the charge that the West is stealing the children of Russian elites is one of the principal tenets of

Kremlin anti-Westernism, driving its attempts to repatriate the country's foreign-domiciled business classes. The country's leaders fear that Russia, as in imperial times, may end up being governed by native-born citizens contaminated by Western culture who could then conspire to prevent today's privileged groups from continuing to live in the style to which they have grown accustomed. If in the West 1968 represented the revolt of children against the oppressive values and choices of their parents, in Russia the 2010s represent the protest of parents against the unfamiliar social and cultural values of their Western-educated children.

Today it is fashionable to interpret Putin's policies as an attempt to restore the geopolitical influence of the Soviet Union, if not the Soviet Union itself.[82] Other commentators emphasize Russia's role as a conservative power seeking to remake Europe in its own image as a crusading opponent of modern decadence.[83] Alarming statements by Aleksandr Dugin, the pop star of Russian Eurasianism, are frequently recycled in Western media. This is all very misleading. The Kremlin is making conservative noises and tries to look imperial, but Putin's policies have almost nothing to do with Russia's traditional imperialism or expansionism. Nor are Putin's supporters about to turn their backs on modern rationalism and individualism to embrace an idealized vision of medieval peasant communities and the organic oneness of traditional rural life. Resemblances between Putin's anti-Americanism and nineteenth-century Slavophile hostility to *zapadnichestvo* (westernism) are therefore superficial at best. Moreover, for someone who came of age in the Soviet Union, ethno-nationalism cannot possibly be such a decisive factor as many commentators allege. And although he used nationalistic rhetoric in justifying the annexation of Crimea, he is too acutely aware that nationalism destroyed the Soviet Union to be serious about celebrating the kind of ethnic homogeneity which would explode the multi-ethnic Russian Federation too.

Putin does not dream of conquering Warsaw or re-occupying Riga. On the contrary, his policies, to repeat, are an expression of aggressive isolationism, an attempt to consolidate one's own civilizational space. They embody his defensive reaction to the threat to Russia posed by global economic interdependency and digital interoperability as well as the seemingly unstoppable diffusion of Western social and cultural norms. In this sense, Kremlin policy reflects a general trend that can be observed in the self-insulating, barricade-erecting and de-globalizing behaviour of other global actors in the wake of global financial crises as they have unfolded since the 1980s. Superficially, it's true, Putin's actions resemble nineteenth-century Russian imperial politics. But they are much better understood as part of a worldwide 21st-century resistance to unfettered, open-for-business but under-governed globalization. Foreign travel has not been restricted for Russians able to afford it. But Putin, not unlike Trump, wants to insulate the country from the liberal West. This is more important to him than annexing adjacent lands. By crudely threatening the West, he may even hope to force the West 'to pay for the Wall', that is, to invest heavily in sealing itself off from Russia's cyber interferences in US and European politics. These attacks, among other things, represent a doomed attempt to resurrect the information borders between states at a moment when governments around the world are losing their monopoly control over the national information space as a result, for example, of gradual improvements in Google Translate.

We can, of course, speculate about historical parallels explaining Putin's move to close Russia off. Whenever Russia opens itself to the world, there seems to be a point when panic sets in and the country's authoritarian leaders hysterically return to isolationism with a vengeance. Something of this sort happened after Russia's victory over Napoleon in the nineteenth century. In 1946, Stalin launched his infamous campaign against cosmopolitanism, and hundreds of thousands of Soviet soldiers were sent to the camps because the regime feared that they had seen too much of Europe. Perhaps we are witnessing something similar, though less murderous, today. Then again, Stalin had an ideology and a mission, not to mention an appetite for mass murder, which have no counterpart in the Putin system. It is nevertheless fair to say that the Kremlin remains convinced that the survival of the regime depends on undermining the global hegemony of the liberal West.

IMITATION AS UNMASKING

In 2012, just as the Kremlin was discovering the dangerously subversive potential of imitating the West's domestic institutions, it also came to appreciate the utility of imitating American foreign policy as an offensive weapon, and as a way to de-legitimate the liberal world order. A classic example of imitation in the service of undermining the enemy is the Nazi plot to collapse the British pound by flooding the UK with forged banknotes.[84] But this is very different from holding up a mirror to force one's foes to see their brutality and hypocrisy. Russia's post-2012 policies show how such mirroring can be employed by a much weaker party to attack, confound and demoralize its ostensibly stronger adversary.

The most dramatic recent non-Russian example of this kind of aggressive imitation is the decision by media-savvy ISIS propagandists to dress ISIS captives in orange jumpsuits before executing them.[85] The gruesome pantomime represents a conscious attempt to imitate America's humiliation of Muslim prisoners at Guantanamo. The jihadists sought to provide a mirror-image of the way America violates the basic human dignity of Muslim prisoners. They obviously believed that this cruelly scornful mimicry exposed the hollowness of the West's claims to moral superiority.[86]

Since 2014 Putin has repeatedly resorted to this kind of violent parody of US foreign policy in order to reveal America's congenital hypocrisy to the world. Because hypocrisy helps us avoid conflict by hiding beliefs that are insulting and hurtful, attacks on hypocrisy often signal a desire to fight. This is what makes Russia's switch from simulation to mockery – from counterfeiting democratic accountability domestically to holding up a mirror to US misbehaviour internationally – so dangerous. The change was possible, presumably, only because the aspiration to become like the West was never genuinely internalized by powerful forces inside Russia.

A good example of aggressive imitation is Putin's March 2014 speech announcing Russia's annexation of Crimea. This official address lifted whole passages from speeches by Western leaders justifying the dismantling of Serbian territory in Kosovo and applied them to the Crimean case.[87] Thus, what most Western observers took to be the first step in Putin's attempt to restore Moscow's empire was explicitly justified by the rhetoric of US President Woodrow Wilson extolling the fundamental right of popular self-determination.

What sets foreign-policy mimicry apart is arguably the way it is designed to show the absurdity of the bad original. By clothing its own violent actions in an idealistic rhetoric borrowed verbatim from the US, Moscow aims to unmask the Age of Imitation as an Age of Western Hypocrisy. Vaunted Western values, such as the self-determination of peoples, are simply Western interests in disguise. The implication is that the entire post-Second World War international system will collapse if other nations start imitating the *real* West. One might even suggest that Putin imitated Bush's America for reasons similar to those that impelled Charlie Chaplin to imitate Adolf Hitler in *The Great Dictator*. He wanted to weaken and demoralize the enemy nation by holding up a mirror in which enemy leaders are stripped of their pretensions. We are not saying that this mirroring tactic is necessarily effective in a strategic sense, only that it is meant to undermine the enemy's self-image as well as its allegedly undeserved good name in the rest of the world. But as an attempt to rip off the West's liberal mask and expose its alleged hypocrisy, mirroring savours more of backward-looking revenge than forward-looking policy.

The primary objective of the Kremlin's foreign policy today is to unmask the West's purported universalism as a cover for the promotion of its narrow geopolitical interests. The most effective weapon in this campaign to reveal the enemy's irredeemable bad faith is sarcastic imitation. The Kremlin presumably believes that its mirror-imaging of real or imagined American misdeeds is the highest form of pedagogy. Like revenge, of which it is a variant, it may taste 'sweeter than honey', but it is also making the world a much more dangerous place.

In response to Western complaints about Moscow's aggressive interventions abroad, Russians repeatedly claim they are doing to the West only what the West has been repeatedly and insultingly doing to them. A minor but telling example is the Dima Yakovlev Act, named after an adopted Russian child who died from criminal negligence by his adoptive American parents and explicitly designed to mirror the Magnitsky Act, a US law aimed at punishing Russian officials involved in the death of a Russian tax accountant in a Moscow prison in 2009, by imposing sanctions on US citizens involved in 'violations of the human rights and freedoms of Russian citizens'.[88] But other examples are legion. Just as NATO violated the territorial integrity of Serbia in 1999, so Russia violated the territorial integrity of Georgia in 2008. Just as the United States is flying long-range bombers close to Russia's borders, so Russia is now flying long-range bombers close to America's borders. Just as the American administration has blacklisted some prominent Russians, preventing them from entering the US, so the Kremlin has blacklisted some prominent Americans, preventing them from entering Russia. Just as Americans and Europeans celebrated the dismantling of the Soviet Union, so Russians now celebrate Brexit and the potential dismantling of the EU. Just as the West has supported liberal NGOs inside Russia, Russians are financing far-right and far-left groups in the West to undermine NATO, block US missile defence programmes, weaken support for sanctions and sap European unity. Just as the West (in Moscow's view) lied brazenly to Russia about its plans for NATO expansion and about the UN-sanctioned attack on Libya, so Russia lies brazenly to the West about its military incursions into Ukraine. And just as the US is aiding the military of Ukraine (traditionally in Moscow's sphere of influence), so Russia is aiding the military of Venezuela (traditionally in Washington's sphere of influence). The end result of this mirror-imagining is deepened mistrust, conspiracy thinking and the loss of any basis for mutual accommodation.

This brings us to the allegation that Russia intervened in the 2016 presidential elections in the United States, something that the Kremlin officially (if inconsistently) denies and that American intelligence officials adamantly affirm. That the United States has regularly meddled in foreign elections is well known.[89] This includes at least one important Russian case: the 1996 election that returned Yeltsin to the presidency. Without help from a team of American political consultants and especially without a Clinton-arranged loan from the IMF coming on the eve of the elections, it is very likely that Boris Yeltsin would have lost his bid for re-election in 1996.[90] If Russia was going to undertake a policy of aggressive imitation against the United States, it would make perfect sense for the Kremlin to focus on meddling in

an American election. Since Putin sees 'private' American organizations involved in Russian elections as arms of the American state,[91]
he would have no patience with hypocritical outrage on the US side
about Russia messing around in America's domestic affairs. Indeed,
using 'cut-outs' to hack and release embarrassing Democratic Party
emails covertly, giving the Kremlin deniability, would, from the Russian perspective, be a well-deserved tit-for-tat retaliation for what
they believe Washington did to Moscow clandestinely and presumably
without a twinge of conscience. According to the US intelligence agencies tasked with assessing Russian interference in the 2016 presidential
campaign, 'Putin publicly pointed to the Panama Papers disclosure
and the Olympic doping scandal as US-directed efforts to defame
Russia', suggesting that Russia in turn would 'use disclosures to discredit the image of the United States and cast it as hypocritical'.[92] Why
leaking the Panama Papers was good while hacking Democratic Party
emails was bad is the Russian question, however arbitrary the comparison may seem from a Western point of view. Interfering covertly
and deniably in the American elections was presumably Putin's way of
correcting the asymmetrical relationship between Washington and
Moscow created at the end of the Cold War. Instead of propping up a
flimsy democratic façade in Russia, the Kremlin decided to show the
world that American democracy itself was nothing but a flimsy façade.
This is why the Kremlin was not especially shy about making their
electoral interference 'known', despite their pro forma denials that it
ever occurred. In other words, Russia was meddling in the American
elections not so much because they hoped that they could elect Donald
Trump but because meddling in American elections – doing to America what America was doing to them – was a cheap way for Moscow
to reclaim its lapsed status as a global force to be reckoned with. As
Nina Khrushcheva, a professor of international affairs at the New
School for Social Research in New York and the great-granddaughter
of Soviet premier Nikita Khrushchev, said to the *New York Times*:
'This operation was to show the Americans – that you bastards are
just as screwed up as the rest of us.'[93]

Like much of Putin's anti-American foreign policy, the value of the
Kremlin's interference in the American election was expressive and
retaliatory rather than instrumental or strategic. One thing Putin was

trying to communicate to Western leaders was that the West should fear a world populated by copies of the 'real' West.

THE BLIND ALLEY OF
SUBVERSIVE IMITATION

In March 2014 the United States government elevated outrage to the point of poetic inspiration: 'As Russia spins a false narrative to justify its illegal actions in Ukraine' – so read a press release from the State Department – 'the world has not seen such startling Russian fiction since Dostoyevsky wrote: "the formula two plus two equals five is not without its attractions".'[94] And Washington was not the only government to feel poetically inspired. On Sunday 2 March 2014, after talking to President Putin, German Chancellor Angela Merkel made a telephone call to President Obama and, according to the information leaked, said she doubted that Putin was in touch with reality. Indeed, according to Merkel, Putin 'lives in another world'.[95] The confrontation between Russia and the West was no longer about who lived in a better world and who owned the future. That had been the logic of the Cold War confrontation. Now the conflict between Russia and the West was about who inhabits a real rather than a make-believe world.

Washington seemed shocked: Russia was denying obvious facts! American officials could not understand why Putin was claiming that 'It is "citizens' defence groups," not Russian forces, who have seized infrastructure and military facilities in Crimea',[96] or why Putin denied that Russia had anything to do with hacking the emails of the Democratic Party. What sense did it make to say such things when images of Russian Special Forces capturing the public buildings in Crimea were all over the TV and the internet and when the FBI has identified the intelligence officer who did the hacking? Putin's lies seemed absurd in the age of involuntary transparency. So why were Russian officials lying so blatantly when they knew perfectly well that their lies would be exposed a few hours after they were uttered? Putin's barefaced mendacity ran counter to a basic assumption of realpolitik, namely that 'lying is only effective when the potential victim thinks that the liar is probably telling the truth' and that 'nobody wants to be called a liar, even if it is for a good cause'.[97]

Putin's lies about the absence of Russian troops in Crimea were bluntly stated and effortlessly exposed. But he was not afraid to be called 'liar'. This was because Western expressions of shock and outrage made the West's practical impotence in the face of Russia's only thinly veiled misdeeds impossible to overlook. In the 1990s, Russia itself had experienced the frustrating effect of outrage that leads to nothing. Now it was America's turn.

Putin's strategy of flatly denying Russia's responsibility for any of the acts of which it was accused cannot be understood as a simple act of deception. Rather, it strongly resembles a certain type of behaviour typical of hardened criminals who, when sentenced to prison, proudly display their total disrespect for civilized rules and norms and whose underworld reputation depends on their refusing even minimal cooperation with prison authorities. In Russian criminal slang such a behaviour is known as 'otritsalovo', which roughly translates as 'defiant stonewalling' with an element of 'omertà'.

But Putin's untruths also served another purpose. Every counter-attack provoked by Putin's blatantly mendacious behaviour was, from his perspective, a way to remind the world and especially America how often the West had lied to Russia in the past. The goal was less to achieve a strategic advantage than to change the mental state and self-image of the Main Enemy, that is, to make Americans painfully remember what they had so conveniently forgotten. Explicitly echoing the behaviour of the enemy in such contexts always implies a derogatory commentary on the original.

James Jesus Angleton, chief of CIA Counterintelligence from 1954 to 1975, would be less scandalized by Putin's behaviour than his successors in charge of America's intelligence agencies today. He was convinced that 'deception is a state of mind – and the mind of the state.' He spent his free time in his orchid garden. What enchanted him was that 'with most species of orchids, it is not the fittest but the most deceptive ones that survive'. The problem is that most orchids are too dispersed through the jungle for the wind to carry pollen to them; they depend on insects or birds for this crucial service. But since they do not provide any food or other nutrients for these carriers, orchids have to trick them into perpetuating their species. It was taking care of the orchids and exposing Soviet double agents that made Angleton believe that 'the essence of disinformation is provocation, not lying.'[98] When denying the well-documented presence of Russian Special Forces in Crimea and Eastern Ukraine, Putin was not lying. He was provoking, that is goading and needling and poking at the West to elicit a sub-rational, stammering response. He was trying to destabilize and demoralize the West by forcing it to confront the limits of its power.

After Russia's annexation of Crimea, Western commentators were obsessed with the Kremlin's 'hybrid war', the unprecedented mixture of military, informational and other resources intended to break the political will of the enemy. Analysts linked this new strategy back to Soviet 'playbooks'. They were wrong. 'Hybrid war' was the result of reverse engineering. Russians were doing to the West what they were rightly or wrongly convinced the West was doing to them. They had painstakingly reconstructed the way the West, in their opinion, orchestrated the 'colour revolutions' and come up with an instruction manual for organizing similar ones. Just as the West has supported liberal NGOs, Russians decided to finance far right and far left groups in the West. After 2012, Russia's leaders concluded that the major weakness of their country's policies in the post-Cold War period was that they were not imitating the *real* West. Examined closely, their imitations of Western democracies were perfunctory and cosmetic. So now they were hell-bent on imitating Western hypocrisy for real. Whereas it was previously obsessed with its own vulnerability, Russia has now discovered the vulnerability of the West and has mobilized all its resources to expose this vulnerability to the world. The paradox is that conspiracy-minded Russian leaders, by acting on their conspiratorial beliefs, have succeeded in making many people around the world look at world politics as nothing but a vast conspiracy.

Russian satirist Viktor Pelevin's absurdist novella *Operation Burning Bush* (2010)[99] displays this understanding of world history as a series of undercover plots and machinations. The story follows a humble Russian English-language teacher, endowed with a powerful voice, who is recruited for a special intelligence operation to speak with President George W. Bush through an implant in the president's tooth. Following the Kremlin's instructions, the teacher, pretending to sound like God, encourages the forty-third President to invade Iraq. Later in the novel we discover that in the 1980s the CIA had conducted a similar operation – this time posing as Lenin's spirit to convince Mikhail Gorbachev to initiate perestroika, setting off a chain of events that ended with the disintegration of the Soviet Union. What you once did to me, I will now do to you.

Russia is driven to mirror Western aggression and especially Western hypocrisy by more than a desire for revenge. The Kremlin also hopes to recreate, at least superficially, the symmetry between Russia and the United States that it lost when the Cold War ended. This hope to reclaim lost symmetry with the US, rather than restoring Moscow's lost status as a global superpower, is what explains Russia's resort to asymmetrical forms of warfare that have proven their effectiveness when used by weak powers against strong powers in the past. Washington experienced the end of the Cold War as victory and vindication, while Moscow experienced it as disorientation, demoralization and the loss of its superpower status. Yet Russia was a defeated country even before Putin decided to admit it. Instead of two victorious powers facing off after 1989–91 (as after 1945), a self-satisfied winner presided over the stumbling recovery of a loser dazed by geopolitical humiliation and territorial amputation. This inherently unstable asymmetry was papered over but not redressed by the unconvincing storyline of a victory without losers.

What it is most difficult for Western analysts schooled in the Cold War to grasp is that Putin is not attacking the American-made world order on behalf of any ideological or organizational alternative. Unlike communism, authoritarianism is not an ideology. It is simply a form of government that can exist within different ideological frameworks. So Putin is attacking liberal democracies without any ambition to make them into Russia-style authoritarian states. He is attacking the international liberal order for pedagogical reasons, to make a point and teach the West a lesson, to reveal its hypocrisy and hidden vulnerability, and to make its defenders weaker still. The non-ideological Putin is challenging the international order in much the same way as the deeply ideological ISIS and with the same lack of

realism and forethought about a positive goal to be attained. He is
engaged in subversion by emulation. In other words, Russia's recent
turn to foreign adventurism is a classic case of imitation used as a
weapon to subvert the imitated and destroy America's reputation and
self-understanding as a model to be imitated. But to what end?

Putin may be playing a weak hand skilfully but the fact remains
that the hand he is playing is demonstrably weak. This raises the
question of why America is so obsessed with Putin's Russia when it is
the rise of China that is remaking the geopolitical landscape of the
twenty-first century? Answering this question can help us explain
why Putin, for the moment, feels victorious in his imitation war.

Suspicions of collusion are obviously a factor. But the clue to a
deeper dynamic can be found in classic Russian literature, namely in
Dostoevsky's novel *The Double*, the story of a low-level clerk who
ends up in a madhouse after meeting his double, a man who looks
like him, talks like him, but who displays all the charm and self-
confidence that the tortured protagonist profoundly lacks; and who,
step by step, is becoming 'him'.

When it comes to Russia, the West feels like Dostoevsky's protagonist in the presence of his double. The difference between the novel
and our reality is significant, however. In Dostoevsky's novel, the
double looks like a person who the protagonist always wanted to be.
For the West, by contrast, Russia has become the double the West
fears it might become. While some years ago Russia was perceived by
the Western public as a museum piece from the past, now it looks like
a time-travelling guest from the future. Americans and Europeans
have started to fear that what happens in Russia today could take
place in Western countries tomorrow.[100] The politics of imitation
has destroyed the sense that we live in a common reality but it has
increased the fear that we are becoming much more alike – that is,
equally unprincipled and cynical – than we would ever before have
believed.

In the days of the Cold War, historian Robert Conquest insisted
that 'a science-fiction attitude is a great help in understanding the
Soviet Union. It isn't so much whether they're good or bad, exactly;
they're not bad or good as we'd be bad or good. It's far better to look
at them as Martians than as people like us.'[101] Today, this advice

seems dated. We now realize not simply that Russians are more like Westerners than Conquest claimed but that Westerners are more like Russians than he would have allowed himself to imagine.

During the first two post-communist decades, Russia was a classic example of a non-democracy functioning behind the institutional façade of democracy: a political regime in which elections were regularly held but in which the ruling party never risked losing power. This is true even today, at least to some extent. In the Putin system, periodic pseudo-competitive elections still serve as instruments for disempowering, rather than empowering, citizens. So the story of Russia's stage-managed elections provides a historically vivid illustration of the way in which institutions and practices that originally emancipated citizens from the whim of unaccountable rulers can be refashioned into pseudo-democratic institutions that effectively disenfranchise citizens. This brings us back to 'contagious imitation'. Disillusioned with their democracies, Westerners are now beginning to see their own political systems as not much more genuinely democratic than the Russian one. A recent study has revealed that in the last decade trust in democracy has declined in the West's developed democracies, and that levels of mistrust towards democracy as a political system are highest among younger people.[102] A central pillar of Putin's anti-Western policy is to nourish these seeds of doubt, giving American and European citizens ever more reasons to disbelieve that periodic elections in the West work to the public's advantage. That the people's voice was heard in the Brexit referendum, for example, does not mean that the consequences of the decision were thought through in advance. Whether Russian interference in Western elections has had a significant influence on outcomes is debatable. But the West now shares Russia's post-Cold War fears of polarization, ungovernability and disintegration. In this case, too, the imitator–imitated relationship, as understood immediately after the communist collapse, seems to have been brutally reversed.

Putin's Mirror is an 'active measure'. It is designed less to reflect accurately than to dishearten morally. The principal purpose of the Kremlin's meddling in American elections is to reveal that competitive elections in the West – shaped by the manipulative power of money, disfigured by growing political polarization and emptied of meaning by a lack of genuine political alternatives – resemble Kremlin-engineered elections more than Westerners would like to think. This is how Putin is trying to kill the West's victory narrative that took shape after 1989. The global spread of democracy signals not the liberation of the enlightened masses from elite domination but the manipulation of the masses by dark forces operating behind the scenes. His efforts have been abetted by radically changing perceptions of the role of social media in politics. If, in the initial euphoric days of the Arab Spring, social media were seen as 'liberation technologies'[103] and Facebook, Google and Twitter were signs of the coming democratic future of the world, these same social media are now universally associated with post-truth fragmentation, polarization and the coming end of democracy.

Post-communist Russia illustrates how a handful of politically unaccountable and self-enriching rulers have, despite internal rivalries, managed to stay atop the country's fragmented society without resorting to historically significant levels of mass violence. Economist Gabriel Zucman calculated that, in 2015, 52 per cent of Russia's wealth resided outside of the country.[104] This political model, neither democratic nor authoritarian, neither exploitative of a working-class majority in the Marxist sense nor repressive of all individual freedoms in the liberal sense, is an image of the future that should keep us awake at night. This is the nightmare the Kremlin wants us to have.[105]

What is causing anxiety among some Western liberals is not the fear that Russia will run the world, but that much of the world will be run the way Russia is run today. What is disturbing is that the West has started to resemble Putin's Russia more than we are ready to acknowledge. The resemblance includes a tendency to see democracy's downward spiral in the West as the result of a conspiracy orchestrated by the West's adversaries. Like many other countries, America has always been conspiracy-minded. Some researchers even argue that the myth of national exceptionalism welcomes conspiratorial thinking. If a nation has a mission, it is logical to assume that the nation's enemies will try to make that mission fail.[106] But if conspiracy theories used to be consigned to the basement of American politics, they are now welcomed across the political spectrum (with more justification in some cases than in others).

But Moscow's resentment-fuelled policies – however emotionally satisfying they may feel to the Kremlin leadership and whatever desires for vindication they fulfil – don't rise to the level of a well-considered, long-term strategy. Indeed, Russia's policy of ironic mimicry and reverse engineering of American hypocrisy may be slowly nudging the world towards disaster.

Aggressive imitation assumes, in a self-fulfilling way, that all grounds for trust between Russia and the West have been fatally eroded. Alternative explanations for the West's failures to live up to its own ideals – such as poor planning, muddling through and lack of professional coordination on the Western side – are downplayed in order to impute unhelpful behaviour on America's part to implacable bad faith. Unmasking hypocrisy attributes malicious intentions (rather than naïveté, self-deception, bureaucratic infighting or incompetence) to the adversary. Distinguishing public justifications from hidden motivations is only common sense. But focusing dogmatically and obsessively on this distinction, as Putin seems to do, is a slippery slope.

An obsessive focus on the West's hypocrisy has encouraged a ratcheting up of strategically pointless malice on the Russian side. Because they spy cynicism behind every American invocation of humanitarian ideals and want to prove that they are no longer as naïve as they were when they believed America's two-faced promises not to expand NATO eastward, they have thrown themselves into a strutting disregard for elementary humanitarian values, as if jettisoning moral inhibitions in the siege of Aleppo, for example, made them into worthy counterparts to the amoral America whose purported villainy they love to revile.

Relying on exposure of the enemy's hypocrisy to justify one's own aggressive acts makes it possible to attack the existing world order without offering any positive alternative that can be put in its place. This is not a formula for a sober foreign policy that channels limited means towards achievable objectives. True, Putin can snub the US and get away with it or parody US foreign policy in order to expose its hypocrisy. But there is no way he can turn any of this to the benefit of Russia's development. Russia became richer and more stable under his tenure between 2000 and 2008 because he was able to balance his desire to limit Western influence (though not to isolate Russia entirely) against lucrative cooperation with the West. Since 2012, this balance has been lost. A backward-looking not forward-looking policy, aimed basically at sticking a finger in America's eye, is the result. Intervening in Syria and eastern Ukraine to show that a renewed Russia can do anything that America can do has entangled the Russian military in bloody struggles that seem to contribute nothing to the country's national security and have no obvious endgame or exit strategy.

Russia's attempt to justify its aggressive actions abroad as mere replicas of Western aggression has created a situation where, for the purpose of self-preservation, the West is now starting to imitate Russian actions in turn. In November 2016, for example, the European Parliament adopted a resolution aimed at countering Russian propaganda. It stated:

> The Russian government is employing a wide range of tools and instruments, such as think tanks ... multilingual TV stations [e.g. Russia Today], pseudo-news agencies and multimedia services [e.g. Sputnik] ... social media and internet trolls, to challenge democratic values, divide Europe, gather domestic support and create the perception of failed states in the EU's eastern neighbourhood.[107]

Based on these allegations, the Parliament asked EU member states to react. It is very likely that European governments will respond in kind, that is, with policies that basically replicate Russia's 'foreign agents' legislation, including restrictions on foreign ownership of media adopted some years ago as a response to the West's allegedly subversive activities on the territory of the Russian Federation. The United States' policy of sanctions, while targeting Russia, also helps disassemble the infrastructure of open global trade that Russia, too, wants to destroy.

Cold War era 'convergence theory' postulated that technological developments would end the split between capitalism and socialism by forcing all industrial societies into the same format. This prediction seems to be coming true but for different reasons and in an ironic sense. Russia and America have indeed started to resemble each other. This time, however, it is America that is remaking itself along lines suggested by Putin's Mirror. This reverse imitation is not only shocking. It may bring momentary smiles to the Kremlin, but it is unlikely to underwrite global stability and peace. It is much more likely to fuel escalating rivalry and increased violence. Unlike the Soviet Union, the Russian Federation cannot hope to defeat the West. What it does hope to do is to bring the West to the point of breaking into pieces, just as happened to the Soviet bloc and the Soviet Union itself in 1989–91. That the result will be a stable world in which Russia's interests will be protected is impossible to imagine.

3

Imitation as Dispossession

They say 'America First,' but they mean 'America Next!'
                                          Woody Guthrie

In Agatha Christie's gripping whodunnit of 1934, *Murder on the Orient Express*,[1] renowned Inspector Hercule Poirot brilliantly unravels the mystery behind the killing of a malevolent American passenger whose dead body, knifed multiple times, has been discovered on the train. After an exacting inquiry, he learns not only that each passenger has personal reasons for wanting the dubiously named Samuel Ratchett dead but also that they all colluded knowingly in the plot, each conspirator taking turns to stab their quarry to death.

In the previous two chapters, we have examined the culprits co-responsible for the strange death of what we used to call the liberal international order.[2] We have analysed the resentments, aspirations and chicanery of both the Central European populists and Vladimir Putin. But they plainly did not act alone. Indeed, no Poirot-style sleuthing is required to discover that the current President of the United States has been their willing accomplice.[3] His motives for turning his back on America's allies, disavowing multilateral treaties, and trying to wreck the international institutions created by the US after the Second World War are a matter of controversy. But whatever his motives, he has been an eminent confederate in the gang-slaying of the 'liberal hegemony' that characterized international politics for three decades after 1989.

Although criminal conspiracy has its fascinations, we are not asking, in the footsteps of Poirot: Why did Trump do it? We are asking, instead: Why have substantial swathes of the American public and the

US business community as well as most Republican leaders aligned themselves so uncritically with the project of dismantling what the neoconservative historian Robert Kagan, with good reason, has called 'the world America made'?[4]

To answer such political, as opposed to criminological, questions, it won't suffice to examine the Trump revolution in a narrowly conspiratorial and solely American setting. Situating it in the context of the various anti-liberal movements and tendencies afoot elsewhere in the world can help us get to the bottom of what might otherwise seem accidental and inexplicable. The common theme that we have found running through the Central European, Russian and American cases, making a comparative analysis possible and fruitful, involves the politics of imitation and its unintended consequences. Trump, too, came to power by exploiting disillusion and resentments that arose in the unipolar Age of Imitation.

Trump's willingness to flirt with white nationalism has obviously contributed to his popular appeal. But we want to widen the focus and ask how his supporters view the rest of the world. Why have so many citizens of the dominant power in the West, under a 'legally and legitimately' elected president, come to distrust countries that have traditionally seen America as an exemplar nation and long viewed liberal democracy as *the* political model most worth imitating? Explaining the stored-up resentment of the imitators towards the imitated is relatively easy, especially when the moral hierarchy implicit in the imitative relationship is exacerbated by lack of alternatives, moralistic monitoring and dubious success. But why would the imitated resent their imitators?

This fertile question spawns various others: Why do Trump's supporters see the Americanization of the world as a catastrophe for America? Why do they agree that the United States, rather than benefiting handsomely, has suffered miserably from the central role it has played in global trade, international organizations and the Atlantic Alliance? And why have so many Americans rallied to a President who describes the dividing of the West against itself and the deglobalization of the American economy as America's revenge for decades of national humiliation?

Trump has retained a non-negligible level of support among many of his fellow citizens even after attacking America's closest allies and publicly embracing leaders who routinely denounce America in the shrillest terms. More mysterious still, many Americans accept and even celebrate the leadership of a man who, in an extraordinary act of imitative reversal, seems to be cribbing his public rhetoric from the xenophobic nativism of Central Europe and the belligerent anti-Americanism of the Kremlin. How can these oddities be explained?

THE AXIS OF RESENTMENT

A major obstacle to properly appreciating Donald Trump's political significance is that he is a gauche, opportunistic and boorish individual with whom almost none of the commentariat shares any aesthetic or ethical sensibilities. The offence he causes to the morals and tastes of well-educated analysts encourages them to take literary revenge by disparaging him as a pathological idiot and fool. But this jeering attitude gets in the way of plumbing the sources of Trump's shocking political success.

Situating the Trump revolution in the context of a contemporaneous worldwide revolt against liberal democracy and liberal internationalism helps us see through the clutter. Our focus will be on the way the Trump movement fits into the global culture of grievance and victimhood that is led and manipulated by the leaders of formerly communist countries, notably Viktor Orbán and Vladimir Putin. This approach will not provide the last word on the Trump era. But it can help us understand him not as a brief deviation from a purportedly normal order that will snap back into place once he is gone, but as the radically transformative political figure he is. The changes that Trump has wrought will be difficult to reverse because they are rooted not in one individual's sleazy and lawbreaking behaviour but in a global revolt against what is widely perceived to be a liberal Imitation Imperative of which he is merely one gaudy expression among others.

Because Trump is anti-intellectual to the point of illiteracy as well as erratic in his policy pronouncements, liberal commentators also assume that he has no coherent project that needs to be theorized and opposed as such. But a world-view can be intuitive rather than ideological and philosophical. And a strategy can be instinctive rather than clear-headed and thought through. This provides another rationale for our comparative approach. Trump's eccentric ways of thinking about America's place in the world, not his cloakroom conspiracies and schemes for self-enrichment, explain whatever popularity he retains. And his intuitive, not ideological, world-view comes into sharper focus when his statements and actions are compared with those of his post-communist peers and shown to stem from shared resentments at the unipolar reordering of the world after 1989.

While instinctively disparaging US allies, the US president is loath to criticize authoritarian rulers, including those in Russia and Central Europe, who rally domestic support by attacking the American model of liberal democracy. It isn't merely that he gets along better with 'tough' dictators rather than 'soft' allies, as he puts it.[5] It's that he thrives in the company of authoritarian rulers devoted to denigrating the United States for its double standards and hypocrisy.

To a political establishment used to basking in its global leadership role, Trump's idea that America is the world's greatest 'victim' has been difficult to absorb. Whether or not Trump turns out to be a world-historical figure, he may well be, in columnist Gideon Rachman's words, 'the kind of instinctive statesman . . . who has harnessed and embodied forces that he himself only half-understands'.[6] The challenge for us is not to unearth proofs of collusion but to uncover the sources of illiberalism's contemporary power. We all feel that something deep is shifting in the global political architecture and atmosphere, and the capture of the American presidency by such a disrupter is part of it. If Napoleon was the heroic world spirit on horseback, then perhaps Trump can be considered the anti-liberal zeitgeist on Twitter.

If it were not for Trump's elective affinity with this wider anti-liberal revolt, we might have been tempted to dismiss his presidency as a fluke, without either majority support or lasting historical significance. That would be a mistake. The changes he has wrought in America's self-understanding and reputation in the world are not only radical. They also reflect the same ethos of provincial resentment against a cosmopolitan world that invites you in without letting you in that we encountered in Central Europe. Just like his soulmates, Orbán and Putin, moreover, Trump adamantly rejects America's traditional self-image as an exemplary nation. He has therefore attacked, with substantial public support, a conceit that goes back to the founding of the country, namely that 'the world will bless and imitate ... our example.'[7] The Trump revolution represents much more than a switch in policy, therefore. It registers and presages a difficult-to-reverse transformation in the way America defines itself and its historical role.

Although his capacities for forethought should not be overstated, Trump seems to have set out to 'normalize' Hungary, Russia and other illiberal regimes not, like past presidents, by encouraging them to adopt liberal-democratic norms, but on the contrary by encouraging America to become their double. We might even say that he is orchestrating 'regime change' in reverse, shattering so many informal norms that he is redesigning the US Constitution piecemeal along illiberal lines. And if his domestic agenda mirrors Hungary's, his international agenda closely tracks Russia's. Trump, too, has cheered the possible dismantling of the EU. And he continues to flirt with the Kremlin dream of an American withdrawal from NATO, making Trump and Putin co-revolutionaries, whether or not they turn out to be co-conspirators.[8]

Trump's expressed fondness for Central European illiberalism and childlike awe before Putin's strongman image no doubt reflects private discomfort with liberal constitutionalism's idea of accountable government. But he does not denigrate the rule of law only because it threatens him personally.[9] He also rejects it because the very idea of impartial justice makes America seem historically unique, morally superior, and a shining example to the world.

WHO DO WE THINK WE ARE?

In a 2013 op-ed, published by the *New York Times,* Vladimir Putin took aim, with tongue-in-cheek religiosity, at the starry-eyed legend of American exceptionalism:

It is extremely dangerous to encourage people to see themselves as exceptional, whatever the motivation. There are big countries and small countries, rich and poor, those with long democratic traditions and those still finding their way to democracy. Their policies differ, too. We are all different, but when we ask for the Lord's blessings, we must not forget that God created us equal.[10]

There is nothing unusual about the leader of a rival nation criticizing America's exaggerated sense of its own uniqueness and moral superiority. What was peculiar and remarkable, in this case, was the enthusiasm with which private citizen Donald Trump praised and echoed Putin's slap-down of one of America's most deeply cherished myths. The term American exceptionalism, Trump concurred, is 'very insulting and Putin really put it to [Obama] about that'.[11] This splashy endorsement of Putin's attack on American exceptionalism, although originally provoked by a petty need to dispraise Obama, provides an important clue to both Trump's intuitive vision of political life and the psychological sources of his popular appeal.

The centrality of his attack on American exceptionalism to Trump's world-view is clear from the frequency and enthusiasm with which he reverts to it. In 2014, responding to a reporter's question about the meaning of American exceptionalism, he summarized his two main objections to the idea. His typically meandering, stream-of-consciousness response bears so centrally on our argument that it is worth citing at length:

Well, I think it's a very dangerous term in one way, because I heard Putin saying, 'Who do they think they are, saying they're exceptional?' You can feel you're exceptional, but when you start throwing it in other countries' faces or other people's faces, I actually think it's a very dangerous term to use. Well, I heard that Putin was saying to somebody ... 'Who do they think they are, saying they're exceptional?' And I understand that. You know, he said, 'Why are they exceptional? They have killings in the streets. Look at what's going on in Chicago and different places. They have all of this turmoil, all of the things that are happening in there.' And I can tell you that there are many countries throughout the world that are extremely angry with that term American Exceptionalism. Countries that are doing better than we are – far better than we are. You're looking to get along with the world, and you say you're exceptional? So I never particularly liked the term. I think you can think it, but I'm not sure it's something that you should necessarily be talking so much about.[12]

This rambling monologue, replete with made-up Putin quotations, suggests two surprisingly good reasons for Trump's agreement with the Russian President about American exceptionalism. First, it is insulting to tell foreigners that your country is superior to theirs. Saying that America is by far the best country that has ever existed on God's earth is ungracious and bound to provoke unwelcome counter-measures. As a gratuitous affront to other countries' sensibilities, it needlessly complicates America's efforts to achieve favourable outcomes internationally.[13] Second, and somewhat inconsistently, the United States is no longer the envy of the world and therefore should stop pretending to be so. Far from resembling a shining city on a hill, much of America now displays the crumbling infrastructure of a third-world country. Indeed, the American dream has become the laughing stock of all those countries 'that are doing better than we are – far better than we are'.

The Russian president's legendary resentment at being lectured to, especially by Americans, makes perfect sense to Trump: 'I don't know that we have a right to lecture.' Violence in the streets, more imagined than real, is one of the main reasons why, in his opinion, America should get out of the preaching business: 'Just look about what's happening with our country. How are we going to lecture when people are shooting our policemen in cold blood? How are we going to lecture when you see the riots and the horror going on in our own country?'[14] To explain why Americans have no right to lecture foreigners, Trump manages to sound both calculatingly alarmist and uncharacteristically self-effacing. But the revolutionary nature of the claim should not be overlooked. He is announcing that he will be the first president in American history to scrap the conviction that America stands for a teachable idea. To make America great is to ensure that America stands for nothing uplifting and inspiring. That is a shrewd move, because a country that sticks faithfully to a moral idea will attract imitators and hangers-on who are bound to spell trouble down the road.

Trump's boast about putting America first is not inconsistent with his repudiation of American exceptionalism. That is because 'America First' means caring nothing for the welfare of other countries while angling to best them in international trade negotiations. There is nothing exceptional about that. 'Winning' is the opposite of 'leading by example'. The latter, for Trump, is worse than a waste of time. It means training others to overtake you.

Central to Trump's radicalism is his idea that the Americanization of foreign countries, especially former enemies, is bad for America. Such talk represents a tectonic shift. Among other things, it involves a wholesale renunciation of the idea that America is an exceptionally good and innocent nation and that its exceptional goodness is what gives it the right and duty to spread its influence abroad.[15] He has explicitly renounced, as no previous American President ever has, the deep-seated American belief that the United States has a historical mission to teach the inhabitants of foreign countries about how to organize their societies and live their lives.[16] Trump is arguably the first American President who could never, under any conditions, echo the famous words of Woodrow Wilson: 'you are Americans and are meant to carry liberty and justice and the principles of humanity wherever you go.'[17]

Trump not only opposes all proselytizing for democracy and human rights. He consistently disregards the boundary between countries that respect and countries that violate human rights and democratic norms. America has no mission and is nobody's model, just as human history has no 'end' in the sense of a moral purpose or goal. This is why he persistently rejects America's messianic self-understanding as well as the idea that the United States is a beacon of liberty and justice for all mankind, a model to which all developing countries should aspire.

After his election, one of Trump's harshest critics remarked, in a way not meant to be flattering, that 'America may once again start behaving like a normal nation.'[18] To make America normal again does not entail returning to Reagan-era boosterism, however. On the contrary, it means reconfiguring the country's international image as no better or worse, in a moral sense, than any other country. Prior to the 2016 election, Mitt Romney warned that if Trump became president, 'America would cease to be a shining city on a hill', apparently without realizing that this was precisely Trump's intention.[19] Jettisoning the contrast between America's innocence and decency and the sinfulness and indecency of other countries, Trump wants the rest of the world to know that America not only is, but also sees itself as being, just as unprincipled as any other country.

For Trump, normalization means 'the restoration of the US as a selfish state among selfish states'.[20] America can only come out on top if it stops standing for airy ideals such as democracy and human rights, intended to benefit other peoples. Previous American presidents professed to believe in American exceptionalism. But that was a dangerous form of self-hypnosis, a self-laid trap into which naïve Americans periodically fall. What could be stupider than committing the United States to acting selflessly for other countries?

A Darwinian vision of life as a ruthless, amoral war-of-all-against-all underpins this rejection of the myth of American exceptionalism. When television journalist Joe Scarborough remarked that Putin 'kills journalists who don't agree with him', Trump famously replied: 'Well, I think that our country does plenty of killing too, Joe.'[21] America is a normal country. It murders innocent people, like any other country, and often for no good reason.[22]

Trump wants America not only to recognize but also to embrace its lack of innocence. Compare this cynical amoralism with similar-sounding denials of America's innocence by his liberal predecessors. When Bill Clinton and Obama spurned the idea of American innocence, they did so for reasons completely contrary to Trump's. They both admitted serious wrongdoing by their country, but without abandoning the conceit that America represents a globally admirable moral ideal.

In 1999, for example, to show that he was not coming to Ankara to preach or crow about America, President Clinton spoke to the Turkish Grand National Assembly as follows:

> Keep in mind, I come from a nation that was founded on the creed
> that all are created equal; and yet, when we were founded, we had

slavery; women could not vote; even men could not vote unless they owned property. I know something about the imperfect realization of a country's ideals. We have had a long journey in America, from our founding to where we are, but the journey has been worth making.[23]

The rhetorical point of this confession of America's imperfection was to persuade his listeners to *imitate* America's 'long journey'. If the Turks would only follow America's lead, they could eventually overcome ethnic discrimination in their own country. The United States is still far from reaching the goal of liberty and justice for all. But that takes nothing away from the country's exceptional nature. What makes America exceptional is precisely that an American president can travel abroad and, without feeling defensive, openly admit his country's failings. This heartfelt guilty plea indirectly implied that the lecturing Americans were further down the pathway towards moral improvement than the listening Turks.

Ten years later, Obama delivered a similarly subtle paean to America's exceptionalism in Cairo.[24] What made America unique was the willingness of its leaders to come clean about its past sins. This disarming candour was evidently why the country remained a moral beacon for mankind. This is why its representatives retained the right and duty to tell others what chores they 'must' perform and what best practices they 'must' copy. For Clinton and Obama, disclaiming America's innocence was an indirect way of salvaging America's widely contested exceptionalism and especially America's status as a moral exemplar for the rest of the world.

Trump admits America's sins for a less confessional and more nefarious reason. In a ruthless and competitive world, only the naïve would strive for innocence and only a loser would go on an apology tour. Awareness of one's own lack of innocence, as a result, is no cause for feeling guilty or regretful. On the contrary, it's a sign of savoir faire. After all, why be the only honest player at the poker game? For him, disclaiming American righteousness is a first step towards escaping the self-defeating do-gooder illusions induced by the myth of American exceptionalism.

Trump's 'charisma', if we can call it that, is largely based on his mould-breaking ways. And the most exceptional thing about his exceptional presidency is his rejection of the myth of American exceptionalism.[25] He has accomplished something which would have been previously thought impossible. He has reconciled America's most jingoistic citizens to the idea that America can be 'great' without being an international leader, without being morally superior, without being especially innocent, and without having any right to lecture other countries. He has detached America's congenital self-love from the idea that America is 'special' in the sense of morally superior. It is worth noting in this context that only the most left-wing members of the Democratic Party deny that 'the US stands above other nations.'[26] This provides a good measure of Trump's hypnotic powers. He has charmed his nationalistic base into thinking exactly like the most liberal of self-doubting Democrats without obliging them to abandon their intolerant and xenophobic fantasies.

Trump's battle cry is: 'We need somebody that can take the *brand* of the United States and make it great again.'[27] This is a paradoxical slogan because he explicitly aims to rebrand America as no better or worse than any other country. Because it has nothing to do with American exceptionalism, his kind of American 'greatness' is historically unprecedented. He says great *again* but he cannot really be looking back to the 1950s and 1960s when America out-produced a world devastated by war, solved its labour–business conflicts, and 'saw the emergence of beatniks and civil rights',[28] for that was clearly a heyday of American exceptionalism. Trump's 'greatness' is altogether something else. It involves the obliteration of America's self-professed uniqueness and its assimilation to the rest of the mundane world. This should have been a shocker since 'Americans are not accustomed to thinking that theirs is a country like any other.'[29] But the leaders of the Republican Party, among others, have accepted this 'normalization' of their country largely without struggle or qualification.[30] To understand this lack of resistance is to go a long way towards comprehending the secret of his extraordinary political success. How has he been able to convince America's flag-waving nationalists to abandon the idea that the United States is morally better than other countries?

'WONDERFUL DEMOCRACY'

Why were Americans prepared to accept political views so radically dissonant with many of their country's deepest cultural traditions? The election of a figure so openly hostile to America's moral leadership of the world suggests that dark currents are swirling around in the depths of American public opinion. When Trump began arguing that America is a 'loser' nation in the 1980s, almost no one paid attention.[31] What has changed in the interim is not Trump's thinking but the susceptibility to his message of important forces in American society. But why would the implausible notion that America is the greatest victim of the Americanization of the world suddenly gain the political traction that it never before enjoyed? To deepen our answer to this question, we should revisit the way the occupation of Iraq and the War on Terror helped prepare public opinion to sympathize with Trump's radically revisionist way of thought.

During his campaign for the presidency, Trump routinely denounced the 'dangerous idea that we could make Western democracies out of countries that had no experience or interests in becoming a Western democracy'.[32] He was obviously thinking about Iraq. Already in 2004, he was expressing doubts that Iraq would become a 'wonderful democracy', predicting instead that 'two minutes after we leave, there's going to be a revolution', during which power will be seized by 'the meanest, toughest, smartest, most vicious guy'.[33] And, as President, he has made it clear that the United States was finally and definitively getting out of the imitation-promotion business.[34]

That America is the greatest loser from the Americanization of the world may be Trump's oddest intuition. But he found a much more receptive audience for his assertion that America had no business trying to democratize Iraq than for his earlier suggestion that America had had no business helping transform Germany and Japan into functioning capitalist democracies.[35]

Times have changed. But a more specific reason for the divergent public responses to these two claims is that the United States was able to initiate and steer the democratization of former enemies after 1945 because of its economic and military domination of the world

in the wake of a war that had reduced most previously industrial
ized countries to rubble. America obviously no longer enjoys such a
disproportionate share of global power. And the American public's
enthusiasm for remaking the world in America's image was destined
to fade after it became clear that it no longer had the capacity to do
so.[36] Seen from abroad, too, American-style liberal democracy was
bound to lose its canonical status once America itself lost its global
dominance. This relative decline in power made imposing American
interests and value judgements on the rest of the world seem hopeless.
There is no point in trying to achieve what one lacks the capacity to
achieve. In this sense, Trump's 'un-American' rejection of American
exceptionalism is more realistic than Robert Kagan's typically American belief that 'decline . . . is a choice. It is not an inevitable fate'.[37]
Relative decline *is* America's fate. The choices that remain only concern how wisely or foolishly this decline is managed.

It is also worth recalling that Trump was right when he said, in his
Inaugural Address, that 'America's infrastructure has fallen into dis-
repair and decay.'[38] The plausibility of clothing America's foreign-
policy choices in the language of a universal mission on behalf of all
mankind was bound to founder once America lost its self-confidence
as the cutting edge of modernity. A realistic recognition of America's
dwindling relative power and global prestige helps explain why a significant swathe of the American electorate was willing to embrace a
candidate who openly mocked the country's 'calling' to spread, by
example if not by force, its political and economic model around
the world.

After 1989, many prominent members of the American foreign-
policy establishment believed 'that a global democratic capitalist
revolution led by and modeled on the United States was imminent'.[39]
Lingering over-confidence of this sort does not explain the invasion
of Iraq, but it does explain the publicly promulgated rationale for
undertaking it. After it became clear that Saddam Hussein possessed
no weapons of mass destruction, the George W. Bush administration
shifted to justifying the war solely on liberal humanitarian grounds,
to protect the human rights of Iraqi civilians and to promote democracy at the point of a gun. These were ambitions that the American
public had become used to supporting. The actual motivations of the

war, as the administration's many critics leapt to point out, were quite different.[40] But whatever the motivations, the war was publicly justified by a moral duty to generalize liberal-democratic norms and institutions around the world.

Fast-forward to today. Trump's anti-missionary message has been strengthened by the fact that America's image in the world was seriously tarnished by its government's irrational response to 9/11, including not only America's unsuccessful wars but also the photographically documented mistreatment of prisoners in Abu Ghraib and the decade-long arbitrary detention of random captives in Guantanamo Bay. Such abuses encouraged even parts of the world that once looked up to the United States as a liberal 'beacon' to entertain doubts not only about America's 'crusader' ambitions but also about the imitability of America's example. The readiness of many Americans, including those of a liberal persuasion, to accept Donald Trump's abandonment of the moral high ground can be most economically explained by America's objective loss of the moral high ground. This is how, in the first decade of the twenty-first century, America forfeited much of its previously boasted 'influence of example'. Trump did not instigate a global disenchantment with the US's global leadership. Instead, he became electable only when his own instinctive hostility to America's missionary tradition began to resonate with the wider public.

This brings us back, once again, to the way in which 1989 radically altered America's posture in world affairs. For the previous four decades, the Soviet Union had not only been America's principal military adversary. It had also been its ideological and moral 'other'. Both left and right in America defended their competing visions of a liberal society in reaction to the Stalinist nightmare. In this sense, the Cold War profoundly shaped America's public philosophy. Indeed, we might say that the Cold War was America's public philosophy. The demanding contest with Soviet communism guided how Americans thought about the core principles underlying their basic institutions. For American liberalism was, or appeared to be, Soviet totalitarianism turned inside out. Freedom of speech and the press as well as freedom of conscience were idealized precisely because they were cruelly repressed under Moscow's sway. In the same spirit, Americans underscored the freedom of movement, the right to form private associations, the right to a fair trial, and the right to vote in competitive elections where incumbents might be toppled from power. Likewise emphasized was the latitude to accumulate private wealth, on the assumption that a decentralized and unplanned economy alone could provide the basis of both prosperity and political freedom. In 1989, the question was: Would these 'American values' survive the geopolitical contest that had made them strategically vital?

Ironically, the superpower that prevailed in the Cold War was the one ideologically devoted to the supreme value of political and economic competition. Having always celebrated the beneficial effects of competition, the West no longer had a peer competitor with an equally international vision to encourage its laboured efforts to comply with its own publicly proclaimed ideals.[41] Having gained a monopoly on superpower status, a victorious America became the unique supplier not only of security but also of political values. Most of those who welcomed this development did not take seriously what liberal theory would have predicted, namely that monopoly suppliers, freed from competitive pressures, begin to behave wastefully, recklessly, and without much regard for the costs of their behaviour, especially to the consumers of what they and only they supply.

This is one reason why American liberalism, once 'freed' from its Cold War competition with Soviet communism, began to lose its bearings. Democracy and human rights began to seem less central to the nation's identity because Americans no longer defined their public philosophy in contrast to the model espoused by a lethally armed and existentially threatening peer competitor. Universal human rights had been considered a strategic asset during the Cold War. During the War on Terror, by contrast, freedom from arbitrary arrest and the right to a fair trial began to be seen as strategic liabilities, overly restricting the harsh methods by which US officials believed they needed to attack the country's new-found jihadist enemies. Thus, spreading human rights abroad became as politically suspect as spreading democracy.

Similarly, 'the open society', including the freedom to travel freely across national borders, became less of a promise than a threat. Reagan's demand that the Soviet's 'tear down that wall' gave way to a new valorization of hardened barricades and barbed-wire-strewn frontiers as the only feasible method for protecting the embattled liberal world from the jungle out there. Such were the fears that gave birth to Donald Trump and his promise of salvation-by-wall.

AMERICA'S GLASS HOUSE

A helpful way to approach the paradoxical idea that imitation seriously threatens the imitated, leaving them disoriented and disinherited, involves the global spread of the English language. Central European populists regularly accuse Anglophone elites of being traitors to the nation, monopolizing the emergency exits and willing to abandon their fellow citizens at a moment's notice. Here we approach the topic from the opposite perspective.

A decade or two ago, non-Americans assumed that the spread of English meant that American values and ideas were conquering the world.[42] In his theory of linguistic justice, the philosopher Philippe Van Parijs suggested that a special language tax should be imposed on members of Anglophone communities to subsidize the costs of English learning by members of non-Anglophone communities.[43] The justification offered for such a transfer programme was that English speakers reap massive unearned benefits from having been raised with English as their mother tongue.

In a way it is true that American English serves as the world's 'reserve language' just as the American dollar serves as the world's reserve currency, giving Americans an unfair leg-up in all kinds of international transactions. But after the transformation of Washington into the centre of worldwide instability, the idea that the spread of English provides an indisputable advantage for native speakers seems less intuitively plausible. To be sure, Americans remain proud that people everywhere learn English and want to study at American universities. But it has become increasingly obvious that the global spread of the English language in many ways puts Americans at a competitive disadvantage in an interconnected world. It even poses a strategic threat to American security.

To start with the obvious: Americans are less motivated to learn foreign languages than non-Americans. According to a Gallup poll, only about a quarter of Americans can converse in any language other than English. Among that quarter, 55 per cent are Spanish speakers, for many of whom Spanish is actually their first language rather than a second. The head of the American Council for the Teaching of Foreign Languages reports that Americans are 'at the bottom' of the world in foreign-language ability.[44]

This subordinate ranking of the allegedly top country has unfortunate consequences. The asymmetry between monolingual Americans and those whose mother tongue is not English but who nevertheless speak English with relative fluency is one of the most important power asymmetries in a world where education is the key to social mobility and adaptability to rapid change. As Amin Maalouf has written, 'It will always be a serious handicap not to know English, but it will also, more and more, be a serious handicap to know English only.'[45] Burdened with a parochial media culture and deprived of the ability to enter into and make sense of complex local realities through language-enabled learning, Americans have become increasingly out of touch. The world-views of non-Americans are increasingly incomprehensible to business, diplomatic, journalistic and even academic elites. All too often they are told by the people they speak to abroad only what they are presumed to want to hear.[46]

It is frequently argued that the worldwide popularity of American culture is a sign of America's global pre-eminence and power. Here is a representative example:

> During the apogee of Western liberal democracy, the United States – and, to a lesser extent, western Europe – was home to the most famous writers and musicians, the most watched television shows and movies, the most advanced industries, and the most prestigious universities. In the minds of many young people coming of age in Africa or Asia in the 1990s, all these things seemed to be of a piece: the desire to share in the unfathomable wealth of the West was also a desire to adopt its lifestyle, and the desire to adopt its lifestyle seemed to require emulating its political system.[47]

The well-respected authors go on to claim that such 'cultural clout' allowed the United States 'to influence the development of other countries'.[48] But such claims about America's 'soft power' are dubious. Indeed, the global diffusion of English-language proficiency, and the global familiarity with American culture that it enables and encourages, means that citizens of the United States now live in a glass house. The world knows America much better than America knows the world. This raises the question: Who is best able to manipulate and outmanoeuvre whom?

The world watches US movies and follows US politics, it is true. But this gives foreign powers, such as Russia, an immense advantage when they decide, for instance, to interfere covertly in American politics. It's reported that President Putin instructed his defence minister, Sergei K. Shoigu, that if he wanted to understand how America worked, the only thing he needed to do was watch the Netflix series *House of Cards*.[49]

While the citizens of other countries know a lot about Americans, Americans have little idea of how the rest of the world thinks and lives. Americans have never heard of non-Anglophone movie stars and have only the vaguest idea of what's at stake in other countries' political conflicts. This gross asymmetry of understanding creates a strategic vulnerability. For instance, twenty-year-olds in Jeddah or Karachi can surf the internet and enroll in flight lessons in Oklahoma, but hardly any twenty-year-old from Oklahoma could learn what is on offer in Jeddah or Karachi, because they don't speak the languages there.

When WikiLeaks released the secret cables of the American State Department, it became a global news sensation and a major embarrassment for American diplomacy. In contrast, the Chinese diplomatic cables leaked a few years ago, although no doubt very interesting to professionals, could never become a worldwide human-interest story, nor a serious setback for Chinese foreign policy, because relatively few people read Chinese fluently, except for the Chinese themselves and a handful of experts abroad.

The United States may currently enjoy a significant military advantage over China. But the asymmetry represented by a culturally and politically transparent America and a culturally and politically opaque China casts doubt on America's superior leverage in trade disputes. As Bob Woodward remarks in discussing the Sino-American trade war that began in 2018:

The Chinese knew exactly how to inflict economic and political pain. The United States was in kindergarten compared to China's PhD. The Chinese knew which congressional districts produced what products, such as soybeans. They knew which swing districts were going to be important to maintain control of the House. They could target tariffs at products from those districts, or at a state level. The Chinese would target bourbon from McConnell's Kentucky and dairy products from Paul Ryan's Wisconsin.[50]

There are not only many more Chinese students of America than American students of China, but they are, on average, much better informed.

Although the transformation of English into the global lingua franca once seemed like a signal example of America's soft power, it now appears to have created a world in which America's military dominance and economic success are undermined by cultural illiteracy, incurious parochialism and indifference.[51] The problem is exacerbated by the tendency for State Department specialists who know the languages and cultures to be sidelined by Defense Department heavyweights who do not. In any case, lack of familiarity with the language, history and politics of other nations naturally engenders suspicion and fear of what one only dimly comprehends. It also raises the chances of being deliberately deceived by carefully tailored, agenda-driven disinformation. When American military personnel in Afghanistan or Iraq report about locals that 'the only language they understand is force', they are revealing more about their own monolingual provincialism and tunnel-vision than about the country in which they are stationed and whose domestic conflicts they struggle vainly to decipher.[52] Failure to grasp how others think makes strategic action difficult, since strategy requires an ability to foresee how others are likely to react to one's initiatives. It is impossible for the US government 'to influence the development of other countries' so long as Americans remain hamstrung by a monolingual education and inherited cultural blinders that have become dangerously anachronistic in an irreversibly globalized world.

As Alexander Voloshin, former Chief of the Presidential Administration of Russia, told one of the authors, imitators know those they imitate much better than the imitated know those who imitate them.[53] Successful predators know their prey better than their prey know themselves. Rather than walling itself off from competitors, the United States has created and sustained a wide-open world without walls that makes monolingual America an easy target for multilingual foreign raiders. The suspect interlopers include countries which, attempting to conform to the expectations of the world's liberal hegemon, have for many decades been conscientiously studying America's politics and culture. As China's economic clout continues to grow at the West's expense, business executives apprehensive about technology transfer and populist voters apprehensive about job loss are both rallying around the paranoid fear of foreign competition that Trump espoused for many decades to near-universal indifference. As the US's relative power declines, more and more national politicians, including Democrats, have become wary of international interdependence. Trump's rise was primed by this cultural shift. Foreign understanding of the American scene, enabled by the globalization of English, is now widely feared as an instrument for political subversion and technological larceny.

IMITATORS AS COMPETITORS

The Age of Imitation pretended to be a win-win world. The faux morality of such naïve liberalism, according to its populist critics, is 'do unto others as you would have them do unto you.' Such a moralistic imperative is an invitation to let down your guard. America First is the anti-Golden Rule. This means, on a geopolitical level, that all of its commercial rivals are scheming to cheat America and that America must pull no punches in striving to come out ahead in every bilateral deal. Winning means besting, and losing means being bested. So a win-win world, even if it were possible, would be a world in which America never 'wins' anymore, which is exactly Trump's never-ending complaint.

Within our framework, an obvious question to ask is this: What would make Trump intuitively uncomfortable with the distinction between imitators and the imitated? One answer is that it obscures what he considers a much more meaningful distinction, that between victory and defeat. Trump's biographers seem to agree about his 'simple mind-set, winners versus losers', and his 'zero-sum world of winners and losers'.[54] This is how he (or his ghost writer) put it: 'You hear lots of people say that a great deal is when both sides win. That is a bunch of crap. In a great deal, you win – not the other side. You crush the opponent and come away with something better for yourself.'[55] Either dominate or be dominated. That is the law of the jungle. As a one-time confidant also explained:

> It was a binary, zero-sum choice for him: You either dominated or you submitted. You either created and exploited fear, or you succumbed to it . . . In countless conversations, he made clear to me that he treated every encounter as a contest he had to win, because the only other option from his perspective was to lose, and that was the equivalent of obliteration.[56]

On a more mundane level, Trump naturally feels uncomfortable with the politics of imitation because, from a businessman's perspective, imitators are threats.[57] American businessmen appreciate Trump's tax cuts and deregulatory moves, but they don't like his erratic and unprincipled imposing and lifting of tariffs. What keeps many of them nevertheless on Trump's side is precisely his fierce insistence that foreign imitators of America are infringing America's patents and copyrights.

If emulators successfully replicate (and improve on) your business model, they will peel away your customers. Successful imitators will steal your thunder and even drive you into bankruptcy. For Trump, Germany and Japan were for years the most scandalous examples. After defeating them decisively in the Second World War, the United States allowed its one-time enemies to become its commercial rivals. The 'Wise Men' in charge of US foreign policy after 1945 considered this an unobjectionable trade-off, since potential trade imbalances seemed preferable, at the time, to potential thermonuclear war. This was deliberate policy not inadvertence. But within a short few decades, America's militarily defeated enemies began beating the United States at its own industrial export game. By encouraging a re-channelling of German and Japanese nationalism away from military competition and into industrial competition on the American model, the United States, according to the zealots of economic protectionism, dug its own grave.

In the interim, from Trump's perspective, Sino-American relations have developed along similar lines. 'We built China', he believes.[58] After encouraging China's economic opening, apparently on the assumption that this would lead to the country's preordained convergence with liberal-democratic capitalism, the West was shocked to find itself confronting a Party-led mercantilist system that is outcompeting the West on multiple fronts. Fortuitously, China's stupendous economic growth coincided with America's futile attempt to Americanize the formerly communist nations of Central and Eastern Europe. In China, by contrast, reform-by-imitation excluded the imitation of Western values such as freedom of the press and checks-and-balances. Democratic participation and electoral accountability were not included either, although it was initially thought by some observers that they might naturally follow, at least in the long run.

For Trump, and not only for him, the Chinese economic miracle has been a disaster for the United States. Precisely because its citizens are world-class imitators, China is stealing or has perhaps already stolen the mantle of economic front-runner from the United States. Indeed, Reagan was the last president who was justified in talking of American exceptionalism because he had not yet seen the effects on the US economy of China's rise.

Trump and his business supporters like to point out that the US has created and maintained an open world trading system free of charge. This helped transform first Germany and Japan and now China into turbo-charged, export-oriented capitalist economies. For economic nationalists, the fact that American managerial styles and industrial production methods were transferred to former and future adversaries is a national embarrassment. Giving them security for free was bad enough. But America encouraged them to divert their scarce resources and energy to economic development, helping them channel their nationalistic ambitions into manufacturing high-end products for global, including American, markets. This misbegotten policy has purportedly led to the disastrous de-industrialization of the United States.

What originally irked Trump most was that Germany and Japan, after being crushed militarily, developed copy-cat automobile industries that succeeded in beating their American forerunners on the world consumer market. His famous fondness for Cadillacs and dislike of their competitors helps explain his otherwise inexplicable obsession with German luxury cars in particular. In his famous 1990 interview with *Playboy*, Trump said that, if it were possible, 'I'd throw a tax on every Mercedes-Benz rolling into this country.'[59] Twenty-five years later, in the same speech in which he famously remarked that Mexico was sending the US its rapists, Trump complained: 'When did we beat Japan at anything? They send their cars over by the millions, and what do we do? . . . They beat us all the time.'[60] America's fabled love affair with the automobile makes consumer preferences for foreign cars seem like a disloyal attack on America's entrepreneurial pre-eminence. In the summer of 2018, absurdly but revealingly, 'Trump ordered Commerce Secretary Wilbur Ross to investigate auto tariffs and probe whether car imports are a danger to national security.'[61]

It bears repeating that America's post-1945 national-security establishment *deliberately* set about to replace the war-prone militarized nationalism of Germany and Japan with peaceful commercialized nationalism. Encouraging and subsidizing the emulation of America's postwar export-led industrialization in both Germany and Japan was meant to avert a Third World War which, given the development of compact weapons of mass destruction, might have led to the real 'end of history'. Because they would be diverting their energies into becoming economic rather than military powerhouses, these two former enemies of America would be willing to forgo the development of nuclear weapons and would accept an American nuclear umbrella in exchange for joining America's anti-Soviet system of alliances. Whatever else 'the liberal world order' represents, it includes the post-Second World War exclusion of Germany and Japan from the club of nuclear-armed nations.

But Trump seems utterly unconcerned about nuclear winter or a Third World War. He has other dragons to slay, namely the stupendous successes of export-led economic growth in Germany and Japan after the Second World War and in China after the Cold War. America won the wars but lost the post-wars by exporting its capacity to export to foreign competitors. It is ridiculous to see the economic miracles in post-fascist Germany and Japan and post-communist China as victories for America, he contends, because 'to the victor belongs the spoils'[62] and the spoils of global trade were grabbed by the US's one-time adversaries, to the shame of America's policy makers who were perhaps too wracked by liberal guilt to devour the fruits of domination. It is as if avoiding a Third World War was too great a price to pay for a cross-border 'invasion' of Toyotas and Mercedes-Benzes.

Many of the businessmen who stand with Trump agree that the most consequential form of transnational imitation is copyright infringement. When you allow others to imitate you, you risk losing your competitive edge. That worry, as much as tax cuts and deregulation, explains how Trump has managed to rally a significant portion of the American business community to his side.

Trump's bigoted remarks about Mexicans and Muslims lend some credence to the idea that he aims to revive the Nazi-friendly and isolationist politics of the America First movement of the 1930s.[63] There is no reason to doubt his subliminal sympathies for white supremacy. But his version of America First is about American products beating all rivals on the global marketplace. In a beauty contest between Cadillac and Mercedes, the American car should 'win'. In other words, 'First' means 'in first place', not 'über Alles', since dominating others means interacting with them, a prospect that holds little lure for an instinctual xenophobe (and germaphobe) like Trump, who always prefers to take the money and run rather than hanging around to govern other peoples, a task he would consider burdensome and pointless.

In his view, America's brand, and brands, will never come out first so long as other countries free-ride on American ingenuity. Americans were the principal architects of global dispute-resolution mechanisms; but arbitration tribunals now often and ungratefully rule against the United States. Even more scandalously, America gave the internet to the rest of the world for free. Afterwards, the US has looked on passively as its very creativity was expropriated. It no longer controls the internet, which was originally an invention of the country's defence establishment. Gifted freely to the world, the internet has been mastered by America's rivals and is now being used to outshine the country which created it. Something similar can be said of GPS and other globalization-friendly products of American inventiveness. America has lost control of its own creations. Anger at China's underhanded acquisition of Western technology via obligatory joint venture arrangements which disclose industrial secrets to Chinese firms is widespread. It is one of the principal reasons why the country proved receptive to Trump's message that America has been despoiled of its rightful inheritance and dispossessed by the Americanization of the world.

Several commentators have noticed Trump's 'complete lack of interest in the Cold War contest, which was at its height when Trump first entered the fray in 1980, and was a battle which [at the time] the United States was widely perceived to be losing'.[64] A possible reason for his insouciance in this regard was that the Soviet Union, unlike Cold War Germany and Japan, was no imitator of American-style capitalist democracy. The USSR was never integrated into the global trading system. Unlike today's China, therefore, it was in no position to outdo or underbid American firms and lure away their customers. Something similar can be said about Russia today which, although no longer a communist country, is still not bristling with export industries that compete for market share with American firms. What this suggests is that Trump had a post-Cold War outlook at least a decade before the end of the Cold War. He consistently gave, and still gives, absolute priority to commercial competition over national-security threats. Unlike the Republican Party's now silenced national-security hawks, he is in sync with 21st-century American public opinion, where kitchen-table issues preoccupy voters more than a few terrorists in East Africa or a few artificial islands in the South China Sea.

Trump does not see the transformation of America's former authoritarian and militaristic enemies into peaceful capitalist democracies as a victory for American foreign policy. Rather than being 'the sincerest form of flattery that mediocrity can pay to greatness', as Oscar Wilde claimed, he sees German-style imitation as a con game that undermines America's economy. Already in the 1980s, Trump stated, and still evidently believes, that America has been betrayed by the imitation game. The country has been bamboozled by its imitators, whose fake flattery also conceals behind-closed-doors laughter which is the ultimate sign of disrespect.

IMMIGRATION AS IDENTITY THEFT

It would be an exaggeration to claim that imitation-anxiety alone explains the resonance of Trump's message in the American heartland. But it certainly plays a pivotal role. His popular constituency, as opposed to his adherents in the business community, feels endangered by imitation in two senses. In both cases, fear of being imitated hinges on fear of being replaced.

For Trump's supporters, 'globalization' is a dirty word because it connotes job loss and the drop in social status and self-esteem that accompanies unemployment and precarious part-time work. Trump speaks directly to these existential anxieties: 'They are taking our jobs. China is taking our jobs . . . India is taking our jobs.'[65] That this metaphor of global job theft resonates in the American heartland is beyond doubt.[66] In reality, Trump's trade policy is more concerned with preventing China from stealing America's job-killing robots than from stealing American jobs. The cry that his supporters want to hear, however, is that 'The wealth of our middle class has been ripped from their homes and then redistributed across the entire world.'[67] The middle classes in China and India have expanded exponentially while the American middle classes have proportionally shrunk. Globalization does not merely spell job loss, therefore. It entails the wholesale transfer of middle-class status from the United States to its economic imitators abroad.[68]

The second form of imitation-anxiety afflicting Trump's base is even more serious and multi-layered. It is the fear that America, as an exemplar nation, will serve as an irresistible magnet for non-white immigrants from south of the border. Fear-mongering about 'job theft' is an appealing political tactic for populist politicians because it melds fear of foreign invasion with fear of foreign competition. The prospect of more people competing for fewer jobs naturally distresses those whose employment prospects are visibly shrinking.

But immigration panic has roots deeper than fear of losing jobs and status. It touches on loss of identity.

Alongside contempt for so-called 'establishment elites', hatred and fear of immigrants represents the most salient point of convergence between American and Central European populisms. 'The United States will not be a migrant camp,' Trump has promised, 'and it will not be a refugee holding facility.' Referring to 'what's happening in Europe', he continues, 'we can't allow that to happen to the United States. Not on my watch.'[69] The 'big mistake made all over Europe' was 'allowing millions of people who have so strongly and violently changed their culture!'[70] The idea that non-European immigrants, with the connivance of post-nationalists in the European Union, are infiltrating Europe and gradually erasing European culture and civilization from the book of history is the core of the ultra-nationalist nightmare of a 'Great Replacement' of Europeans by non-Europeans.[71] Trump's willingness to echo such far-right tropes, which have provided rhetorical justification for murderous violence,[72] suggests that the mass appeal of his brand of populism, too, lies in demographic anxiety. If his business supporters fear copyright infringement and technology theft, his enraptured crowds fear cultural infringement and identity theft.

Both Trump and Orbán enflame visceral hostility to political refugees as well as economic migrants by waving the bloody shirt of an imaginary slow-motion 'invasion'.[73] Their aim is to foment demographic panic among their followers and thereby awaken primitive longings for a last-ditch saviour of white identity. Trump warns that 'large, well-organized caravans of migrants are marching towards our southern border. Some people call it an "invasion". It's like an invasion.'[74] Similarly, in a speech from July 2016, during which he fulsomely praised Donald Trump, Orbán reminded his audience of an earlier 'Great Replacement': 'I can even understand the Americans' positive point of view on migration because that is how the United States came to be, but they have to be able to see that in this situation we are the Indians.'[75] Like Central European populists, in fact, America's white supremacists see themselves as the new Native Americans, 'indigenous' peoples being overrun by foreign invaders and threatened with ethnic extinction. What we once did to the Indians, the

Mexicans are now trying to do to us. For America's white nationalists, this is reason enough to reject the Golden Rule.

These fantasies of invading hoards also explain how crowds that
chant 'USA! USA!' can also accept Trump's denial that America is
an exceptionally good country. His most ardent supporters are intuitively sceptical of the Reagan-era picture of America as an
imitation-worthy 'shining city on a hill', sensing correctly that Reagan used the image to reiterate that America was 'still a beacon, still
a magnet for all who must have freedom', which for populists includes
non-white immigrants from south of the border scrambling to displace and dispossess white Americans.[76]

Anti-immigrant politics is highly emotional because mass immigration, whether real or fictional, threatens to wash away the last
remnants of an imagined community that, for historically contingent
reasons, is already coming unstitched. This analysis assumes that
identity is experienced most vividly in feelings aroused by perceptions
of otherness and belonging. In modern societies, to be sure, most
individuals inhabit multiple reference groups defined by religion, age,
gender, class, metropolitan versus non-metropolitan residence, mari-
tal status, level of education and worldliness. Identity collapses into
clannish antagonisms and even murderous social conflict only when
one affiliation, usually a sectarian or ethnic one, plays such a prominent role in an individual's self-understanding as to eclipse all rival
affiliations.[77] Tribalism and fundamentalism are such effective political mobilizers because they define 'who we are' based on a starkly
one-dimensional distinction between 'them' and 'us'. This distinction
increases its grip on human motivation under conditions of economic
stress or rapid and unpredictable social change.

Samuel Huntington was among the first to express America's growing reluctance to see itself as an immigrant nation. He notoriously
doubted that any culturally heterogeneous country could be politically well-organized.[78] This was very bad news for an increasingly
multicultural America. Huntington blamed decades of liberal immigration policy for his country's political incoherence and dysfunction.
The liberal elite's commitment to universalism and individualism had
led them to deny that citizenship in a liberal state could and should
be awarded exclusively to individuals of a specific race, ethnicity or

culture. Their anti-racism and reluctance to discriminate against non-whites marks liberal policy makers as 'rootless cosmopolitans' who are actually or potentially disloyal to the majority of their co-nationals. During the run-up to the 2018 midterms, Trump asserted that Democrats and coastal elites 'want Open Borders and Unlimited Crime, well into the future'. This, he implied, is why they should be classified as traitors to the true American nation.[79]

Huntington did not speak this way, but the gist of his thinking tracks Trump's cruder intuitions fairly well. As a result of liberalism's profligate hospitality, the United States has become a cultural hybrid or mishmash, unified only by principles, such as the rule of law, that are too abstract to bind together people who have arrived from a multitude of countries across the world. But here comes an important nuance. In *Who Are We?*, Huntington suggests that the cohesion of the American 'we' depends not only on cultural assimilation but also on a homogeneity of ethnic descent.[80] But he also recognized that, having sacrificed the coherence it once enjoyed when a common ancestry and posterity were shared by the vast majority of its citizens, the US can never regain its lost soul, no matter how tightly it seals its borders. Nostalgia is possible but going back is not. By pretending to turn nostalgia for an irretrievable past into a partisan political pro-gramme, by contrast, Trump is leading his compatriots off a cliff. He can't make America white again. All he can do is destroy America's post-Second World War self-image as a country uniquely able and will-ing, over time, to assimilate immigrants from everywhere in the world.[81]

Trump has capitalized on a cultural shift, most prominent in pro-vincial America, away from an open and welcoming to a closed and unwelcoming definition of 'who we are'. Given that 13.7 per cent of the American population is now foreign-born, that the rate of increase in this percentage is slow, and that demography has a remorseless logic of its own, there are basically two options for dealing with immigration into the US. The first is to create a clear path to citizen-ship for the millions of illegal aliens already living and working in the country, thereby reaffirming America's image as a nation of immi-grants, while investing heavily in programmes to integrate those already in the country, thereby preserving America's self-image as an inclusive, welcoming and culturally mixed nation. The second is to radically redefine America as a barricaded, inhospitable, mono-ethnic society, belonging essentially to its 50 per cent white Christian inhabitants, closed to subsequent non-white immigration and unfazed by discrimination inside the country against black, Hispanic and Muslim citizens, and perhaps against Asians and Jews.

Rhetorically, at least, Trump has chosen this second, logistically unworkable, politically incendiary and morally repugnant option.

In Chapter 1 we explained the emergence of anti-immigrant politics in Central Europe, even in the absence of actual immigrants, as a roundabout expression of the demographic anxiety caused by cata-strophic depopulation throughout the region. In the American case, the first-hand experience fostering hostility to immigrants is not depopulation as in Eastern Europe but de-industrialization.[82] With-out being the cause of economic insecurity, illegal immigration has been turned by populists into a focal point around which those suf-fering most from the loss of jobs and opportunities can rally.

During the two decades after the Second World War, when the United States was the world's sole industrial powerhouse, working-class America did extraordinarily well. In the two decades after the end of the Cold War, by which time the US example had inspired legions of industrial imitators abroad, these same working-class families began to struggle. In these latter years, to maintain the façade of a middle-class existence to which they had become accustomed, many Americans went on a profligate borrowing spree. Then came the financial crash of 2008. The burden of their credit-card-enabled imitation game became unsustainable and the precipitous loss of status subsequently experienced by those unable to pay their debts fuelled the anti-liberal revolt in America just as it did in Hungary. Populist demagogues exploited these conditions to convince voters whose fortunes were sinking and who saw few prospects for their children to blame a con-spiracy of immigrants and multicultural elites, even though their misfortunes actually stemmed from a combination of automization and the planetary redistribution of middle-class reputability (and faith in the future) from America and Europe to India and China.

The loss of high-paying and secure employment by lower-middle-class American whites delivered a rude blow to their self-respect as well as their material well-being. Precisely because they pose threats to social status, outsourcing and robotization have prepared the ground for us-versus-them demagoguery. In this context, the role of China's rapid integration into the world trading system is especially important because it associates the decline of American primacy with the end of communist ideology, something for which Americans had been ardently struggling. The end of the Cold War seriously reduced anti-oligarchic pressures inside the liberal West, since capitalists no longer felt compelled to curry favour with workers in the hopes of reducing the appeal of a militarily powerful egalitarian alternative to the liberal order.[83] Without a formidable communist enemy, American capitalism abandoned what little concern it had for the well-being of working stiffs and wholeheartedly embraced an essentially unlimited concentration of wealth at the top. As economic disparities grew and chances for upward mobility shrank, America's Cold War victory continued to buoy up the lucky few. But to the new plutocracy's 'forgotten man', it began to feel like a post-Cold War defeat.

Some portion of white working- and middle-class resentment can be explained as a hostile reaction not to illegal immigrants but to perceived contempt from America's increasingly wealthy and insulated liberal establishment.[84] The distress of lower-middle-class and working-class whites with only a high-school degree at their perceived political invisibility made them an easy touch for Trump, whose rhetorical attention to their plight, however opportunistic and insincere, stood out among the general indifference of political elites in both parties. A classic treatment of the dangerous untethering of the American establishment from the bulk of the population, a disengagement which prepared the country for Trump, is Christopher Lasch's 1995 book, *The Revolt of the Elites*. America's 'privileged classes,' Lasch explains, 'have made themselves independent not only of crumbling industrial cities but of public services in general'. They see private doctors, send their children to private schools, have private security guards and live in gated communities. Having 'ceased to think of themselves as Americans in any important sense', they are 'deeply indifferent to the prospect of American national decline'.[85] In a democracy, this self-absorbed inattentiveness of the political, economic and cultural elite to the preoccupations of the majority opens up a door for a populist counter-elite willing to listen (or pretend to listen) to the woes of those who feel ignored and unheard. As Republican pollster Frank Luntz says about Trump's message to his base: 'He tells them they matter. He tells them their votes count. They're either forgotten or fucked and they've been waiting to be told their existence matters.'[86]

The anti-elitist strand running through the anti-liberal backlash in America closely parallels what we witnessed among the Central European populists. After being told to reform their politics and economies along Western lines in order to join the European Union, Hungarians and Poles came to resent being alternately ignored and looked down upon as second-rate replicas of advanced liberal democracies. The presumed existence of an Imitation Imperative obliged them to embrace a metric of respectability which doomed them to feelings of perpetual inadequacy. Orbán has responded as the theory of resentment would predict, by a revaluation of values: that is, by declaring Western standards of merit and success to be biased and bogus. He repeatedly attacks the very idea of 'meritocracy' as a Western ideology meant to discredit the merit of indigenous Hungarians by imposing a foreign value hierarchy on the country. This is part of his rationale for driving the Central European University founded by Hungarian-American philanthropist George Soros from the country.[87] Populism cannot abide the idea that the best academic training available in Hungary is a college education seemingly transplanted lock, stock and barrel from America, and to which the vast majority of Hungarians can never aspire.

In America, similarly, the populist backlash reflects a transformation of what should have been a working-class party, the Democrats, into the party of educated elites. Both Bill Clinton and Barack Obama seemed to be saying: Imitate us! Get a college education. Or better, a post-graduate one. To white high-school graduates who were already feeling superfluous in the new Knowledge Economy, such an Imitation Imperative felt like an existential reproach. They were in no position to imitate the urban elite and its liberal values. They weren't going to college and were therefore naturally looking for a politician who would fight back, who would tell them they weren't lost simply because they didn't have a college degree, who would assure them that they didn't have to imitate the well-educated but could just go on being themselves. For this subgroup, Trump is the President who has liberated them from a meritocratic value hierarchy that left them feeling deprived of all socially acknowledged merit. Just as some Hungarian and Polish populists brag about their refusal to copy the liberal West, so Trump supporters feel liberated when told that Harvard-educated elites, far from being role models, aren't even Americans in a fundamental sense.

IMITATION AS INFILTRATION

Reasons why the imitated may reasonably fear their imitators are legion. Imitation can be feared, for example, when the imitators are impostors who, beneath the radar, infiltrate a group with hostile intent. Wearing a lookalike uniform to gain a split-second advantage in a terrorist ambush is much easier than sustaining a false identity for months at a time to garner useful intelligence, Donnie Brasco style, inside a criminal or terrorist organization. But both are forms of belligerent and justifiably dreaded imitation.[88] An example of unwished-for imitation more closely related to our theme is provided by those Russian hackers who so successfully impersonated Americans online that they may have helped elect Trump.[89] They regarded their bold gambit of identity mimicry as an amply justified act of retaliation, while Americans tend to see it as wholly unprovoked. Yet both agree that it involved acts of aggressive imitation intended to inflict serious harm by destroying public confidence in democratic elections.

Keeping such examples in mind opens up a little explored perspective on the anti-immigrant strand in today's populist revolution. It suggests that white nationalism in America, rather than being fuelled by a fear that new immigrants will fail to assimilate into American culture, is fuelled by a fear that they will assimilate all too successfully. The Belgian classicist Marcel Detienne argued that national identity revolves around a mythical belief in the blood bond connecting living generations to their deceased ancestors.[90] Successful assimilation severs this mystical and pseudo-biological linkage. The implication of successful assimilation is that the cultural identity of natives is not a genetic inheritance but, instead, something disturbingly superficial and relatively easy for newcomers to adopt. If those with an entirely different genetic inheritance can internalize the cultural legacy of multi-generational inhabitants of their host country, then national identity does not really reflect a blood bond tying the current generation to its dead forefathers. If true, Detienne's thesis helps explain the roiling emotionalism of anti-immigrant politics. It stems, on this account, from an unspoken fear of identity theft. Subconsciously, we can speculate, white nationalists fear that recent arrivals, with biologically unrelated ancestry, will expose the embarrassingly shallow roots of their cherished but fictional national identity.

The Nazis' anti-Semitic rage and hysteria was famously exacerbated by the intermarriage of German Christians and Jews. Such marriages and their progeny, the *Mischlinge* with mixed ancestry, were seen as blurring, diluting and insidiously contaminating the ideal of pure-blooded Aryan identity.[91] Such fears are not unknown among American racists today. Indeed, Spike Lee's 2018 film, *BlacKkKlansman*, is an extended reflection on the threat posed by cultural assimilation (a.k.a. imitation) to exclusive racial and ethnic identity. It is based on the real story of an African-American detective, Ron Stallworth, who managed to infiltrate the Ku Klux Klan. Responding to a newspaper advertisement placed by the Klan in search of recruits, Stallworth is able, over the phone, to persuade Walter Breachway, the white nationalist president of the Colorado Springs chapter, that he, Stallworth, is white.

But this deceptive mimicry of a white man's diction, vocabulary and cadence is only the beginning of the hoax. Stallworth then persuades a fellow detective, Flip Zimmerman, who happens to be Jewish, to impersonate Stallworth at a Ku Klux Klan meeting. What makes this undercover operation so deeply subversive is the utter inability of the white supremacists to detect in person (or by phone) the boundaries between whites and blacks, Christians and Jews, or insiders and outsiders around which their entire lives revolve. In particular, the ability of Jews to 'pass' as Gentiles enrages Christian nationalists precisely because it shows the untethered transferability of an identity that they thought was rooted in non-transferable consanguinity. Successful assimilators turn out to be identity sappers. They expose family tales of consanguinity to be little more than comforting lies.[92] For racist bigots, the revelation is demoralizing because it blurs the sharp distinction between 'them' and 'us' that offered them false certainty about who they are.

BlacKkKlansman demolishes the myth of biologically rooted national identity by revealing how easy it is for those who do not share local ancestors to assimilate smoothly to the local culture and to fly under the radar unseen. The ease with which white non-Christians can imitate white Christian patterns of thought and behaviour makes Trump's bigoted supporters feel dispossessed of what they believed was their deepest identity. They react by taking the accusation of 'cultural appropriation', used to bar white Christians from decorating themselves with the identity symbols of ethnic minorities, and turning it against their non-white and non-Christian accusers. This mirror-imaging can be violent, which was the case during the 2016 'Unite the Right' white supremacist rally in Charlottesville, Virginia. Lee meant his film to be a sardonic reply to this event, where marchers notoriously announced their fear of identity theft by chanting 'Jews will not replace us!'[93]

But the rallying cry that best summarizes the populist attack on political correctness in America is 'White Lives Matter'. A mirror-image of the Black Lives Matter slogan used to protest repeated police killings of young black males, it is a classic example of racism mimicking anti-racism for racist ends.[94] The left's perceived coddling of marginalized minorities apparently triggered a counter-reaction among many economically distressed voters who claimed victim status for their own white nationalist identity in turn. To imply that discrimination against whites in America is as serious as discrimination against blacks is surprising enough. But it sometimes seems that Trump's aggrieved white nationalist supporters also think that, under his presidency, they are finally 'reclaiming agency' and 'emerging into history' for the first time. Not satisfied with imitating marginalized minorities, they also aspire to imitate post-colonial peoples liberated, at long last, from the grievous oppressions of a 'foreign-hearted' elite.

LYING IS THE MESSAGE

For many America Firsters there was no debating (even with the facts).

Philip Roth[95]

In the famous Long Telegram he sent from Moscow in 1946, American diplomat George Kennan wrote that 'the greatest danger that can befall us in coping with this problem of Soviet communism, is that we shall allow ourselves to become like those with whom we are coping.' The Soviet habit that he was most concerned for Americans to avoid imitating was the 'disrespect of Russians for objective truth – indeed, their disbelief in its existence' which 'leads them to view all stated facts as instruments for furtherance of one ulterior purpose or another'.[96] What distinguished Western liberalism from its enemies on both the left and the right, according to Kennan, was its commitment to unbiased information, especially when that information challenges fundamental preconceptions.

Hannah Arendt defended a similar view when she claimed that totalitarian elites displayed an 'ability to dissolve every statement of fact into a declaration of purpose',[97] implying that political freedom presupposes an ability to distinguish the desirable from the likely and to describe reality without twisting it to serve partisan or personal agendas. Trump is no totalitarian, but Arendt's analysis can be fruitfully applied to his rhetorical style since he regularly reduces statements of fact, made by allies or adversaries, to declarations of political purpose or instruments in the service of ulterior motives. That, indeed, may well be the essence of his instinctual or intuitive illiberalism.

Behind his constant complaints about 'fake news', we can discern a very specific and very peculiar attitude towards the truth. Here again, associating Trump with post-communist leaders such as Putin, known for publicly denying easily checkable facts, helps illuminate behaviour that would otherwise seem anomalous. As the Russian-born American journalist Masha Gessen argues, Trump and Putin share a similar contempt for objective truth. 'Lying is the message,' she writes. 'It's not just that both Putin and Trump lie, it is that they lie in the same way and for the same purpose: blatantly, to assert power over truth itself.'[98] Curiously, they both tell lies that can be quickly and effortlessly exposed as false. The purpose of their lying, given that much of their intended audience has access to alternative sources of information, cannot be to deceive. One aim, at least, is to show that leaders can prevaricate without suffering untoward consequences. Paying no price for telling easily exposable untruths is an effective way to display one's power and impunity. This brings us back to the American president's baseline distinction between winning and losing.

When deciding what to say, Trump always asks whether truths or untruths are more likely to help him 'win'. In his mind, obviously, there is no reason to believe that truth-tellers are more likely to get what they want than liars. It's an open question and, as an empirical matter, the opposite is often the case. But if his blatant lies betray consciousness of guilt, his sometimes surprising truths (that elected politicians are owned by their donors, for example)[99] do the same, since he is retailing such truths not because they are true but only to dramatize his defiance of political correctness and to throw his enemies off balance.

A passage from Bob Woodward's *Fear*, describing Trump's advice to a friend who acknowledged treating women badly, helps convey the gist of Trump's attitude towards truths and lies:

> 'You've got to deny, deny, deny and push back on these women,' he said. 'If you admit to anything and any culpability, then you're dead. That was a big mistake you made. You didn't come out guns blazing and just challenge them. You showed weakness. You've got to be strong. You've got to be aggressive. You've got to push back hard. You've got to deny anything that's said about you. Never admit.'[100]

Truth-tellers can inadvertently give aid and comfort to their enemies. That is why they often lose, and why liars often win. This has evidently been Trump's personal experience. It makes no sense for a public figure with powerful enemies to commit suicide by impaling himself on the sword of truth.

On the surface, it might appear that Trump believes the flattery dished out by his political allies at Fox News and disbelieves the criticisms levelled by his political enemies at CNN and MSNBC. But it isn't a matter of believing or disbelieving. It is, once again, a matter of besting or being bested. Loyal friends are those who help you win by lying shamelessly on your behalf. Enemies and 'rats' are those who publicize truths selectively and instrumentally to harm your reputation and even put you in legal jeopardy for personal or partisan gain. Seeing life as war[101] and the world as 'a jungle full of predators who were forever out to get him',[102] Trump instinctively gravitates towards lying as a legitimate defence against enemies who would weaponize truth to bring him down.

The American minister Norman Vincent Peale, who preached 'the power of positive thinking', apparently taught Trump that brashly exaggerating one's own talents and achievements was a formula for success in life.[103] The current president also learned the art of strategic falsehood from the world of New York City real estate. Salesmanship, after all, can mean exploiting the gullibility of buyers for a handsome profit. Banks are more likely to lend you money if they believe you are solvent. As a practical matter, Trump found that this gambit worked perfectly well.[104] Like sellers scheming to scam their buyers, insolvent borrowers, confident of impunity and lacking moral scruples, have a strong incentive to provide potential lenders with made-up appraisals of their existing assets.

An even deeper secret of lying is that it pulls those who are duped by lies into an echo chamber where the original prevarication is repeated back to the liar. For example, if I sell you a very expensive apartment which turns out to be much less desirable than you thought and therefore worth much less than you paid, you may decide to hide the truth and repeat the original over-valuation in order to resell the apartment to another naïve buyer. Similarly, if you owe several billion dollars to a bank, the bank will conspire with you to maintain your false reputation for solvency in the hopes that you will stay in business long enough to repay some of what you owe. Dishonest real-estate agents can therefore take solace from the fact that their victims have every incentive to perpetuate their most unprincipled deceits.

Not only does Trump see brazen lying as a perfectly legitimate way to prevail in life's multiple competitions. He also believes that his enemies speak truths not because they have some sort of impartial devotion to veracity but because (and when) it serves their interest to do so. Shifting opportunistically between telling truths and telling lies, he is always 'projecting his own unruliness' onto others,[105] and that means assuming everyone else does the same. This is why he refuses to consider truth-tellers in any way his moral superiors. Whether right or wrong, his critics have partisan agendas. When he denies their manifest truths, he is not espousing a relativist philosophy or rejecting Truth as Such. He is counter-punching, opposing their one-sided partisan agenda with his own.[106]

This brings us back to Masha Gessen's comparison between Trump and Putin. When Putin denies that Moscow had anything to do with the poisoning of former spy Sergei Skripal and his daughter in Salisbury, he is obviously defending his country's sovereignty, which includes the right to deny the validity of 'truths' that are used by political adversaries to attack Russia. Any Russian who provides corroborating evidence of such acts is guilty of 'objective complicity' with the enemy. Collective self-defence is more important than a mere recital of facts, especially if these facts play into the hands of hostile forces.

Liberals initially believed that they could erode Trump's popularity by unmasking his innumerable lies. But the avalanche of disclosures had no effect. To understand the willingness of Trump's supporters to accept his lying ways, it will help to draw on the distinction, developed by the British philosopher Bernard Williams, between 'accuracy' and 'sincerity'.[107] People can be truthful about two states of affairs: about what occurs out there in the world and about what they feel inside. Statements about the former are judged by criteria of accuracy or inaccuracy. Statements about the second are judged by criteria of sincerity or insincerity. The former can be fact-checked, the latter cannot.

Trump's most zealous fans are wholly indifferent to revelations that his statements are very often inaccurate because they believe that these statements are sincere, and thus 'true' in a deeper sense.[108] Trump is constantly telling demonstrable lies. But he has been totally candid about one thing. Everything he does, including telling lies, is meant to help him 'win'. He says this clearly. So when his supporters hear him lie, they know he is doing so to gain a strategic advantage, because that is exactly what he said he would do. Since his lies presumably serve this honestly stated purpose, they are basically truthful in an indirect sense.

His supporters' acceptance of Birtherism, a conspiracy theory claiming inaccurately that Obama was not born in America, might also be explained this way. Trump and his supporters genuinely 'feel' that a black man should not become President of the United States. When they allege that Obama's presidency was illegitimate, they are reporting sincerely on their mental and emotional state. They believe that most of Trump's rivals for the Presidential nomination in 2016 felt the same way but were constrained by political correctness from expressing how they genuinely felt.

While Williams's distinction between accuracy and sincerity helps clarify certain aspects of Trump's popularity, it falls short in important respects. For one thing, it has always seemed that Birtherism was more cynical than sincere. We propose a modified distinction, therefore: not between accuracy and sincerity but between accuracy and loyalty. To paraphrase Arendt, for Trump and his supporters, *every statement of fact dissolves into a declaration of membership or allegiance.*

Why reiterate endlessly that Obama was foreign-born? This lie not only crystallized white nationalist disappointment that a highly educated black president had upended the racial hierarchy on which the country had been based since its founding. It was also Trump's gift to bigots, a rallying cry they could repeat aloud to alert other Obama-haters of their partisan affiliation. Giving membership priority over verifiable reality or objective truth makes it psychologically impossible to acknowledge the factual evidence presented by one's partisan enemies (such as Obama's authenticated birth certificate), for that would risk the obliteration of one's publicly announced partisan identity. Such deeply felt loyalty to a leader or a movement cannot be shaken by official documents or other such bureaucratic niceties. The willingness to repeat such factual untruths is a test of loyalty. It represents an existential decision to burn all bridges to the world of over-educated elites who still think that accuracy matters more than loyalty.

The willing sacrifice of accuracy in the name of loyalty to one's partisan faction brings us to one of the most dramatic transformations wrought by Trump in American public life. He has turned the Republic of the Citizens into a Republic of Fans. Enthralled fans, with their critical faculties switched off, are central to Trump's understanding of politics as centred less on policy-making than on a series of raucous campaign-style rallies. Citizens, by contrast, are devoted to their country, but their loyalty is contingent and critical.[109] Indeed, their readiness to point out and correct mistakes is a sign of their patriotic liberalism. They are ready to challenge their government if they believe that it is betraying the country's principles. The loyalty of fans, by contrast, is zealous, unthinking and unswerving. Their cheers reflect their sense of belonging. Trust-but-verify is replaced by rowdy adoration. Those who refuse to applaud are traitors.[110]

Trump's novel understanding of the remade Republican Party as a giant football club (recalling Berlusconi's Forza Italia), and of its citizens as fans, best explains why Trump feels no obligation to represent Americans who do not admire and respect him. Why should he trust the American intelligence professionals who criticize him and not trust President Putin who prayed that Trump would win the election? Admittedly, a degree of loyalty is critical for the success of any state and that includes any democracy. But Trump has redefined the role of loyalty in American democracy. For him, a loyalist is not someone who supports you when you are right, even against the political headwinds, but someone who supports you when you are wrong, whatever the costs.

Why would anyone believe Trump's claim that 'Some of the most dishonest people in media are the so-called "fact-checkers" '?[111] The answer again is that it is less a matter of belief than of loyalty, membership and allegiance. Conspiracy theories, like conspiracies themselves, cut their adherents off from the surrounding society. Etymologically, 'conspiracy' means 'breathing together'. And conspiracy theorists, too, shut the door on those who find their speculations implausible. This is why Trump's supporters are unmoved by the revelations of his mendacity. The acoustical separation between his populist supporters and their liberal opponents is more important to Trump than the Wall he has promised to erect on America's southern border. The fifty per cent of Republicans who assert (sincerely or wilfully) that Trump won the popular vote and the majority who refuse to acknowledge any Russian interference at all in the election dismiss all evidence to the contrary as maliciously fabricated propaganda.[112] They thereby renounce the possibility of inhabiting a common world with fellow citizens of the contrary persuasion. In this way, they are destroying the possibility of offering and accepting mutual concessions to adjust political differences peaceably. They deliberately insulate themselves, fraternizing solely with other converts, to consolidate their comfortingly exclusive and partisan identity. Demographic change has discoloured the uniformly white ethnicity of their neighbourhoods, schools, churches and shopping venues. But Trump's most zealous fans can recapture a kind of reassuring homogeneity by associating solely with fellow believers. They share 'alternative facts' and are not about to subject pro-Trump spin to falsifying evidence. To do so would involve a loss of partisan identity. By making such a choice, they are repudiating the very idea of deliberative politics at the heart of liberal democracy.

A well-known French engraving of 1848, the year France introduced universal male suffrage, epitomizes democracy's commitment to resolving domestic differences non-violently. It pictures a worker with a rifle in one hand and a ballot in the other. The message is clear: while bullets are reserved for the nation's enemies, ballots will decide differences among the nation's citizens. In Trump's post-Cold War world, however, it is the internal enemy, rather than the external enemy, who poses the gravest existential threat. If the French engraving were to be reworked today, a Trump supporter would hold a list of tariffs in one hand and a list of partisan lies in the other: tariffs for trade competitors and lies for political foes.

DROPPING THE PRETENCES

A politically inspired focus on Trump's instinctive illiberalism and chronic mendacity deflects attention from a final paradox: namely, that he is inflicting the greatest and most enduring damage on American democracy not by lying continuously but by telling truths selectively, especially half-truths with which liberals are inclined to agree. Understanding this characteristically populist gambit will help explain why the liberal response to Trump, while often admirably professional and intellectually persuasive, has been so disappointingly weak politically.

Liberals despise Trump for pulling out of the Paris Accord and the Iranian nuclear deal, trying to destroy Obamacare, giving generous tax cuts to the rich while withdrawing funding from programmes that benefit the poor, putting underage children separated from their parents at the Mexican border into cages, making light of the abominations committed by autocrats he admires, using the term 'globalist' to suggest that Jewish Americans are disloyal, and so forth. But principled liberals have a hard time disagreeing with a statement like the following: 'Globalization has made the financial elite who donate to politicians very wealthy. But it has left millions of our workers with nothing but poverty and heartache.'[113] As the liberal writer John Judis says: 'for all his casual bigotry and corruption, at least he has fairly accurately identified the damage wrought by globalization.'[114]

Other liberal commentators even make positive comments about some aspects of Trump's erratic foreign policy. Trump's decision to pull US troops out of Syria, for instance, while it loosed a torrent of criticism from American hawks and conservatives, was generally greeted with praise by liberals: 'when it comes to a dysfunctional Middle East, some of his instincts are right on target.'[115] Similarly, in national security meetings, Trump has been so strongly opposed to a continuing US military presence in Afghanistan that, according to Bob Woodward: 'His antiwar argument [was] practically ripped from a Bob Dylan song lyric.'[116]

But Trump's selective echo of liberal verities (and lyrics) extends far beyond the observation that globalization favours business over labour and that regime change and nation-building are beyond America's capacities and not in America's interest. One of his most persistent themes, that 'the system' is not fair, is a liberal platitude. The same can be said of his claim that democratic politicians are in the pocket of lobbyists and donors. And what liberal would disagree with the following: that turning Iraq into a functioning liberal democracy after a six-week military campaign was a fool's errand, that dark money flowing into political campaigns is corrupting American democracy, that the Washington swamp needs to be drained, that the

US electoral system is biased, that Congress can misuse the impeachment power to harm a sitting president of the opposite party, that reporting is often one-sided, that the CIA and FBI cannot always be trusted to act in the public interest, and that the justice system is discriminatory or skewed for and against identifiable groups? Given that the American print and broadcast media are partly responsible for Trump's election, liberals might even be tempted to agree that the press is the enemy of the people.

Naturally, we need to distinguish between the meaning (or lack of it) with which Trump invests such statements and what liberals have in mind when asserting something similar. For the most part, he is cynically parroting liberal talking points not converting to a liberal philosophy. We have already encountered one example of how the borrower of phrases differs from the original phrase-maker when contrasting the way Trump, on the one hand, and Clinton and Obama, on the other, denied that America is an 'innocent' nation. For liberals, confessing America's faults is a prelude to trying to improve. For Trump, admitting that Americans are just as amoral as Russians, Saudis and others is a prelude to casting off whatever inhibitions remain.

By taking up, twisting, and exaggerating the liberal truth that American elections are unfair, given the realities of gerrymandering and voter suppression, Trump is both normalizing the rigging of elections by Republicans and laying the ground for casting a shadow of illegitimacy over future Democratic victories. Such weaponizing of half-truths is a hallmark of populist demagoguery. Why lift a finger to protect the integrity of America's electoral system, given that it has no integrity to lose?

An even better example is the dispute between Trump and Chief Justice John Roberts about the partisan character of the American bench. Responding to Trump's claim that a judge who ruled against the administration was 'an Obama judge', Roberts issued this statement:

> We do not have Obama judges or Trump judges, Bush judges or Clinton judges. What we have is an extraordinary group of dedicated judges doing their level best to do equal right to those appearing before them. That independent judiciary is something we should all be thankful for.[117]

Noteworthy here is not only that Trump was telling the truth and the Chief Justice was lying, but that they were doing so for the same reason. Both of them understand that the legitimacy and therefore effectiveness of the American judiciary depends on its reputation for impartiality. If you want to destroy the prestige of the American legal system in the eyes of the public, the best way to do so is to convince people that judges are nothing but party hacks implementing partisan agendas. If you want to preserve that prestige, by contrast, it is crucial to deny that judicial decisions are driven by factional interests rather than neutral considerations of right and wrong. From this we can conclude that Trump is deploying a liberal truth or half-truth to erode the legitimacy of the American legal system which threatens him personally as well as his family.

That American justice is far from perfectly impartial is a central theme of liberal scholarship and commentary on racial and class bias in legislation, adjudication and policing. Trump has taken this accurate observation and, once again, warped it to serve his own ends. To justify refusing to cooperate fully with the Mueller investigation, he said that he was not obstructing justice but only fighting back.[118] This remark implies that impartial justice does not exist. What counts as justice in ordinary parlance is merely the power of a social faction attempting to impose its interests and biases on the rest of society. There is no justice; there are only organized interests trying to dominate, outmanoeuvre and exploit each other. This is how he saw the Mueller investigation. Partisan enemies had taken hold of the justice system and were attempting to use it to bring him down. Far from impeding the workings of impartial 'justice', he was (and is) simply parrying a partisan attack. These comments probably have more in common with the cynical view of Western law shared by radical jihadists and Russian mobsters than with the usual liberal criticism of legal bias.

Let's return in conclusion to the theme of political hypocrisy. Trump is a stellar exemplar of what the French call *la droite décomplexée* (conservatism without hang-ups). That is to say, he is a bigot who feels disinhibited enough to express his bigotry without embarrassment. This can be disarming or alarming, depending on how you look at it. But there is no doubt that his disavowals of the ordinary hypocrisies made him stand out among the other Republican candidates for the party's nomination to the presidency in 2016. He seemed spontaneous, while they seemed scripted, precisely because he was willing to dance shamelessly with white supremacists in a way that none of the others could imagine doing. He was the only candidate willing to express openly what anti-immigrant white-nationalist voters inwardly believe. So he was seen as authentic. If the other candidates felt any sympathy for racial prejudice, they carefully hid it, adopting politically correct anti-racist language in conformity with the reigning liberal culture. Mainstream Republicans would sometimes sidle up to racism, coming just close enough to titillate their supporters. But they would never cross the line. But their liberal masks made them come across as 'fake' in a deeply human sense. Republican primary voters may not have agreed with all of Trump's prejudices, but they watched him rip up all the elementary rules of decorum and, as a consequence, they understood that, in some perverse way, this weirdly hollow man was free.

People who are privately comfortable with ethnic stereotypes can nevertheless refrain from tossing around offensive epithets in public. Such etiquette can be disparaged as hypocrisy or political correctness. But it is also a socially productive form of conflict avoidance. That is why attacks on hypocrisy can sometimes double as incitements to violence.

The corrosive impact of Trump's casual dropping of all pretence is hard for American liberals to resist because liberals, too, have been unmasking more or less the same political hypocrisy for years with little or no political impact. Liberals, for instance, excoriated the George W. Bush administration for invoking human rights and democracy to justify the 2003 invasion of Iraq. Trump's enthusiasm for unmasking American hypocrisies is therefore an important reason why liberals continue to find him an elusive target. To straighten out this confusion, we need to distinguish between two styles of unmasking, one in the service of Enlightenment values and the other in the service of a cynical and unprincipled abandonment of values.

'Tearing away the mask' assumes a sharp distinction between private motivations and public justifications. This distinction is overdrawn. In fact, what looks like the same policy, if it is justified differently, turns out to be a different policy. This suggests that moral justifications cannot be simply dismissed as deceptive pretexts and tossed away in the name of a greater realism. Here is an example. Obama took a tough line on expelling illegal aliens from the United States.[119] But he never justified this policy by claiming that America would not be America if it became a mixed-race nation. A good reason for not invoking such a justification is that America has irreversibly become a mixed-race nation. Denying that the country can be what it manifestly already is would be a recipe for violence. What makes Trump unique, and uniquely dangerous, is not the hard line he takes on expelling illegal aliens, but his willingness to justify this policy on racist grounds. More generally, for the President of the United States to publicly justify a restrictive immigration policy by invoking the need to keep America as white as possible has several knock-on effects. Perhaps the worst is that it legitimates the idea that white people are the only real Americans and that discrimination against non-whites is perfectly acceptable for American patriots.

This is no slip of the tongue on Trump's part. Obama's optimistic embrace of cultural and ethnic diversity is precisely what drove so many Trump supporters crazy. For some of them, America is fundamentally a white nation whose nature has been distorted by an imprudent admixture of non-whites. What this strongly suggests, once again, is that ripping off the mask of liberal toleration and concern for human rights does not bring American foreign and domestic policy back to a sober approach of putting the country's real interests first. Once these values are cast aside, what we get are not sensible and corrigible policies but a delirium of racial animus.

Trump's response to the killing of Saudi journalist Jamal Khashoggi in October 2018 provides a final chilling example of what it means in practice to jettison liberal hypocrisy. He could have easily justified his refusal to break with Mohammed bin Salman, the crown prince of Saudi Arabia, by citing the need for Saudi support in the coming conflict with Iran and perhaps also in helping de-escalate Israeli–Palestinian tensions. But instead, Trump consciously chose to speak only about the money Riyadh promised to spend in the United States, especially on the purchase of American arms.[120] This conveyed the impression that he was *selling* the right to strangle and dismember a *Washington*

Post columnist to the highest bidder. If so, it's a particularly grue-some example of the Art of the Deal. But it would be a mistake to interpret his covetous reflex, in this instance, as proof that Trump is interested only in money. On the contrary, the purpose of such state-ments is, first, to wallow vicariously in the savagery of non-democratic strongmen who casually kill annoying journalists and, second, to communicate that America will henceforth empty its foreign policy of any shadow of 'human decency' as commonly understood. Aban-doning talk of values does not bring you to honesty about interests. Instead it opens the door to 'revolutionary cynicism', or the intoxica-tion of being able to live without ethical illusions. When Trump drops the liberal pretences that offend liberals, far from settling down into cool-headed *raison d'état*, he sinks ever deeper into an abyss of capri-cious volatility, unprincipled incoherence and predatory malevolence.

CODA

The crowning irony of Trump's attack on liberal democracy's preten-sions to be an example for the world is that his own words and actions are now bound to be imitated. The election to the Brazilian presi-dency of Jair Bolsonaro, a far-right populist who models himself on Trump and rode to power on a wave of anti-establishment rage, is just one example among many. Similarly, the day after Trump declared that he was ordering the army to shoot at 'stone throwers' approaching America's southern border, the Nigerian military, responding to an accusation of crimes against humanity, declared that the civilians it had killed were also throwing stones, as if cold-blooded killing in such circumstances has become the new normal.[121] The Age of Liberal Imitation is over, but the Age of Illiberal Imitation may have just begun. After 1989, formerly communist countries were challenged to reform themselves in the light of an ostensibly higher liberal-democratic ideal. Today, as America disowns its traditional self-image as an exemplary nation, countries around the world have Washington's blessing to retrogress complacently into the most bru-tal, unprincipled and rule-breaking versions of themselves.[122]

The motivations of the Central European liberals who aimed to imitate the US in the 1990s differed fundamentally from the motivations of populists who pretend to be following in Trump's footsteps today. The Central Europeans imitated America in the hopes of becoming like America, and that meant becoming better. Theirs was an imitative project imbued with ameliorative ambitions. When reactionary authoritarian leaders around the world imitate Trump today, they do it simply to lend a patina of worldly legitimacy to what they independently want to do. Brazil's right-wing president does not imitate Trump because he wants to be Trump. He does it because Trump has made it possible for Bolsanaro to be himself.

The Closing of an Age

*A state may borrow from another useful information,
without imitating the other's customs.*

Nikolay Karamzin[1]

In 1959 a Soviet spacecraft crash-landed on the Moon. As the first manmade object to touch down on another celestial body, it demonstrated to the world Moscow's unrivalled technical and military prowess, even though it broke into pieces on impact, scattering its remnants across the lunar surface. A decade later, in 1969, the US re-took the lead in the race for the future when Neil Armstrong and Buzz Aldrin became the first human beings to set foot on the Moon.

A popular Soviet joke summarizes how this Cold War contest turned out. At a certain point, Soviet cosmonauts call Moscow to report proudly that they have not only reached the lunar surface but have painted it red so the world will understand that mankind's future is in communist hands. A month later, Soviet euphoria yields to despair. The Americans, too, have landed on the Moon and they 'have brought white paint and written "Coca-Cola" on it'.[2]

Fast forward to 2 January 2019. On that date, the Chinese spacecraft Chang'e made a soft lunar landing on what is usually referred to as the Moon's 'dark side' because it wasn't observed until photographed by a Soviet space probe in the late 1950s. The geopolitical implications of this unprecedented achievement of space exploration by a country that wasn't even a competitor in the Cold War space race are momentous.[3] The Chinese are now laying claim to the far side of the future, one that is neither dyed utopian red nor has the brand name of a globally marketed soft drink blazoned profanely across it.

China's meteoric transformation into a geopolitical superpower has made the Soviet–American rivalry seem like ancient history. It has also finished off the Age of Imitation that began in 1989 and came to an end sometime between 2008 and 2016. This historically unique period had two defining features: first, the Cold War competition between two proselytizing ideologies was definitively over, and second, the West's project of spreading abroad its own values and institutional models found for several years more willing takers than ever before. The world was divided anew, this time between relatively stable and prosperous liberal democracies and countries that hoped to emulate them. This troubled asymmetry of the imitated and their imitators has now also come to an end. Among the forces that colluded to destroy it, the most important is the resentment it naturally engendered. But an additionally decisive factor is the emergence of China as a major player in global affairs.

BEIJING's 1989

To understand China's crucial role in wrapping up our story, we need to revisit 1989 from a Chinese point of view.

In the early summer of that pivotal year, the Chinese leadership dispatched several divisions of the Chinese Liberation Army to crush with tanks and live ammunition the pro-democracy movement on and around Tiananmen Square. Deng Xiaoping's radical economic reforms, launched in 1978, had provided some of the most persuasive evidence for the prediction that free markets were bound to prevail everywhere over chronically inefficient command economies. But new opportunities for private gain created by market liberalization also fomented social unrest over flagrant inequalities, rampant inflation, favouritism and corruption. Student discontent, in particular, eventually sparked the occupation of Tiananmen Square, perceived by key Party leaders as an imminent threat to their hold on power.

To justify the imposition of martial law, Deng and his fellow hardliners accused the demonstrators of worshipping Western lifestyles and betraying their country by imitating bourgeois liberalism, even to the point of advocating political pluralism, freedom of the press, freedom of assembly, and accountable government. Directly facing the enormous portrait of Mao at the Gate of Heavenly Peace, they had scandalously erected a statue of the Goddess of Democracy, 'a figure of a defiant woman holding high a torch' which bore a striking resemblance to the Statue of Liberty. Some of the protesters called it 'the Goddess of Liberty and Democracy', immediately seen as a symptom of 'overt Americanization'.[4]

Speaking a few days after the Square was cleared, Deng said of the Westernizing protesters: 'Their goal was to establish a bourgeois republic entirely dependent on the West.' He also comparted 'bourgeois liberalization' to 'spiritual pollution'.[5] In other words, he justified the 4 June crackdown by citing the Party's moral duty to crush a mass movement of students and workers who hoped to drag China into the Age of Imitation.[6]

This violent repression, precisely in 1989, of a movement aimed at imitating Western-style freedoms raises the question: Why didn't the Tiananmen events lead more Western commentators to doubt that the end of Eastern European and eventually Soviet communism had in fact established liberal democracy as the only viable model for political reform?

One reason is that, coincidentally, June 1989 also witnessed Solidarity's victory in the first free elections in Poland. This small triumph of the Polish opposition kick-started a process that led to the dissolution of the Soviet Union itself in December 1991. The dramatic cascade of events unfolding on Europe's eastern frontier contributed significantly to the impression that, while it was a tragedy and a political setback, Tiananmen was of negligible importance to world history. Political repression in China was generally viewed not as a sign of strength but as a symptom of the leadership's weakness and insecurity. It was therefore thought to have little significance for who controlled the future. And control of the future was the prize for which Soviets and Americans had gone to the brink.

The Cold War had been a potentially apocalyptic contest for the right to shape the world to come. The Soviets had lost this struggle and the Americans had won it. These two superpowers were the

'Main Enemies', and Europe was the major theatre of confrontation. In the eyes of the West, therefore, what happened in China in 1989 was a sideshow staged in a backwater.

Even if liberalism's cheerleaders had taken it more seriously, the Tiananmen crackdown would not have forced them to rethink their expectations for the post-Cold War world. The claim that liberalism had become the only viable political ideology never involved a wager on the success of poorly organized and sporadic democratization efforts in China. A few optimists argued that the gradual adoption of Western habits of consumption would eventually lead to the emergence and stabilization of democratic governance there.[7] But most of those who wrote of liberalism's new global pre-eminence did not have the political makeover of China in mind. What they meant was that, after the defeat of fascism in the Second World War and the defeat of communism in the Cold War, no ideology other than liberal democracy would be able to capture the imagination of the world and particularly of the non-Western world.

The end of communism did not foretell a democratic China any more than it predicted a liberal Russia. It simply implied that no non-liberal and undemocratic state could henceforth serve as a model worth imitating. As Fukuyama wrote at the time, 'the People's Republic of China can no longer act as a beacon for illiberal forces around the world, whether they be guerrillas in Asian jungles or middle-class students in Paris.'[8] But to say that China after Mao was no longer going to be a beacon for revolutionaries abroad was not to predict that America's liberal beacon would light China's path towards democratic reforms.

That is because the West can be imitated in non-political ways as well. To appreciate the importance of the distinction between imitating ends and imitating means, we need only contemplate Deng's response to the protesters on Tiananmen Square. While they wished to imitate Western values, he presided over China's imitation of Western-style economic growth. He was helped in this project, it should be said, by Western businesses who re-engaged in China soon after Tiananmen. By ducking controversies over political freedom, they were able to focus narrowly on lucrative trade and investment opportunities. The Party had driven the would-be imitators of

Western liberalism and democracy underground, but the country was still open for business, including the business of swiping Western technology and adapting Western methods of industrial production. None of this has anything to do with democratic accountability. On the contrary, importing, copying and improving Western face-recognition technology has reduced the privacy of citizens while doing nothing to permit them to examine or question the actions of their government.[9] Multinational corporations, for their part, had no problem turning a blind eye to Beijing's harsh treatment of domestic admirers of Western liberal and democratic values and focusing instead on deepening China's integration into the global economy. This is how Western business helped Beijing skip over the Age of Imitation.

PARTY OVER IDEOLOGY

Contemporary Western commentators on the events of 1989 paid scant attention to the different ways in which Soviet and Chinese elites interpreted the failure of the communist system. They focused on the commonalities. Both the Russians and the Chinese, for example, had stopped seeing the future as an extended struggle to build a communist society. And both had abandoned efforts to spread their now-discredited models abroad. With the benefit of hindsight, however, these parallel responses have come to seem less consequential than the sharp divergence between Soviet and Chinese understandings of the communist collapse.

Gorbachev and his allies traced the downfall of communism to the Communist Party's failure to fulfil the inspiring promises of Marxism. Worth saving in socialism, in the Kremlin's view at the time, were its ideas of social equality and working-class empowerment. But they repudiated the Stalin-era commitment to the transformative power of state violence and the repression of political pluralism as mistakes of tragically epic proportions.

For Gorbachev, socialism was morally unsalvageable if saving it would have required the government to massacre hundreds of pro-democracy demonstrators in Red Square. He also believed that his historic mission was to rescue the idea of socialism from the corrupting influence of the Communist Party. He was naturally impressed by the Chinese leadership's success at pushing through economic reforms. From his perspective, in fact, the chronic inertia of his own Party apparatus, including the central-planning bureaucracy, remained the major obstacle to any meaningful modernization of the Soviet economy and society.

The Russians under Gorbachev abandoned the Party in an attempt to save what was most universally appealing in communist ideology, and ended up losing both Party and ideology. The Chinese under Deng and his successors abandoned the export of communist ideology and retained the Party's dominant role nationally, allowing it to manage the most remarkable story of economic development in world history.

Although Chinese leaders had become increasingly sceptical of the major economic ideas of Marxism, they remained impressed by the capacity of the Communist Party to exercise power, to organize society around shared long-term aims, and to defend the territorial integrity of the state. As Xi Jinping has recently remarked, looking back on four decades of economic development: 'It was precisely because we've adhered to the centralized and united leadership of the party that we were able to achieve this great historic transition.'[10]

Committed to avoiding what they saw as Gorbachev's fatal mistakes, Chinese leaders became the most serious students of the Soviet collapse. They continued to speak like Marxists, but not because they were convinced by Marxism's 'science of history' or its fortune-cookie futurology. They appreciated Marxism, instead, as a shared idiom for helping the Party to distinguish loyalists from renegades and to discipline, coordinate and mobilize millions of Party members to advance the top leadership's chosen goals. This explains their zealous adherence to 'the centralized and united leadership of the party'.[11]

Gorbachev believed communism had failed because it had not managed to build a socialist society. For the Chinese leadership, communism had succeeded because the Communist Party had managed, against formidable odds, to unify both the Chinese state and Chinese society. Given this deep discrepancy between the Chinese and Soviet understandings of the roles played by party on the one hand and ideology on the other, we should not be surprised when we discover that, according to his youngest son, Deng thought Gorbachev was 'an idiot'.[12]

IMITATION AS APPROPRIATION

The difference between post-communist China, post-communist Central Europe and post-communist Russia closely tracks the distinction between three styles or strategies of development: namely, imitating the means (or borrowing), imitating the ends (or converting), and imitating the appearances (or simulating). Central European elites, at first, genuinely embraced imitation of Western values and institutions as the quickest path to political and economic reform. They were aspiring *converts*, whose identification of normalization with Westernization eventually allowed a reactionary counter-elite to capture the most politically potent symbols of national identity. In Russia, by contrast, post-Soviet elites merely pretended that they were imitating Western norms as well as Western institutions, when they were only using the façade of democratic elections and voluntary market exchanges based on legally secured private-property rights to preserve their power, pocket the country's wealth, and block the kinds of democratic reform that would have threatened insider privilege and perhaps led to state collapse and further territorial disintegration. They were strategic *impostors*.

China, by contrast, was both openly and clandestinely borrowing from the West while insisting that the country's developmental trajectory retained its 'Chinese characteristics'. They were ingenious *appropriators*. Employing joint-venture agreements to force Western firms to transfer innovative technologies to their Chinese partners neither involves democratic hypocrisy nor puts national identity at risk. Similarly, while one-third of all foreign students at American universities are from China, they study mostly science and engineering, not liberalism and democracy.[13] Such developments are crucial because Xi Jinping's effort to safeguard Chinese identity by preventing 'foreign ideas and influences from permeating Chinese society' lies at the heart of the current regime's legitimacy.[14] More than any previous Chinese leader, Xi has turned Marxism into a nationalist ideology, designed to fortify domestic resistance to foreign pressure and influence. In Xi's own words: 'No one is in a position to dictate to the Chinese people what should or should not be done.'[15] What the Party promises society is not that tomorrow will be a communist paradise but that the Communist Party alone can fend off pernicious forms of Western influence.

His unflinching resistance to Westernization is essential to Xi's project of restoring China to its rightful place as a global superpower. It has been observed that he 'believes in ideology and its value, but would probably not pass the kind of intermediate exam on elements of Marxism–Leninism that is sometimes set at Party schools and universities'.[16] But what does it mean to 'believe in ideology' under such conditions? The answer can be sought in 'Xi Jinping Thought', now part of the Chinese constitution.[17] The core of his 'ideological' vision is the mission to re-establish China's lost pre-eminence in the world, a mission that can be accomplished only if the Party retains its total control over civil society.

The Chinese skipped over the Age of Imitation, smuggling Marxist lingo and Communist Party rule into the end-of-history world where all world-spanning ideological conflicts are over and post-ideological nationalistic forces compete for influence, resources, markets and turf. As China's export-led industrial economy boomed, in the decades after Tiananmen, its political system did not, by some imaginary law of social development, become more liberal and more democratic. Far from remaking themselves in the image of the West, the Chinese resolutely refused to convert to America and Western Europe's liberal-democratic system of values, opting instead to borrow or steal from the economically more advanced West.

When 'means are adopted and the goals pertaining to them are rejected,' as two insightful sociologists have speculated, 'the borrowing of means is frequently understood only for the ultimate purpose of turning the tables on the lender'.[18] This seems to fit the Chinese case perfectly. The Chinese are among the most relentless and accomplished imitators of the West when it comes to technology, fashion, architecture and so forth, but they have explicitly rejected the imitation of Western-style liberal democracy naïvely favoured by the

Tiananmen protesters. They *borrow* exuberantly but refuse to *convert*. Nor have they felt Moscow's need to *fake* Western-style democracy or to expose American hypocrisy by *mirror-imaging* the US's brazen international rule-breaking. Borrowing or stealing technology makes you richer, in any case, while imitating moral values threatens your identity and faking democracy or exposing hypocrisy seems pointless.

After 1989, unlike Central Europe's would-be converts to liberal democracy, the Chinese have developed their society without putting their cultural identity at risk and therefore without ever feeling like cultural phonies and impostors. Memories of nineteenth-century humiliation at the hands of Western powers, deliberately kept alive by school textbooks, continue to shape the thinking and decision making of the country's leaders. The refusal to play the liberal game of identity mimicry has not eliminated resentment from Chinese foreign policy, therefore. But it has conceivably played a role in their visible reluctance to engage in imitation-promotion themselves.

This brings us back to our main question: In precisely what sense does the rise of China signal the end of the Age of Imitation?

POWER WITHOUT CONVERTS

Most scholars who speculate about what will happen when China rules the world, tend to picture a Sino-centric world as a facsimile of America's liberal hegemony. China, they imagine, is destined to occupy the place which will be vacated sooner or later by a declining United States. China watchers today no longer believe that China's opening to global economic exchange is slowly nudging the country towards a system of political competition and the free exchange of ideas. What many of them fear, instead, is that a Sino-centric world will be populated by Chinese-style authoritarian, amoral and mercantilist regimes. A common view today is that the Chinese are not simply exporting consumer goods, capital and surveillance technologies but are also encouraging the development of their own brand of ideologically coherent and universally exportable illiberal authoritarianism.

Along these lines, many recent books and reports have tried to frame the escalating confrontation between China and the West as a new Cold War. The National Endowment for Democracy published a report that coined the term 'sharp power' in order to explain the ideological offensive of various new authoritarians.[19] The report rightly stresses the strategy of the authoritarian governments: first, to close their own societies to liberal ideas emanating from outside; second, to highlight the palpable failures of liberal democracies; and third, to take advantage of the open-door permeability of liberal societies in order to subvert them from within. But none of these strategies involves any hint of the competitive proselytizing that characterized the Cold War.

The tendency of authoritarian rulers to close their own societies to liberal ideas emanating from outside seems perfectly exemplified by today's China. Xi apparently thinks he can consolidate the unity of the country by shielding Chinese youth from the corrupting influence of Western values by asking the Ministry of Education, for example, 'to restrict the use of Western textbooks that advocated Western political values'.[20]

Xi's campaign against the 'incorrect path' of imitating the West echoes Deng's response to the Tiananmen protests. But the flipside of this desire not to imitate a foreign model turns out to be the lack of any desire to be imitated by others. Xi is uninterested in forcing peoples at the other end of the stick to undergo identity-transforming Chinese indoctrination. Exporting made-in-China goods is a priority. Exporting Chinese ideology is not. What this means is that we are not about to embark on a New Cold War and that the current Chinese threat to the West will be unlike the Soviet threat in several fundamental respects.

The proliferation of authoritarian regimes is real. But authoritarianism, unlike communism, is not an ideology shareable across borders. It is an oppressive, non-consultative and arbitrary style of rule. The concentration of all power in the hands of a single lifetime president is profoundly illiberal, but it does not constitute an anti-liberal ideology confronting Western liberalism on the plane of ideas. The same can be said of press censorship and the incarceration of regime critics. What unites Putin and Xi is a general belief in the ultimate value of political stability, hostility to the democratic idea that wielders of power should be time- or term-limited, and general mistrust of political competi-tion, accompanied by a firm conviction that the US is covertly plotting regime change for their countries. Beyond these commonalities, Putin and Xi have no shared conception of what a good society looks like. Their actions are driven by national interest and national dreams, shaped by pride and resentment at the humiliations inflicted by West-ern hands, rather than by a universally exportable ideology defining a shared world-view. And while both Chinese and Russian leaders openly argue that Western-style liberalism would not suit their socie-ties, they have now become confident (or overconfident) enough to pretend that Western liberalism has failed just as humiliatingly as communism failed three decades ago.

To say that the rise of China marks the end of the Age of Imitation is to say that there will be no return to a global ideological confronta-tion between two great powers each imposing its social and political model on a group of vassal states and trying to persuade peoples everywhere to adopt its own goals, objectives and vision of man-kind's future. There is no reason to believe that Xi's China will be a particularly benign actor internationally. Its immediate neighbours, many of whom welcome a US naval presence in the South China Sea, justifiably suspect that its economic projection of power may at some point become much more coercive and military. The coming con-frontation between China and the US will no doubt reshape the international order in important and dangerous ways. But it remains misleading to see 'a new economic Cold War'[21] as a rerun of the ori-ginal, ideology-obsessed Cold War. This conflict may turn out to be explosively emotional rather than coolly rational on both sides. But it will not be ideological. It will involve, instead, bitter struggles over trade, investment, currency and technology, as well as international prestige and influence. This is the aim behind the Chinese project to 'de-Americanize' the world.[22] The idea is not to replace a global lib-eral ideology with a global anti-liberal ideology, but to radically diminish the role of ideology, not necessarily domestically, but in the arena of international competition. As a result, a Sino-American power struggle, even if it imposes a 'with us or against us' logic on the rest of the world, will not be an end-times battle between rival world-views and philosophies of history.

CHINATOWN OR MELTING POT?

When comparing yesterday's American world with a possible Chinese world of tomorrow, we should keep in mind the very different ways in which Americans and Chinese experience the lands beyond their borders. America is a nation of immigrants, but it is also a nation of people who never emigrate. Americans living outside the United States are not called emigrants, as a result, but 'expats'. America gave the world the notion of the melting pot – an alchemical cooking device where diverse ethnic and religious groups voluntarily mix and mingle, brewing a new post-ethnic identity. And while critics may justly point out that the melting pot is a national myth, the idea of it has tenaciously informed America's collective imagination. The myth of a melting pot naturally inclines American foreign-policy-makers toward the goal of assimilating foreign cultures to America's own. The Chinese experience of Chinatowns does the opposite, favouring economic integration while preserving cultural insulation. The two exceptionalisms therefore lead to very different strategies for advancing each country's global ambitions.

America's allure lies partly in its ability to transform others into Americans, to induce immigrants to imitate not merely American rituals but also American desires, goals and self-understandings. It should come as no surprise, therefore, that America's global agenda is transformative and generally supportive of regime change. The country's foreign-policy-makers are not just rule-makers. They are missionary proselytizers for the American model, or at least they have been so through much of the country's history until the presidency of Donald Trump.

Deng Xiaoping called off Mao's proselytizing mission. This retreat from an attempt to convert the world may have come naturally because, in its traditional self-understanding, China was the world. It is often remarked that China looks at itself not as a country but as a civilization. One might even say that it sees itself as a universe. China's relationships with other countries in the last two decades are channelled mainly through its diaspora and, as a result, the Chinese perceive the world via their co-nationals' experience as immigrants.

Today, more Chinese live outside China than French people live in France, and these overseas Chinese account for the largest number of investors in China. In fact, only twenty years ago, the Chinese living abroad produced approximately as much wealth as China's entire domestic population. First, the Chinese diaspora succeeded, then China itself.

Chinatowns are the Chinese diaspora's core. As the political scientist Lucien Pye once observed, 'The Chinese see such an absolute difference between themselves and others that even when living in lonely isolation in distant countries they unconsciously find it natural and appropriate to refer to those in whose homeland they are living as "foreigners" '.[23]

While the American melting pot transforms others, Chinatowns teach their inhabitants to adjust – to profit from their hosts' rules and the business opportunities they offer while remaining insular and distinct by choice. While Americans hoist their flag high, Chinese usually work hard to stay invisible, aiming to keep their light under a bushel so long as the surrounding world is dominated by non-Chinese. Chinese communities worldwide have managed to become influential in their new homelands without being threatening; to be closed and non-transparent without provoking resentment; and to be a bridge to China without appearing to be a Fifth Column.

In this sense, a world where China is on the rise and America has become a normal country (that is, where America abandons its traditional claim to be an exemplar nation) will be a world where imitation on a retail level remains common. But it will not be a world divided between two rival models or between a single worthwhile model and its successful or unsuccessful imitators. As Kerry Brown persuasively argues, Xi Jinping is not 'in the business of conversion. There are no illusions in Beijing that the outside world will suddenly embrace modernization of socialism with Chinese characteristics for the new age.'[24] Contrary to the fears of the new Cold warriors, then, China does not see its mission to be populating the world with Chinese clones. This is true even though it may eventually shift from seducing smaller countries into dependency with big loans to using bullying tactics to guarantee compliance with China's foreign-policy aims. During the height of the Cold War, communist China itself was 'an alternative pole of ideological attraction', mostly in the developing world, 'and as such constituted a threat to liberalism'.[25] But by 1989, according to the liberal consensus of the time, 'Chinese competitiveness and expansionism on the world scene have virtually disappeared. Beijing no longer sponsors Maoist insurgencies or tries to cultivate influence in distant African countries as it did in the 1960s.'[26]

Re-read today, this last sentence is a kind of revelation. Plainly, China's competitiveness and expansionism on the world scene have in no way disappeared. What *has* disappeared is China's sponsorship of Maoist insurgencies in Africa. By way of compensation, it is building new bridges, roads, railways, ports and other facilitators of global commerce. Yet this new intrusion onto the African scene involves zero efforts to convert the affected populations to Confucian values or economic mercantilism or one-party rule.

IMITATION'S WOES

China's unhappy historical experiences with the geopolitics of imitation, starting with the arrival of Protestant missionaries in the nineteenth century, may help explain why its new strategy of global power-projection eschews any policies recalling 'the business of conversion'. After the 1911 Revolution overthrew the last of the Qing dynasty emperors, for instance, China was obliged by the expectations of the Great Powers to organize itself as a nation-state. But, as Lucian Pye has argued:

> China is not just another nation-state in the family of nations. China is a civilization pretending to be a state. The story of modern China could be described as the effort by both Chinese and foreigners to squeeze a civilization into the arbitrary and constraining framework of a modern state, an institutional invention that came out of the fragmentation of Western civilization.[27]

To join the international system, the Republic of China had no alternative. It was obliged to present itself to the world in an awkwardly constraining nation-state format, a Procrustean bed that ill-suited its cultural self-understanding as a civilization.[28] And it continues to struggle against the imposition of this mismatched Western political structure today.

China's second modern experience with obligatory imitation came after the Revolution of 1949 when the country reformatted its political system in slavish imitation of the Soviet model of democratic centralism. The Chinese Communist Party not only built Soviet-style concrete buildings, but also set up a Politburo, called Party Congresses, created the post of General Secretary, and designed such vital ministries as the Central Organization Department, responsible for all Party appointments, according to a blueprint provided by the Soviet Orgburo.[29] Through this wholesale import and adoption of Soviet institutions, China learned that imitation as a rule triggers resentment and that the imitator lives in constant vulnerability. The Sino-Soviet conflict of the 1960s can perhaps be understood as an explosive manifestation of China's pent-up resentment against such pressure to follow slavishly in Moscow's footsteps.

Finally, China was the world's most aggressive exporter of ideology in the late Maoist period. This missionary project did not turn out well. 'China supported revolutionary struggle abroad in such an idiosyncratic way,' writes Kerry Brown, 'that by 1967 it had only one ambassador serving overseas – Huang Hua, in Egypt.'[30] So Beijing has learned first-hand the dangers of political and economic isolation that come from the Promethean ambition to export your own value-system and ideological model to others.

Critically important for Xi's foreign policy is not the recruitment of imitators, therefore, but the search for global influence and global recognition. As China's wealth and power has grown, so too has its leaders' desire for the country to be deferred to and admired. But China's aspiration to global pre-eminence is not based on a claim that its culture is universally shareable. It does not expect others to emulate its model, even if it wants them to conform to its wishes. The already legendary Belt and Road Initiative is creating integration, interconnection and interdependence without relying in any way on cross-border indoctrination. There is no reason to believe that the new post-missionary Chinese imperium will be particularly benevolent. But Xi's way of demonstrating China's global stature and projecting

Chinese power, whatever it means for other countries, will not be sustained by ideological conversion.

Although 'One Belt, One Road' has given Xi and his colleagues a grand international narrative, demonstrated Chinese global stature, and dramatically re-injected Chinese influence into Africa, there is nothing further from its organizers' minds than encouraging peasant insurgencies or seeking to induce others to accept a uniquely Chinese system of values as was the case under Mao. China simply wants to multiply its influence and to co-opt or subordinate other countries, not to turn them into miniature clones of China. China wants to be a caller of the shots, and presumably an exploiter, not a beacon or a model. This is because, unlike America in the heyday of liberal hegemony, China has no reason to think that a world populated by copies of itself would be a world congenial to Chinese interests and plans.

China marks the end of the Age of Imitation because both its history and its current success demonstrate that, while a 'no-alternatives' introduction of foreign values predictably sparks a nationalist backlash, the targeted 'borrowing' of technical means brings prosperity, development, social control, and a chance to renew a country's international clout and prestige. Without assaying or feigning a Western-style political makeover, the Chinese are successfully outpacing the West along many dimensions. At the same time, they reveal no inclination to teach other countries how to live. They nevertheless have a compelling lesson to convey. The copious benefits of rejecting Western norms and institutions while selectively adopting Western technologies and even consumption patterns is what China teaches the world.

A ZERO HYPOCRISY WORLD

This is not to deny that China's influence operations abroad have also produced their share of Sinophobia and nationalistic backlash. After all, a refusal to proselytize, based on China's sense of its cultural distinctness and superiority, does not necessarily translate into a capacity for winning friends or mobilizing voluntary cooperation. Moreover, building islands in disputed waters, damming up rivers regardless of the consequences for countries downstream, and constructing far-flung military bases are among the recent assertions of Chinese domination that have frayed nerves in India, Japan, South Korea, the Philippines and Vietnam. The resort to aggressive lending to cash-strapped countries, such as Sri Lanka and Pakistan, which subsequently struggle to repay the loans, is also widely resented as a Machiavellian manoeuvre for gaining control over seaports and other strategic assets abroad. But such resentment of Chinese strong-arming, however real and significant, is not inflamed by additional resentment of American-style moralistic lecturing and imitation-promotion. China's agents abroad are uninterested in selling foreigners on the Chinese model of domestic political and economic organization. Thus, Chinese loans come with no *ideological* strings attached. Needless to say, Chinese officials and NGOs never accompany development projects abroad with lectures about human rights, free and fair elections, transparency, the rule of law and the evils of corruption. But neither do they preach the virtues of Chinese mercantilism, seek converts to Chinese civilization, or idealize lifetime executives in one-party states.

This is why China's rise marks the end of the Age of Imitation. Unlike the West, China expands its global influence without aiming to transform the societies over which it seeks to exercise sway. China is not interested in the structure of other governments or even which domestic faction controls them. It is interested only in the readiness of such governments to adapt to Chinese interests and deal with China on favourable terms.

Admittedly, Beijing yearns to be admired and respected. The proliferation of Confucius Institutes, educational centres affiliated to the Chinese Ministry of Education and established to promote Chinese language and culture abroad, is a clear sign of this. But it is not interested in coaxing or compelling others to daub 'Chinese characteristics' onto their own political and economic systems. The significance of ideology for Chinese domestic politics remains debatable. But the rise of China marks the end of the Age of Imitation because Xi sees the future of global competition with America through purely military and strategic lenses, without regard to ideology or visions of mankind's shared future.

The Age of Imitation was a natural sequel to the Cold War. It retained the Enlightenment's fascination with our common humanity.

The liberal democratic organizational form could be generalized across the world because all people everywhere shared the same basic aspirations. Miraculously, the globalization of communication, transportation and commerce, made possible by the end of the Cold War's bifurcation of planetary geography, allowed peoples from around the world to know each other better. But it seems to have done so at the cost of destroying the idea of a common humanity capable of pursuing common aims. The withdrawal of peoples into barricaded national and ethnic communities is one consequence of today's populist and identity-based war on universalism. We live cheek-by-jowl, but we have lost the capacity to think of our world as shared. A retreat into protectionist communitarianisms, mutually suspicious identity groups, and parochial separatisms may be the indirect price we are paying for the end, in 1989, of a global war between competing universal ideologies.

The rise of a self-insulating but globally assertive China drives home the lesson that the West's victory in the Cold War marked not only the defeat of communism but also a significant setback for Enlightenment liberalism itself. As an ideology celebrating political, intellectual and economic competition, liberalism was fatally weakened by its loss of a peer competitor that boasted the same secular and post-ethnic commitments and equally stemmed from the European Enlightenment. With no alternative centre of power challenging its claim to the future of mankind, liberalism fell in love with itself and lost its way.

The unipolar Age of Imitation was a period when liberalism shed its capacity for self-criticism. The expectation that others should adopt Western-style liberal democratic institutions and norms seemed as natural as the rising of the sun. Not only is this period behind us, but the democratic wave it was expected to unleash has proved disappointingly ephemeral.

The end of the Age of Imitation does not mean that people will stop valuing freedom and pluralism or that liberal democracy will disappear. And it does not mean that reactionary authoritarianism and nativism will inherit the earth. What it signifies, rather, is the return not to a global confrontation between two missionary nations, one liberal and the other communist, but to a pluralistic and competitive world, where no centres of military and economic power will strive to spread their own system of values across the globe. Such an international order is anything but unprecedented, since 'The primary feature of world history tends to be cultural, institutional, and ideological diversity, not homogeneity.'[31] What this observation suggests is that the end of the Age of Imitation is the end of a star-crossed historical anomaly.

In 1890, Rudyard Kipling finished his first novel, *The Light that Failed*. It is a sentimental story of romantic love, artistic ambition and progressive loss of sight. The novel was published in two different versions. The shorter had a happy ending (his mother liked it), and the longer an unhappy one. We don't have the option of publishing this book with two different endings. But we believe that the end of the Age of Imitation will spell either tragedy or hope depending on how liberals manage to make sense of their post-Cold War experience. We can endlessly mourn the globally dominant liberal order that we have lost or we can celebrate our return to a world of perpetually jostling political alternatives, realizing that a chastised liberalism, having recovered from its unrealistic and self-defeating aspirations to global hegemony, remains the political idea most at home in the twenty-first century.

It is our choice to celebrate rather than mourn.

Acknowledgements

The authors wish to thank many generous friends and colleagues and several institutions for making this book possible. We are grateful to all those who contributed their brilliantly stimulating and helpfully monitory comments on an earlier draft of this book. They include Lenny Benardo, Robert Cooper, Beth Elon, Jon Elster, Diego Gambetta, Venelin Ganev, Dessislava Gavrilova, Tom Geoghegan, David Golove, Helge Høibraaten, Scott Horton, Bruce Jackson, Ken Jowitt, Martin Krygier, Maria Lipman, Milla Mineva, James O'Brien, Claus Offe, Gloria Origgi, John Palattella, Adam Przeworski, András Sajó, Judit Sándor, Marci Shore, Daniel Smilov, Ruzha Smilova and Aleksander Smolar. Needless to say, they are absolved, singly and collectively, from responsibility for remaining shortcomings in the analysis, for which the authors alone can be blamed.

We also appreciate the support we received from the Centre for Liberal Strategies in Sofia, the Institut für die Wissenschaften vom Menschen in Vienna and New York University School of Law. Ivan Krastev thanks the Kluge Center at the Library of Congress. The privilege of holding the Kissinger Chair in the Center in 2018–19 was critical for finishing the book. Stephen Holmes is likewise indebted to the regional council of Île-de-France for the privilege of holding the Blaise Pascal Chair in 2017–18. Special thanks go to our agent Toby Mundy and our editor Casiana Ionita for their steady encouragement and thoughtful advice. As usual, Yana Papazova's tireless assistance proved invaluable.

Notes

INTRODUCTION: IMITATION AND ITS DISCONTENTS

1. Robert Cooper, 'The Meaning of 1989', *The Prospect* (20 December 1999).
2. Francis Fukuyama, *The End of History and the Last Man* (New York: Free Press, 1992), p. 46.
3. Larry Diamond and Marc F. Plattner (eds.), *The Global Resurgence of Democracy* (Johns Hopkins University Press, 1996); Timothy Garton Ash, *Free World: America, Europe, and the Surprising Future of the West* (Random House, 2004).
4. Larry Diamond and Marc F. Plattner (eds.), *Democracy in Decline?* (Johns Hopkins University Press, 2015); Larry Diamond, Marc F. Plattner and Christopher Walker (eds.), *Authoritarianism Goes Global: The Challenge to Democracy* (Johns Hopkins University Press, 2016).
5. David Runciman, *How Democracy Ends* (Basic Books, 2018); Steven Levitsky and Daniel Ziblatt, *How Democracies Die* (Crown, 2018).
6. Michael Ignatieff (ed.), *Rethinking Open Society: New Adversaries and New Opportunities* (Central European University Press, 2018).
7. Elisabeth Vallet, *Borders, Fences and Walls* (Routledge, 2018).
8. David Leonhardt, 'The American Dream, Quantified at Last', *New York Times* (8 December 2016).
9. Yascha Mounk, *The People vs. Democracy: Why Our Freedom Is in Danger and How to Save It* (Harvard University Press, 2018).
10. Stephen Smith, *The Scramble for Europe: Young Africa on its way to the Old Continent* (Polity, 2019); Ivan Krastev, *After Europe* (University of Pennsylvania Press, 2017).
11. Michiko Kakutani, *The Death of Truth: Notes on Falsehood in the Age of Trump* (Tim Duggan Books, 2018), p. 26.

12. Ben Rhodes, *The World as It Is: A Memoir of the Obama White House* (Random House, 2018).

13. Francis Fukuyama, 'The End of History?', *National Interest* (Summer 1989), pp. 12, 3, 5, 8, 13; *The End of History and the Last Man* (New York: Free Press, 1992), p. 45.

14. Fukuyama, 'The End of History?', p. 12.

15. If describing American-style liberalism as the final stage of history felt unremarkable to many Americans, it felt the same not only to dissidents but also to ordinary people who grew up behind the Iron Curtain. This was because Fukuyama justified the defeat of the Leninist regimes in the language of Hegelian-Marxist dialectics. Schooled in the idea that history had a predetermined direction and a happy end, many ex-communists, seeing the writing on what was left of the Wall, were conceptually and temperamentally prepared to accept Fukuyama's reading of events.

16. *Inogo ne dano* (Progress, 1988).

17. To 'explain' political trends in the region today by saying that they remind us of political patterns in the past, as do many students of post-communist illiberalism, is to mistake analogy for causality.

18. 'In 2008, the MIT behavioural economist Dan Ariely conducted an experiment in which participants played a computer game that presented three doors on the screen, each of which paid out different sums of money when clicked on. The sensible strategy would have been to identify the highest-paying door and stick to it until the game was up, but as soon as the neglected doors began to shrink – ultimately to disappear – participants started wasting clicks trying to keep the less lucrative options open. It's dumb but we can't help it. Human beings need choice, even just the illusion of it. George Eliot once wrote that choice was "the strongest principle of growth". How can we grow if we can't choose to?' Yo Zushi, 'Exploring Memory in the Graphic Novel', *New Statesman* (6 February 2019).

19. Ryszard Legutko, *The Demon in Democracy: Totalitarian Temptations in Free Societies* (Encounter Books, 2018), pp. 63, 20, 80.

20. Cited in Philip Oltermann, 'Can Europe's New Xenophobes Reshape the Continent?', *Guardian* (3 February 2018).

21. Legutko, *The Demon in Democracy*, p. 41.

22. Gabriel Tarde, *The Laws of Imitation* (English translation: Henry Holt and Company, 1903), p. 74.

23. Not only can the imitative impulse coexist with inventiveness, as Tarde concedes, but under ordinary circumstances imitation can make an

important contribution to creativity and originality. Cf. Kal Raustiala and Christopher Sprigman, *The Knockoff Economy: How Imitation Sparks Innovation* (Oxford University Press, 2012).

24. Wade Jacoby, *Imitation and Politics: Redesigning Modern Germany* (Cornell University Press, 2000).

25. Thorstein Veblen, 'The Opportunity of Japan', *Journal of Race Development* 6:1 (July 1915), pp. 23–38.

26. Trapped in its economics-centred understanding of politics, Brussels finds messianic provincialism in Budapest and Warsaw easy to ridicule but almost impossible to understand. For European bureaucrats, the fact that Poland and Hungary are among the greatest net beneficiaries of EU funding has made their revolt against the EU seem totally irrational. In 2016, for example, Hungary received 4.5 billion euros of European funds, an equivalent of 4 per cent of the country's economic output. Poland received more than 11 billion euros. That such exceptionally favoured beneficiaries have no right to complain is the master premise of the EU's Ostpolitik, such as it is.

27. Ken Jowitt, 'Communism, Democracy, and Golf', *Hoover Digest* (30 January 2001).

28. Ibid.

29. René Girard, *Deceit, Desire, and the Novel: Self and Other in Literary Structure* (Johns Hopkins University Press, 1976); *Battling to the End: Conversations with Benoît Chantre* (Michigan State University Press, 2009).

30. We thank Marci Shore for this example.

31. René Girard, *Violence and the Sacred* (Norton, 1979).

32. Claiming that Dostoyevsky's writings are 'superlatively relevant to the interpretation of a post-communist world', Girard argues as follows: 'Dostoyevsky deeply resented the servile imitation of everything Western that dominated the Russia of his time. His reactionary leanings were reinforced by the smugness of the West, already boasting of its great "advance" over the rest of humanity, which was then called "progress." The West was almost as vulgar as it is today, already confusing its very real material prosperity with a moral and spiritual superiority that it did not possess.' René Girard, *Resurrection from the Underground. Feodor Dostoevsky* (Michigan State University Press, 2012), pp. 88–9.

33. 'According to UN projections, the combined population of Poland, Hungary, the Czech Republic and Slovakia – known as the Visegrad Four, or V4 – will fall from about 64 million in 2017 to just 55.6 million by 2050, or about 13 per cent. Over that period, no region in the

world will experience a faster decline'. James Shotter, 'Central Europe: Running out of Steam', *Financial Times* (27 August 2018).

34. For an expression of the fear that regional traditions are being traduced by the imposition of Western liberalism, consider: 'A wave of opposition in Central Europe to so-called "gender ideology" has led Bulgaria on 15 February, and then Slovakia yesterday (22 February) to oppose ratifying the Istanbul Convention on preventing and combating violence against women and domestic violence.' Georgi Gotev, 'After Bulgaria, Slovakia too Fails to Ratify the Istanbul Convention', Agence France-Presse (23 February 2018).

35. Benjamin E. Goldsmith, *Imitation in International Relations. Observational Learning, Analogies, and Foreign Policy in Russia and Ukraine* (New York; Palgrave, 2005).

36. 'Jim Mattis's Letter to Trump: Full Text', *The New York Times* (20 December 2018).

37. Gáspár Miklós Tamás, 'A Clarity Interfered With', in Timothy Burns (ed.), *After History?* (Littlefield Adams, 1994), pp. 82–3.

1. THE COPYCAT MIND

1. Stendhal, *Scarlet and Black* (Penguin, 1969), p. 75.

2. John Feffer, *Shock Waves: Eastern Europe after the Revolutions* (South End Press, 1992).

3. Cited by Feffer from Nick Thorpe, *'89: The Unfinished Revolution* (Reportage Press, 2009), pp. 191–2.

4. John Feffer, *Aftershock: A Journey into Eastern Europe's Broken Dreams* (Zed Books, 2017), p. 34.

5. Guy Chazan, 'Why Is Alternative for Germany the New Force in German Politics?', *Financial Times* (25 September 2017).

6. George Orwell, *The Collected Essays, Journalism and Letters*, vol. 3 (Harcourt Brace Jovanovich, 1968), p. 244.

7. Ralf Dahrendorf, *Reflections on the Revolution in Europe* (Transaction, 1990); Bruce Ackerman, *The Future of Liberal Revolution* (Yale, 1994).

8. Lawrence Goodwyn, *Breaking the Barrier* (Oxford University Press, 1991), p. 342.

9. Cited in Dahrendorf, *Reflections on the Revolution*, p. 27.

10. Jürgen Habermas, 'What Does Socialism Mean Today? The Rectifying Revolution and the Need for New Thinking on the Left', *New Left Review* 183 (September–October 1990), pp. 5, 7.

11. Jürgen Habermas, *Die Nachholende Revolution* (Suhrkamp, 1990).

12. Hans Magnus Enzensberger, *Europe, Europe: Forays into a Continent* (Pantheon, 1990), p. 97.

13. Roger Cohen, 'The Accommodations of Adam Michnik', *The New York Times Magazine* (7 November 1999).

14. Václav Havel, *The Power of the Powerless: Citizens Against the State in Central-Eastern Europe* (M. E. Sharpe, 1985), p. 89.

15. Cited in Benjamin Herman, 'The Debate That Won't Die: Havel And Kundera on Whether Protest Is Worthwhile', Radio Free Europe/Radio Liberty (11 January 2012).

16. Stanislaw Ignacy Witkiewicz, *Insatiability* (Northwestern University Press, 1996).

17. Czeslaw Milosz, *The Captive Mind* (Vintage, 1990), p. 45.

18. Albert O. Hirschman, *Development Projects Observed* (The Brookings Institution, 1967), pp. 21–2.

19. Ibid., p. 22.

20. Cited in Liav Orgad, *The Cultural Defense of Nations: A Liberal Theory of Majority Rights* (Oxford University Press, 2017), p. 19.

21. 'Why You Are Not Emigrating ... A Letter from Białołęka 1982' in Adam Michnik, *Letters from Prison and Other Essays* (University of California Press, 1987).

22. Ibid., p. 23.

23. Ibid.

24. Albert O. Hirschman, 'Exit, Voice, and the Fate of the German Democratic Republic: An Essay in Conceptual History', *World Politics* 45:2 (January 1993), pp. 173–202.

25. B. Rother, 'Jetzt wächst zusammen, was zusammen gehört' in T. G. Ash (ed.) *Wächst zusammen was zusammen gehört? Schriftenreihe Heft 8* (Berlin: Bundeskanzler Willy Brandt Stiftung, 2001).

26. Joint Statement of the Heads of Government of the Visegrad Group Countries, Prague, 4 September 2015; http://www.visegradgroup.eu/calendar/2015/joint-statement-of-the-150904.

27. Cited in Anne Applebaum, 'A Warning from Europe', *The Atlantic* (October 2018).

28. Viktor Orbán, 'Speech at the Opening of the World Science Forum', 7 November 2015.

29. Raymond Aron, 'The Dawn of Universal History' in *The Dawn of Universal History: Selected Essays from a Witness to the Twentieth Century* (Basic Books, 2002), p. 482.

30. Stephen Smith, *The Scramble for Europe: Young Africa on its Way to the Old Continent* (Polity, 2019).

31. Henry Foy and Neil Buckley, 'Orban and Kaczynski Vow "Cultural Counter-Revolution" to Reform EU', *Financial Times* (7 September 2016).

32. Renaud Camus, *Le Grand Remplacement*, fourth edition (Lulu, 2017).

33. Feffer, *Aftershock*, p. 34.

34. Adam Taylor, 'Hungary's Orbán Wants to Reverse His Country's Shrinking Population Through Tax Breaks', *Washington Post* (12 February 2019).

35. Cf. 'When natives have lots of children of their own, immigrants look like reinforcements. When natives have few children, immigrants look like replacements': David Frum, 'If Liberals Won't Enforce Borders, Fascists Will', *Atlantic* (April 2019). A tacit rationale for Orbán's decision to decertify gender studies programmes in Hungary seems to be that such programmes teach girls not to have children. Owen Daugherty, 'Hungary Ends Funding for Gender Studies Programs, Calling Them "An Ideology",' *The Hill* (17 October 2018).

36. Roger Cohen, 'How Democracy Became the Enemy', *New York Times* (6 April 2018).

37. 'Eastern Europeans Are More Likely to Regard Their Culture as Superior to Others', Pew Research Center (24 October 2018). http://www.pewforum.org/2018/10/29/eastern-and-western-europeans-differ-on-importance-of-religion-views-of-minorities-and-key-social-issues/pf-10-29-18_east-west_-00-03/

38. Milan Kundera, 'A Kidnapped West, or Culture Bows Out', *Granta* 11 (1984), pp. 93–121.

39. Friedrich Nietzsche, *On the Genealogy of Morals*, Book 1, §10 (Penguin, 2013), p. 25

40. Viktor Orbán, 'Day of Honor Speech', 17 March 2018.

41. Mark Lilla, *The Once and Future Liberal: After Identity Politics* (Harper, 2017).

42. David Miller, *On Nationality* (Oxford University Press, 1997), p. 165.

43. Cited in Philip Oltermann, 'Can Europe's New Xenophobes Reshape the Continent?', *Guardian* (3 February 2018).

44. Frantz Fanon, *The Wretched of the Earth* (Grove/Atlantic, 2007), p. 236.

45. Cf. H. Grabbe, 'How Does Europeanization Affect CEE Governance? Conditionality, Diffusion, and Uncertainty', *Journal of European Public Policy* 8 (2001), pp. 1013–31.

46. Cf. 'Byzantium was a true "forestaller" . . . it "held out", despite its weakness, for many centuries against Islam and thereby hindered the Arabs

from conquering all of Italy. Otherwise, as it transpired at the time with North Africa under the extinction of the ancient Christian culture, Italy would have been incorporated into the Islamic world.' Carl Schmitt, *Land and Sea: A World-Historical Meditation* (Telos Press, 2015), pp. 17–18.

47. Valerie Hopkins, 'Hungary's Viktor Orbán blasts " United States of Europe" ', *Financial Times* (16 March 2019).

48. Foy and Buckley, 'Orban and Kaczynski'.

49. Jason Horowitz, 'Steve Bannon Is Done Wrecking the American Establishment. Now He Wants to Destroy Europe's', *The New York Times* (9 March 2018).

50. Griff Witte and Michael Birnbaum, 'In Eastern Europe, the E.U. faces a rebellion more threatening than Brexit', *Washington Post* (5 April 2018).

51. Vaclav Havel, 'Ce que j'ai cru, ce que je crois', *Le Nouvel Observateur* (19 December 19, 2011).

52. Michnik, *Letters from Prison*, p. 314.

53. Michnik, 'Letter from the Gdańsk Prison' (1985), in *Letters from Prison*, p. 81.

54. In the social-science literature, a classic example of the insensitivity of outside observers to the historical connotations in the region of the word 'normality' is a well-known essay by Andrei Shleifer and Daniel Treisman, 'Normal Countries. The East 25 Years After Communism', *Foreign Affairs* (November/December 2014).

55. Peter Bradshaw, 'Graduation Review – A Five-Star Study of Grubby Bureaucratic Compromise', *Guardian* (19 May 2016).

56. Ruzha Smilova, 'Promoting "Gender Ideolog" ': Constitutional Court of Bulgaria Declares Istanbul Convention Unconstitutional', *Oxford Human Rights Hub* (22 August 2018); http://ohrh.law.ox.ac.uk/promoting-gender-ideology-constitutional-court-of-bulgaria-declares-istanbul-convention-unconstitutional/.

57. Václav Bělohradský, *Společnost nevolnosti* (Slon, 2007).

58. Ryszard Legutko, 'Liberal Democracy vs. Liberal Democrats', *Quadrant Online* (April 2015).

59. Thomas Bagger, 'The World According to Germany: Reassessing 1989', *Washington Quarterly* (22 January 2019), p. 54.

60. Ibid.

61. 'While many other countries around the globe would have to transform, Germany could remain as is, waiting for the others to gradually adhere to its model. It was just a matter of time.' Bagger, 'The World According to Germany', p. 54.

62. Returning to the tangled meanings of 'normality' in the region, it is worth recalling that, in post-WW2 West Germany, 'normalization' referred to the bid by Ernst Nolte and other conservative writers to cast off inherited German guilt for the Holocaust, a move strongly opposed by left-leaning democrats such as Habermas, for whom it is a holy truth that Germany can never become 'a normal country' in the sense of a country unburdened by historical contrition for Nazi crimes. None of this has prevented non-Germans from viewing today's Germany as an essentially 'normal' country in a less morally and emotionally fraught sense.

63. 'I've only ever been afraid of signs and symbols, never of people and things,' wrote Sebastian at the start of *For Two Thousand Years*, the marvellous 1934 book that conveys his country's suffocating atmosphere of antisemitism and toxic nationalism between the two world wars.

64. '*On n'intègre pas les peuples comme on fait de la purée de marrons.*' ('We don't unite peoples the way we purée chestnuts.') Cited in 'La Vision européenne du général de Gaulle', *L'Observatoire de l'Europe* (27 January 2010).

65. President Richard von Weizsäcker, 'Speech during the Ceremony Commemorating the 40th Anniversary of the End of War in Europe and of National-Socialist Tyranny' (8 May 1985), https://www.bundespraes ident.de/SharedDocs/Downloads/DE/Reden/2015/02/150202-RvW-Rede-8-Mai-1985-englisch.pdf?—blob=publicationFile.

66. The fact that Germany led the EU in pushing for Croatian independence suggests the limits, or perhaps hypocrisy, of this anti-nationalistic commitment, it should also be said.

67. This includes Russia, where liberals such as Yegor Gaidar, Anatoly Chubais, Andrey Kozyrev and Boris Nemtsov lost public support even more quickly and more radically than did their counterparts in Central and Eastern Europe.

68. Elzbieta Stasik, 'Stoking anti-German sentiments in Poland', *Deutsche Welle* (15 December 2012); https://www.dw.com/en/stoking-anti-german-sentiment-in-poland/a-16456568.

69. Gabor Halmai and Kim Lane Scheppele, 'Living Well Is the Best Revenge: The Hungarian Approach to Judging the Past' in A. James McAdams (ed.), *Transitional Justice and the Rule of Law in New Democracies* (University of Notre Dame, 1997), p. 155.

70. Ivan Berend, *Decades of Crisis* (University of California Press, 2001).

71. Arthur Koestler in Richard Crossman (ed.), *The God that Failed* (Columbia University Press, 1951), p. 2.

72. 'A Public Opinion Survey about János Kádár and the Kádár Regime from 1989', *Hungarian Spectrum* (28 May 2013); https://hungarianspectrum. wordpress.com/2013/05/28/a-public-opinion-survey-about-janos-kadar-and-the-kadar-regime-from-1989/.

73. This is one of the themes of Ryszard Legutko, *The Demon in Democracy: Totalitarian Temptations in Free Societies* (Encounter Books, 2018), an attack on the 'disease' and 'mental enslavement' of liberal democracy, by a writer who manages to recycle, without citation, every trite simplification and stereotype from the long history of European anti-liberalism.

74. Paul Lendvai, *Orbán: Hungary's Strongman* (Oxford University Press, 2018), p. 13.

75. Zoltán Kovács, 'Imre Nagy Reburied, Viktor Orban's Political Career Launched 25 Years Ago Today', *Budapest Beacon* (16 June 2014).

76. Aviezer Tucker, *The Legacies of Totalitarianism: A Theoretical Framework* (Cambridge University Press, 2015).

77. 'Full Text of Viktor Orbán's Speech at Băile Tuşnad (Tusnádfürdő) of 26 July 2014', *The New York Times* (29 July 2014), emphasis added.

78. Ibid.

79. Ibid.

80. Enzensberger, *Europe, Europe,* p. 109.

81. Elisabeth Zerofsky, 'Is Poland Retreating from Democracy?', *New Yorker* (30 July 2018).

82. 'Orbán Viktor's Ceremonial Speech on the 170th Anniversary of the Hungarian Revolution of 1848' (16 March 2018).

83. 'Full Text of Viktor Orbán's Speech at Băile Tuşnad (Tusnádfürdő) of 26 July 2014', *The New York Times* (29 July 2014).

84. Marc Santora and Helene Bienvenu, 'Secure in Hungary, Orban Readies for Battle with Brussels', *The New York Times* (11 May 2018).

85. 'In the Nick of Time', *The Economist* (29 May 2008).

86. Corentin Lotard, 'Le temps de la colonisation de la Hongrie est terminé!', *Le Courrier de l'Europe Centrale* (3 March 2014).

87. Stephen Holmes, 'A European Doppelstaat?', *East European Politics and Society*, 17:1 (2003), pp. 107–18.

88. Amin Maalouf, *In the Name of Identity: Violence and the Need to Belong* (Arcade, 2000), pp. 74–5.

89. Cited in Sławomir Sierakowski, 'How Eastern European Populism Is Different', *The Strategist* (2 Feb 2018).

90. Maria Schmidt, cited in Oltermann, 'Can Europe's New Xenophobes Reshape the Continent?'.

91. 'Polish President Likens EU Membership to Past Occupations', Agence France-Presse (14 March 2018).

92. Applebaum, 'A Warning from Europe'.

93. Adam Leszczyński, 'Poland's Leading Daily Feels Full Force of Jarosław Kaczyński's Anger', *Guardian* (23 February 2016).

94. Cited in Oltermann, 'Can Europe's New Xenophobes Reshape the Continent?'.

95. Viktor Orbán, 'Speech at the Annual General Meeting of the Association of Cities with County Rights' (8 February 2018).

96. Cf. Zoie O'Brien, 'EU Starting to Resemble Old Soviet Union with its DICTATED Rules and Values', *Daily Express* (31 December 2016).

97. Ken Jowitt, 'Setting History's Course', *Policy Review* (1 October 2009).

98. François Jullien, *Il n'y a pas d'identité culturelle* (Paris: L'Herne, 2018).

99. Kim Lane Scheppele, 'The Rule of Law and the Frankenstate: Why Governance Checklists Do Not Work', *Governance* 26:4 (October 2013), pp. 559–62.

2. IMITATION AS RETALIATION

1. '*Les seules bonnes copies sont celles qui nous font voir le ridicule des méchants originaux.*'

2. 'The West Doesn't Have to Love Us', Vladimir Surkov in an interview with *Der Spiegel* (20 June 2005).

3. Stephen Kotkin, *Armageddon Averted: The Soviet Collapse, 1970–2000* (Oxford University Press, 2008), p. 5.

4. Thomas Bagger, 'The World According to Germany: Reassessing 1989', *Washington Quarterly* (22 January 2019), p. 60.

5. Alexey Pushkov, 'Russian Roulette', *National Interest* (3 March 2008).

6. Vladislav Surkov, 'Putin's Lasting State', *Russia Insider* (13 February 2019); https://russia-insider.com/en/vladislav-surkovs-hugely-important-new-article-about-what-putinism-full-translation/ri26259.

7. 'Putin's Prepared Remarks at 43rd Munich Conference on Security Policy', *Washington Post* (12 February 2007).

8. Reinhart Koselleck, 'Transformations of Experience and Methodological Change: A Historical-Anthropological Essay', in Koselleck, *The Practice of Conceptual History: Timing History, Spacing Concepts*, trans. Todd Preston *et al.* (Stanford University, 2002), Chapter 4.

9. President Richard von Weizsäcker, 'Speech during the Ceremony Commemorating the 40th Anniversary of the End of War in Europe and of National-Socialist Tyranny' (8 May 1985), https://www.bundespraesident.

de/SharedDocs/Downloads/DE/Reden/2015/02/150202-RvW-Rede-8-Mai-1985-englisch.pdf?—blob=publicationFile.

10. Steven Lee Myers, *The New Tsar: The Rise and Reign of Vladimir Putin* (Vintage, 2016), Chapter 4.

11. Pia Malaney, 'Mortality Crisis Redux: The Economics of Despair', Institute for New Economic Thinking (27 March 2017); https://www.ineteconomics.org/perspectives/blog/mortality-crisis-redux-the-economics-of-despair.

12. Vladimir Yakunin, *The Treacherous Path: An Insider's Account of Modern Russia* (Biteback Publishing, 2018), p. 18.

13. Putin's State of the Union speech of 25 April 2005; David Masci, 'In Russia, Nostalgia for Soviet Union and Positive Feelings about Stalin', Pew Research Center (29 June 2017).

14. Alexei Navalny and Adam Michnik, *Opposing Forces: Plotting the New Russia* (Egret Press, 2016), p. 101.

15. One of the plotters of the failed coup, Soviet interior minister Boris Pugo, fatally shot himself on 22 August 1991.

16. Curzio Malaparte, *The Kremlin Ball* (New York Review of Books Classics, 2018), p. 45.

17. Ilya Yablokov, *Fortress Russia: Conspiracy Theories in the Post-Soviet World* (Polity, 2018).

18. Miriam Elder, 'Vladimir Putin Accuses Hillary Clinton of Encouraging Russian Protests', *Guardian* (8 December 2011).

19. Stephen Holmes, *Benjamin Constant and the Making of Modern Liberalism* (Yale, 1984), p. 207.

20. Susan Glasser and Peter Baker, *Kremlin Rising: Vladimir Putin's Russia and the End of Revolution* (Potomac Books, 2007), p. 7.

21. 'Today in polls, Russians describe the West as coldhearted, lacking in spiritual values, extremely formal and aggressive. Russians no longer believe the Western model is for them – their country has its own "special" path.' Evgeny Tonkonogy, 'The Evolution of *Homo Sovieticus* to Putin's Man', *Moscow Times* (13 October 2017).

22. According to the Russian-born historian of nationalism Leah Greenfeld every society importing foreign ideas and institutions has 'inevitably focused on the source of importation – an object of imitation by definition – and reacted to it. Because the model was superior to the imitator in the latter's own perception (its being a model implied that), and the contact more often than not served to emphasize the latter's inferiority, the reaction commonly assumed the form of *ressentiment*.' Liah Greenfield, *Nationalism: Five Roads to Modernity* (Harvard University Press, 1992), p. 15.

23. Wolfgang Schivelbusch, *The Culture of Defeat. On National Trauma, Mourning, and Recovery* (Metropolitan Books, 2013), pp. 33–4.

24. Martin van Creveld, *The Transformation of War* (The Free Press, 1991), p. 225.

25. As Zbigniew Brzeziński later told a journalist: '*Le jour où les Soviétiques ont officiellement franchi la frontière, j'ai écrit au président Carter, en substance: "Nous avons maintenant l'occasion de donner à l'URSS sa guerre du Vietnam."*' *Le Nouvel Observateur* (15 January 1998).

26. As Putin explained in 2014, the Americans 'once sponsored Islamic extremist movements to fight the Soviet Union. Those groups got their battle experience in Afghanistan and later gave birth to the Taliban and Al-Qaeda. The West if it did not support, at least it closed its eyes, and, I would say, gave information as well as political and financial support to international terrorists who invaded Russia (we have not forgotten this).' Putin's speech at the Valdai International Discussion Club in Sochi (24 October 2014).

27. Masha Gessen, 'Putin's Syrian Revenge', *New Yorker* (8 October 2015)

28. Putin cited 'the well-known Kosovo precedent – a precedent our western colleagues created with their own hands in a very similar situation, when they agreed to the unilateral separation of Kosovo from Serbia, exactly what Crimea is doing now'. Address by President of the Russian Federation (18 March 2014); http://en.kremlin.ru/events/president/news/20603.

29. Simon Waxman, 'Why Did Putin Oppose Clinton? Decades of American Hypocrisy', *Washington Post* (April 20, 2017).

30. Cited in Perry Anderson, 'Imitation Democracy', *London Review of Books* 37:16 (27 August 2015).

31. Lincoln A. Mitchell, *The Color Revolutions* (University of Pennsylvania Press, 2012).

32. Alexander Prokhanov, *Politolog* (Ultra Kultura, 2005).

33. Andrew Wilson, 'Virtual Politics: "Political Technology" and the Corruption of Post-Soviet Democracy', Johnson's Russia List E-mail Newsletter (21 December 2005); www.cdi.org/russia/johnson/9324-5.cfm.

34. Andrew Wilson, *Virtual Politics: Faking Democracy in the Post-Soviet World* (Yale University Press, 2005), p. xiii.

35. James Madison, *Federalist #10* (Cambridge University Press, 2003). The phrase suggests that Paul Manafort-style political shenanigans long preceded the television age.

36. Hannah Arendt, *The Origins of Totalitarianism* (Meridian Books, 1958), p. 155.

37. Ivan Krastev, *Time and Place/Vreme i miasto. A conversation with Gleb Pavlovsky*, in Bulgarian (Trud, 2018).

38. 'The vast majority is completely uninterested in political life. Asked whether they want to be more involved, 85 per cent of people say no. Politics, they feel, has nothing to do with them.' Tonkonogy, 'The Evolution of *Homo Sovieticus*'.

39. Personal communication.

40. One might ask how to differentiate 'no alternatives' as a source of legitimacy in Russia and 'no alternatives' as a source of illegitimacy in Central Europe. Why does the same formula produce resignation in Russia and revolt in Central Europe? The answer is that in Russia, Putin can change government policy but no one can change Putin, while in Central Europe, rulers can be changed but policies stay the same. The latter produces anti-establishment rage because of the expectation, cultivated in the region in the 1990s, that your vote matters, something no Russian voter ever believed.

41. Kirill Rogov, 'Public Opinion in Putin's Russia', NUPI Working Paper 878 (Norwegian Institute of International Affairs, 2017); https://brage. bibsys.no/xmlui/bitstream/handle/11250/2452184/NUPI_Working_ Paper_878_Rogov.pdf?sequence=2.

42. Stefan Hedlund, *Russian Path Dependence* (Routledge, 2005). Cf. 'Russia's behavior has certainly conformed in recent years to the long sweep of Russian history.' Robert Kagan, *The Jungle Grows Back* (Knopf, 2018), p. 107.

43. See also Karl Schlögel, *Moscow, 1937* (Polity, 2014).

44. In Levada-Center polls between 2005 and 2015, around 34 per cent of respondents reported that 'development of democracy' is what 'most accurately describes the situation in the country.'

45. Julia Ioffe, 'The Potemkin Duma', *Foreign Policy* (22 October 2009).

46. Sergei Kovalev, 'Why Putin Wins', *New York Review of Books* (22 November 2007).

47. Alexander Lukin, 'Russia's New Authoritarianism', *Post-Soviet Affairs* 25:1 (2009), p. 80.

48. Michael Schwirtz, 'Russians Shrug at Prospects of Another Putin Term, Poll Shows', *The New York Times* (7 October 2011).

49. The Kremlin's game with United Russia is quite complicated: it should be assured of winning over its nominal competitors, yet in such a way that it never appears a strong force or a genuine 'people's party' – for that might turn it into a challenger or rival to the Kremlin.

50. Jacques Séguéla, *Le Vertige des urnes* (Flammarion, 2000).

51. Cf. Andrew Roth, 'Russian Election Officials Bar Protest Leader Navalny from 2018 Presidential Race', *Washington Post* (25 December 2017).

52. Cited in Anderson, 'Imitation Democracy'.

53. Alexei Slapovsky, *Pohod na Kreml'. Poema bunta* (AST, 2010); http://www.litres.ru/aleksey-slapovskiy/pohod-na-kreml.

54. Julia Ioffe, 'The Loneliness of Vladimir Putin', *New Republic* (2 February 2014); http://www.newrepublic.com/article/116421/vladimir-putins-russia-has-crushed-dissent-still-falling-apart.

55. Mischa Gabowitsch, *Protest in Putin's Russia* (Polity, 2017).

56. Putin's First Inaugural Address, 7 May 2000.

57. Miriam Elder, 'Russian Protests: Thousands March in Support of Occupy Abay Camp', *The Guardian* (13 May 2012).

58. Michael McFaul, *From Cold War to Hot Peace: An American Ambassador in Putin's Russia* (Houghton Mifflin Harcourt, 2018), pp. 335, 280.

59. Ivan Ilyin, *Our Mission*; Timothy Snyder argues that Ilyin is 'Putin's philosopher' in 'God Is a Russian', *New York Review of Books* (5 April 2018). And it is true that Putin, in his 'Annual Address to the Federal Assembly' (10 May 2006), mentioned 'the well-known Russian thinker Ivan Ilyin', citing him to support the view that 'We must be able to respond to attempts from any quarters to put foreign policy pressure on Russia, including with the aim of strengthening one's own position at our expense.' For a counter-argument, see Marlene Laruelle, 'Is Russia Really "Fascist"? A Comment on Timothy Snyder', PONARS Eurasia Policy Memo No. 539 (September 2018).

60. This was Putin's famously tearful 'Election Victory Speech' in Manezhnaya Square (4 March 2012); https://www.youtube.com/watch?v=c6qLcDAoqxQ.

61. Anton Troianovski, 'Putin Claims Russia Is Developing Nuclear Arms Capable of Avoiding Missile Defenses', *Washington Post* (1 March 2018).

62. Putin's first interview on assuming the Presidency, 2000; https://www.youtube.com/watch?v=EjU8Fg3NFmo.

63. David Brooks, 'The Revolt of the Weak', *The New York Times* (1 September 2014).

64. Moisés Naím, *The End of Power: From Boardrooms to Battlefields and Churches to States, Why Being in Charge Isn't What It Used to Be* (Basic Books, 2013).

65. Address by President of the Russian Federation (18 March 2014); http://en.kremlin.ru/events/president/news/20603.

66. Shaun Walker, *The Long Hangover: Putin's New Russia and the Ghosts of the Past* (Oxford University Press, 2018), p. 4, emphasis added.

67. Lilia Shevtsova, 'Imitation Russia', *National Interest* 2:2 (1 November 2006).

68. Julia Ioffe, 'What Putin Really Wants', *The Atlantic* (January–February 2018).

69. Roderick Conway Morris, 'For 12 Jurors in a Conflicted Russia, There Are No Easy Answers', *The New York Times* (14 September 2007).

70. Ruslan Isayev, 'Mikhalkov's Film 12 Screened in Moscow and Chechnya', *Prague Watchdog* (6 November 2007).

71. Luke Harding, 'Putin's Tears: Why So Sad, Vlad?', *Guardian* (5 March 2012).

72. From the transcript of an interview with the American NBC News Channel (2 June 2000); http://en.kremlin.ru/events/president/transcripts/24204.

73. Samuel P. Huntington, 'The Clash of Civilizations?', *Foreign Affairs* 72:3 (Summer, 1993), p. 156.

74. Henry Foy, 'Russia's Trust in Vladimir Putin Falls to At Least 13-year Low', *Financial Times* (21 January 2019).

75. But see Alex Hernand and Marc Bennetts, 'Great Firewall Fears as Russia Plans to Cut Itself Off from Internet: Moscow Says Temporary Disconnection Is a Test of its Cyberdefence Capabilities', *Guardian* (12 February 2019).

76. Nicholas Eberstadt, 'The Dying Bear: Russia's Demographic Disaster', *Foreign Affairs* (November/December, 2011).

77. United Nations, Department of Economic and Social Affairs, Population Division (2017), *World Mortality 2017 – Data Booklet*; http://www.un.org/en/development/desa/population/publications/pdf/mortality/World-Mortality-2017-Data-Booklet.pdf.

78. Michael Smith, 'Pentagon Planned Love Bomb', *Daily Telegraph* (15 January 2005).

79. 'Transcript of Press Conference with the Russian and Foreign Media' (1 February 2007); http://en.kremlin.ru/events/president/transcripts/24026.

80. 'Presidential Address to the Federal Assembly' (12 December 2013); http://en.kremlin.ru/events/president/news/19825.

81. Masha Lipman, 'The Battle Over Russia's Anti-Gay Law', *New Yorker* (10 August 2013).

82. According to Robert Kagan, Putin is attacking the liberal world order in order 'to return Russia to its historical influence on the world stage': Kagan, *The Jungle Grows Back* (Knopf, 2018), p. 111.

83. James Kirchick, *The End of Europe: Dictators, Demagogues, and the Coming Dark Age* (Yale University Press, 2017).

84. Adolf Burger, *The Devil's Workshop: A Memoir of the Nazi Counterfeiting Operation* (Frontline Books, 2009).
85. Dan Lamothe, 'Once Again, Militants Use Guantanamo-inspired Orange Suit in an Execution', *Washington Post* (28 August 2014).
86. Similarly, terrorists often plant bombs not to achieve a tactical advantage but to reverse the roles of victim and victimizer.
87. Bojana Barlovac, 'Putin Says Kosovo Precedent Justifies Crimea Secession', *Balkan Insight* (18 March 2014).
88. Will Englund, 'Russians Say They'll Name Their Magnitsky-Retaliation Law After Baby Who Died in a Hot Car in Va', *Washington Post* (11 December 2012).
89. Scott Shane, 'Russia Isn't the Only One Meddling in Elections. We Do It Too', *The New York Times* (17 February 2018).
90. Michael Kramer, 'Rescuing Boris', *Time* (24 June 2001).
91. Just as his 'chef' Yevgeny Prigozhin is a private individual who is free to act as he pleases 'within the framework of Russian law': Neil MacFarquhar, 'Yevgeny Prigozhin, Russian Oligarch Indicted by US, Is Known as "Putin's Cook"', *New York Times* (15 February 2018).
92. 'Background to "Assessing Russian Activities and Intentions in Recent US Elections": The Analytic Process and Cyber Incident Attribution' (6 January 2017); https://www.dni.gov/files/documents/ICA_2017_01.pdf.
93. Scott Shane and Mark Mazzetti, 'The Plot to Subvert an Election: Unraveling the Russia Story So Far', *New York Times* (20 September 2018).
94. Peter Baker, 'Point by Point, State Department Rebuts Putin on Ukraine', *New York Times* (5 March 2014).
95. Ian Traynor and Patrick Wintour, 'Ukraine Crisis: Vladimir Putin Has Lost The Plot, Says German Chancellor', *Guardian* (3 March 2014).
96. 'US Publishes List of Putin's "False Claims" on Ukraine', *Haartez* (6 May 2014).
97. John J. Mearsheimer, *Why Leaders Lie: The Truth About Lying in International Politics* (Oxford University Press, 2013), pp. 29, 20.
98. Edward Jay Epstein, *Deception: The Invisible War between the KGB and the CIA* (Simon and Schuster, 1989), p. 17.
99. Viktor Pelevin, *Operacija «Burning Bush»*, in *Ananasnaja voda dlja prekrasnoj damy* [Pineapple Water for a Fair Lady] (Eksmo, 2011), pp. 7–144.
100. Charles Kaiser, 'Can It Happen Here?', *Guardian* (8 April 2018).
101. Cited in Sheila Fitzpatrick, 'People and Martians', *London Review of Books* 41:2 (24 January 2019).

102. Yascha Mounk, *The People vs. Democracy: Why Our Freedom Is in Danger and How to Save It* (Harvard University Press, 2018).
103. Larry Diamond, 'Liberation Technology', *Journal of Democracy* (20 July 2010).
104. Gabriel Zucman, *The Hidden Wealth of Nations: The Scourge of Tax Havens* (University of Chicago Press, 2016).
105. Franklin Foer, 'How Kleptocracy Came to America', *The Atlantic* (March 2019).
106. Yablokov, *Fortress Russia*.
107. http://www.europarl.europa.eu/news/en/agenda/briefing/2018-01-15/4/russia-s-propaganda-in-the-eu.

3. IMITATION AS DISPOSSESSION

1. Made into a critically acclaimed film by Sidney Lumet in 1971; Kenneth Branagh's remake appeared in 2017.
2. Graham Allison, 'The Myth of the Liberal Order', *Foreign Affairs* (July/August 2018).
3. David Leonhardt, 'Trump Tries to Destroy the West', *The New York Times* (10 June 2018); Robert Kagan, 'Trump Marks the End of America as World's "Indispensable Nation"', *Financial Times* (19 November 2016).
4. Robert Kagan, *The World America Made* (Vintage, 2012); Kagan, 'Trump Marks the End'.
5. Robert Costa, Josh Dawsey, Philip Rucker and Seung Min Kim, ' "In the White House Waiting": Inside Trump's Defiance on the Longest Shutdown Ever', *The New York Times* (12 January 2018).
6. Gideon Rachman, 'Donald Trump Embodies the Spirit of Our Age', *Financial Times* (22 October 2018).
7. Alexander Hamilton, *Phocion Letters*, second letter (1784).
8. Julian E. Barnes and Helene Cooper, 'Trump Discussed Pulling US From NATO, Aides Say Amid New Concerns Over Russia', *The New York Times* (14 January 2019).
9. Trump, Orbán and Putin have all been described as 'kleptocrats': Paul Waldman, 'Trump Is Still Acting Like a Tinpot Kleptocrat', *Washington Post* (29 May 2018); Bálint Magyar, *Post-Communist Mafia State: The Case of Hungary* (Central European University Press, 2016); Karen Dawisha, *Putin's Kleptocracy: Who Owns Russia?* (Simon and Schuster, 2015). But comparable schemes of self-enrichment, however interesting to investigators, tell us nothing about comparable sources of popular support.

10. Vladimir Putin, 'A Plea for Caution from Russia', *The New York Times* (11 September 2013).

11. Trump, *CNN* interview (13 September 2013).

12. Interview with Jeffrey Lord, 'A Trump Card', *American Spectator* (20 June 2014).

13. This observation indicates that Trump's attempt to shake down America's allies during his appearance at NATO's Brussels headquarters on 25 May 2017 was intended less to encourage burden-sharing than to be insulting, and that he assumed that there was nothing the allies could do to hurt the United States.

14. 'Transcript: Donald Trump on NATO, Turkey's Coup Attempt and the World', *The New York Times* (21 July 2016).

15. See Conor Cruise O'Brien, 'Purely American: Innocent Nation, Wicked World', *Harper's* (April 1980); Anatol Lieven, *America Right or Wrong: An Anatomy of American Nationalism* (Oxford University Press, 2004).

16. Cf. 'no nation in modern history has been quite so consistently dominated as the United States by the belief that it has a particular mission in the world': Russel Nye, *This Almost Chosen People* (Macmillan, 1966), p. 164.

17. Woodrow Wilson, *The New Democracy*, vol. 4 of *The Public Papers of Woodrow Wilson*, ed. Ray Stannard Baker and William E. Dodd (Harper and Brothers, 1926), pp. 232–3.

18. Kagan, 'Trump Marks the End'.

19. 'Transcript of Mitt Romney's Speech on Donald Trump', *The New York Times* (3 March 2016).

20. Janan Ganesh, 'America Can No Longer Carry the World On Its Shoulders', *Financial Times* (19 September 2018).

21. Philip Bump, 'Donald Trump Isn't Fazed by Vladimir Putin's Journalist-Murdering', *Washington Post* (18 December 2015).

22. In February 2017, after he became President, Trump doubled down on this casually cynical confession of America's unrighteous character. On his Fox News show, Bill O'Reilly said to him: 'Putin is a killer.' Trump replied, 'There are a lot of killers. We have a lot of killers . . . you think our country is so innocent?' Cited in Christopher Mele, 'Trump, Asked Again About Putin, Suggests US Isn't "So Innocent"', *The New York Times* (4 February 2017). For Trump's capacity to inspire imitators, see 'Trump Advisor Tom Barrack Says "Atrocities in America Are Equal or Worse" than the Khashoggi Killing', *The Week* (13 February 2019).

23. William J. Clinton, 'Remarks to the Turkish Grand National Assembly in Ankara', 15 November 1999; https://clintonwhitehouse4.archives.gov/WH/New/Europe-9911/remarks/1999-11-15b.html.

24. 'Text: Obama's Speech in Cairo', *The New York Times* (4 June 2009).

25. Diane Roberts, 'With Donald Trump in the White House, the Myth of American Exceptionalism Is Dying', *Prospect* (13 September 2017).

26. Pew Research Center (30 June 2017); http://www.pewresearch.org/fact-tank/2017/06/30/most-americans-say-the-u-s-is-among-the-greatest-countries-in-the-world/.

27. Alexander Burns, 'Donald Trump, Pushing Someone Rich, Offers Himself', *The New York Times* (16 June 2015), emphasis added.

28. Ken Jowitt (personal communication).

29. Ganesh, 'America Can No Longer Carry the World'.

30. Stephen Wertheim, 'Trump and American Exceptionalism', *Foreign Affairs* (3 January 2017). Wertheim's prediction that 'if Trump continues to spurn exceptionalism, he will damage his government's credibility domestically, opening up a legitimacy gap that each of the country's political factions will scramble to fill' has yet to be fulfilled.

31. See the interviews collected in Charlie Laderman and Brendan Simms, *Donald Trump: The Making of a World View* (Endeavor Press, 2017).

32. 'Transcript: Donald Trump's Foreign Policy Speech', *The New York Times* (27 April 2016).

33. 'Donald Trump: How I'd Run the Country (Better)', *Esquire* (August 2004).

34. 'Remarks by President Trump to the 73rd Session of the United Nations General Assembly', *Foreign Policy* (25 September 2018).

35. See Laderman and Simms, *Donald Trump*.

36. Analogously, the Central European rejection of the Imitation Imperative began in earnest once it became clear, after 2008, that the West was losing its dominant position in the world. Viktor Orbán: 'My basic point is that the many changes in today's world all point in one direction. The moment at which everything became clear was the financial crisis of 2008, or rather the Western financial crisis . . . According to a well-known analyst, America's "soft power" is deteriorating because liberal values include corruption, sex and violence. Such "liberal values" discredit America and American-style modernization.' In 'Full Text of Viktor Orbán's Speech at Băile Tuşnad (Tusnádfürdő) of 26 July 2014', *The New York Times* (29 July 2014).

37. Robert Kagan, 'Not Fade Away: The Myth of American Decline', *New Republic* (11 January 2012).

38. Inaugural Address, 20 January 2017.

39. Ken Jowitt, 'Setting History's Course', *Policy Review* (1 October 2009).

40. They included displaying America's military might to any country that might contemplate harbouring 9/11-style terrorists, retaliating for Saddam's attempt to kill Bush's father in 1993, installing a government in Baghdad that would do America's bidding, eliminating a strategic threat to Israel, giving America a seat at the OPEC table, testing the military theory that speed is more important than mass, and demonstrating that the executive branch could brush off Congressional supervision of the presidency with impunity.

41. For a study of the boost given to American liberalism by competition with Soviet communism, see Mary L. Dudziak, *Cold War Civil Rights: Race and the Image of American Democracy* (Princeton University Press, 2011).

42. Jacob Mikanowski, 'Behemoth, Bully, Thief: How the English Language Is Taking Over the Planet', *Guardian* (27 July 2018); Peter Conrad, *How the World Was Won: The Americanization of Everywhere* (Thames & Hudson, 2014).

43. Philippe van Parijs, *Linguistic Justice for Europe and for the World* (Oxford University Press, 2011).

44. Paul Pillar, *Why America Misunderstands the World* (Columbia University Press, 2016), p.12.

45. Amin Maalouf, *In the Name of Identity: Violence and the Need to Belong* (Arcade, 2000), p. 140.

46. Edward Behr, *Anyone Here Been Raped and Speaks English?* (Penguin, 1992).

47. Yascha Mounk and Roberto Stefan Foa, 'The End of the Democratic Century: Autocracy's Global Ascendance', *Foreign Affairs* (May/June 2018).

48. Ibid.

49. Chris Hastings, 'President Putin Thinks House of Cards Is a Documentary', *Daily Mail* (27 May 2017).

50. Bob Woodward, *Fear: Trump in the White House* (Simon & Schuster, 2018), p. 159.

51. Western efforts at democracy-promotion after communism didn't amount to much, but to the extent they existed they confirmed the proposition that a decisive victory leads victors to lose their curiosity. The only thing that interested many foreign visitors about countries exiting from communism was whether or not the latter were inching forward on pre-established pathways of democratic and liberal reform.

It's only a slight exaggeration to say that many government officials and representatives of NGOs ended up visiting post-communist nations the way tourists visit primate enclosures at the zoo. They were fascinated only by what was missing: no opposable thumbs, say, or no rule of law.

52. Mark Thompson, 'The Pentagon's Foreign-Language Frustrations', *Time* (24 August 2011).

53. Personal communication.

54. Michael Kranish and Marc Fisher, *Trump Revealed: The Definitive Biography of the 45th President* (Scribner, 2016).

55. Donald Trump, *Think Big: Make It Happen in Business and Life* (HarperCollins, 2009).

56. Tony Schwartz, 'I Wrote the Art of the Deal with Donald Trump' in Bandy X. Lee (ed.), *The Dangerous Case of Donald Trump* (Thomas Dunne Books, 2017).

57. Paul B. Brown, 'How to Deal with Copy Cat Competitors: A Six Point Plan', *Forbes* (12 March 2014).

58. Interview with Jeffrey Lord, p. 40.

59. 'The 1990 Playboy Interview With Donald Trump', *Playboy* (1 March 1990).

60. 'Full Text: Donald Trump Announces a Presidential Bid', *Washington Post* (16 June 2015).

61. Morgan Gstalter, 'Trump to Impose Total Ban on Luxury German Cars', *The Hill* (31 May 2018). See also Griff Witte and Rick Noack, 'Trump's Tariff Threats Suddenly Look Very Real in the Heartland of Germany's Car Industry', *Washington Post* (22 June 2018).

62. Interview on *The O'Reilly Factor*, Fox News, 31 March 2011.

63. Eric Rauchway, 'Donald Trump's New Favorite Slogan Was Invented for Nazi Sympathizers', *Washington Post* (14 June 2016).

64. Laderman and Simms, *Donald Trump*, p. 73.

65. 'Donald Trump Announces a Presidential Bid'.

66. 'Many Americans believe they have been duped of their birthright by unfair competition from Japan, South Korea, Taiwan, and now China and India.' Edward Luce, *Time to Start Thinking: America in the Age of Descent* (Atlantic Monthly Press, 2012) p. 40.

67. Inaugural Address, 20 January 2017.

68. Francis Fukuyama, *Identity: The Demand for Identity and the Politics of Resentment* (Farrar, Straus and Giroux, 2018), p. 157. Conservative history professor Niall Ferguson similarly argues that the liberal hegemony has committed suicide by facilitating China's rise to superpower status and thereby ruining the Western middle classes which had long provided

the mainstay of Western liberalism domestically. Niall Ferguson and Fareed Zakaria, *Is This the End of the Liberal International Order?* (House of Anansi Press, 2017).

69. Lauren Gambino and Jamiles Lartey, 'Trump Says US Will Not Be a "Migrant Camp"', *Guardian* (19 June 2018).

70. Griff Witte, 'As Merkel holds on precariously, Trump tweets Germans "are turning against their leadership" on migration', *Washington Post* (18 June 2018).

71. Thomas Chatterton Williams, 'The French Origins of "You Will Not Replace Us"', *New Yorker* (4 December 2017).

72. James McAuley, 'New Zealand Suspect Inspired by French Writer Who Fears "Replacement" By Immigrants', *Washington Post* (15 March 2019).

73. Viktor Orbán, 'Speech at the Opening of the World Science Forum', 7 November 2015; Shaun Walker, 'Hungarian Leader Says Europe Is Now "Under Invasion" by Migrants', *Guardian* (15 March 2018).

74. 'Remarks by President Trump on the Illegal Immigration Crisis and Border Security' (1 November 2018); https://www.whitehouse.gov/ briefings-statements/remarks-president-trump-illegal-immigration-crisis- border-security/.

75. Holly Case, 'Hungary's Real Indians', *Eurozine* (3 April 2018).

76. Ronald Reagan, presidential farewell address to the nation (11 January 1989). On Reagan's suggestion that immigrants have 'made America great', see https://www.politifact.com/truth-o-meter/statements/2018/ jul/03/becoming-american-initiative/did-ronald-reagan-say-immigrants- made-america-grea/.

77. Maalouf, *In the Name of Identity.*

78. Samuel P. Huntington, *The Clash of Civilizations and the Remaking of World Order* (Simon & Schuster, 1996), p. 306.

79. Ashley Parker and Amy B. Wang, 'Trump Criticizes Democrats, "Russian Witch Hunt," and Coastal Elites at Ohio Rally', *Washington Post* (4 August 2018); Linda Qiu, 'No, Democrats Don't Want "Open Borders"', *The New York Times* (27 June 2018); Aaron Blake, 'Trump Keeps Throwing Around the Word "Treason" – Which May Not Be a Great Idea', *Washington Post* (15 May 2018).

80. Samuel P. Huntington, *Who Are We?: The Challenges to America's National Identity* (Simon & Schuster, 2005).

81. Populist voters seem more afraid of ethnic and racial diversity than of crimes committed by illegal immigrants. This impression is confirmed when we remember what Obama really meant when he celebrated

American exceptionalism. What made America 'exceptional' after 1965, when racial quotas on immigrants were eliminated, was its optimistic and welcoming attitude towards racial and cultural diversity. Here we confront the dimension of American exceptionalism that Trump and his supporters presumably find most repellent. As Obama remarked in his 2008 speech on race: 'I will never forget that in no other country on Earth is my story even possible.' 'Barack Obama's Speech on Race', *New York Times* (18 March 2008). Cf. 'No American president has talked about American exceptionalism more often and in more varied ways than Obama.' Greg Jaffe, 'Obama's New Patriotism', *Washington Post* (3 June 2015). To many Trump supporters, this reminder was unwelcome. They reject Obama's moral and practical claim that America can be a multi-racial society and still remain America. Since America is an irreversibly multi-racial society, this rejection is either a cry in the dark or an invitation to violence.

82. This is true, even though fertility rates among native-born white Americans are also dropping.

83. Larry Elliott, 'As the Berlin Wall Fell, Checks on Capitalism Crumbled', *Guardian* (2 November 2014).

84. Ed Pilkington, 'Obama Angers Midwest Voters with Guns and Religion Remark', *The Guardian* (14 April 2008); Chris Cillizza, 'Why Mitt Romney's "47 Per Cent" Comment Was So Bad', *Washington Post* (4 March 2013); Aaron Blake, 'Voters Strongly Reject Hillary Clinton's "Basket of Deplorables" Approach', *Washington Post* (26 September 2016).

85. Christopher Lasch, *The Revolt of the Elites: And the Betrayal of Democracy* (Norton, 1995), pp. 44–5.

86. David Smith, ' "Democrats Won the House But Trump Won the Election" – and 2020 Is Next', *Guardian* (10 November 2018).

87. Griff Witte, 'Soros-founded University Says It Has Been Kicked Out of Hungary as an Autocrat Tightens His Grip', *Washington Post* (3 December 2018).

88. To refresh our sense of how imitators threaten the imitated, it will help to glance at the war crime of 'perfidy', which includes the practice of dressing deceptively in the uniform of the enemy. In the age of mass armies, uniforms allow soldiers to distinguish hostile from friendly forces. Naïve reliance on such a simple signal of otherwise unobservable group membership, however, creates an irresistible opportunity for mimics. Indeed, treacherous killing of genuine military personnel by insurgents wearing counterfeit or stolen army uniforms remains the

most consequential form of wartime mimicry in, for example, both Afghanistan and Iraq.

89. For a sceptical and humorous account of this aspect of Russia's aggressive imitation policy, see Jesse Walker, 'How Russian Trolls Imitate American Political Dysfunction', *The Atlantic* (25 October 2018).

90. Marcel Detienne, *L'Identité nationale, une énigme* (Gallimard, 1962).

91. As Ken Jowitt has also pointed out to us, the fact that Jews were represented in the Kaiser's army during the First World War in proportion to their numbers in the population, instead of being evidence of loyalty to the Fatherland, was evidence for the Nazis of how these duplicitous camouflaged aliens created a defeatist Bolshevik mentality in the army.

92. Kwame Anthony Appiah, *The Lies That Bind: Rethinking Identity: Creed, Country, Class, Culture* (Norton, 2018).

93. Yair Rosenberg, ' "Jews will not replace us": Why White Supremacists Go After Jews', *Washington Post* (14 August 2017); Emma Green, 'Why the Charlottesville Marchers Were Obsessed With Jews', *The Atlantic* (15 August 2017). In a similar way, when reflecting on his disillusionment with liberal democracy in post-communist Poland, Ryszard Legutko was shocked at the speed with which the ex-communists remade themselves into good liberal democrats. To Legutko, this proved the superficiality of liberal-democratic identity and made a joke of his decades of resisting communist tyranny: Ryszard Legutko, *The Demon in Democracy: Totalitarian Temptations in Free Societies* (Encounter Books, 2018), pp. 2–3.

94. Liam Stack, 'White Lives Matter Has Been Declared a Hate Group', *The New York Times* (30 August 2016).

95. Philip Roth, *The Plot Against America* (Houghton Mifflin, 2004), p. 13.

96. George Kennan, 'The Long Telegram' (22 February 1946); https://digitalarchive.wilsoncenter.org/document/116178.pdf.

97. Hannah Arendt, *Origins of Totalitarianism* (Meridian Books, 1958).

98. Masha Gessen, 'The Putin Paradigm', *New York Review of Books* (13 December 2016).

99. 'As a businessman and a very substantial donor to very important people, when you give, they do whatever the hell you want them to do.' Peter Nicholas, 'Donald Trump Walks Back His Past Praise of Hillary Clinton', *Wall Street Journal* (29 July 2015).

100. Woodward, *Fear*, p. 174.

101. The idea that lying is perfectly permissible in wartime, far from being singularly Trumpian, is confirmed by Article 37.2 of Protocol I to the Geneva Conventions, which reads: 'Such ruses are acts which are

intended to mislead an adversary or to induce him to act recklessly but which infringe no rule of international law applicable in armed conflict and which are not perfidious because they do not invite the confidence of an adversary with respect to protection under that law. The following are examples of such ruses: the use of camouflage, decoys, mock operations and misinformation.'

102. Schwartz, 'I Wrote the Art of the Deal'.

103. James Barron, 'Overlooked Influences on Donald Trump: A Famous Minister and His Church', *The New York Times* (5 September 2016).

104. David Enrich, Matthew Goldstein and Jesse Drucker, 'Trump Exaggerated His Wealth in Bid for Loan, Michael Cohen Tells Congress', *The New York Times* (27 February 2019).

105. Nancy Pelosi, cited in Jennifer Rubin, 'Trump's Fruitless Struggle to Stop Transparency', *Washington Post* (7 February 2019).

106. It's worth noting that Trump's strategy of domination cannot be captured by Gramsci's concept of 'cultural hegemony'. Trump is not trying to impose a universally valid dominant ideology or *Weltanschauung* to justify the power and privilege of the ruling class or prove that that status quo is natural and inevitable. It's not only that he couldn't care less, but also that destroying the very idea of an official version of reality is essential to his quest for legal and political impunity.

107. Bernard Williams, *Truth and Truthfulness: An Essay in Genealogy* (Princeton University Press, 2010).

108. Cf. Daniel A. Effron, 'Why Trump Supporters Don't Mind His Lies', *The New York Times* (28 April 2018).

109. George Orwell, 'Notes on Nationalism', *The Collected Essays, Journalism and Letters*, vol. 4 (Harcourt Brace Jovanovich, 1968).

110. Gregory Korte, 'Trump Blasts "Treasonous" Democrats for Not Applauding at His State of the Union Address', *USA Today* (5 February 2018).

111. Joe Concha, 'Trump Rips Fact-Checkers: "Some of the Most Dishonest People in Media"', *The Hill* (12 February 2019).

112. Rebecca Savransky, 'Poll: Almost Half of Republicans Believe Trump Won Popular Vote', *The Hill* (10 August 2017); Jacqueline Thomsen, 'Poll: Fewer Than Half of Republicans Say Russia Interfered in 2016 Election', *The Hill* (18 July 2018).

113. 'Full Transcript: Donald Trump's Jobs Plan Speech', *Politico* (28 June 2016).

114. John Judis, 'What Trump Gets Right on Trade', *New Republic* (25 September 2018).

115. Aaron David Miller and Richard Sokolsky, 'The One Thing Trump Gets Right About Middle East Policy', *CNN* (7 January 2019). See also Jon Finer and Robert Malley, 'Trump Is Right to Seek an End to America's Wars', *The New York Times* (8 January 2019).

116. Woodward, *Fear*, p. 125.

117. Adam Liptak, 'Chief Justice Defends Judicial Independence After Trump Attacks "Obama Judge"', *The New York Times* (21 November 2018).

118. Mallory Shelbourne, 'Trump: I'm Not Obstructing Justice, I'm "Fighting Back"', *The Hill* (7 May 2018). 'There was no collusion, there was no obstruction,' he said. 'I mean, unless you call "obstruction" the fact that I fight back. I do fight back. I really fight back. I mean, if you call that obstruction, that's fine. But there's no obstruction, there's no collusion.' Cited in Aaron Blake, 'Trump's Notable "Obstruction" Concession', *Washington Post* (27 September 2018).

119. Maria Sacchetti, 'Trump Is Deporting Fewer Immigrants Than Obama, Including Criminals', *Washington Post* (10 August 2017).

120. Karen DeYoung, 'For Trump, the Relationship With Saudi Arabia Is All About Money', *Washington Post* (19 November 2018).

121. Dionne Searcey and Emmanuel Akinwotu, 'Nigerian Army Uses Trump's Words to Justify Shooting of Rock-Throwers', *The New York Times* (3 November 2018).

122. Cf. 'To Jair Bolsonaro, the new president of Brazil, the US president is a barrier-breaker – proof that incendiary comments about women or minorities and a history of trafficking in conspiracy theories don't need to stand in the way of taking power.' Griff Witte, Carol Morello, Shibani Mahtani and Anthony Faiola, 'Around the Globe, Trump's Style Is Inspiring Imitators and Unleashing Dark Impulses', *Washington Post* (22 January 2019).

CONCLUSION: THE CLOSING OF AN AGE

1. Nikolay Karamzin, *Memoir on Ancient and Modern Russia,* trans. Richard Pipes (Atheneum, 1974), p. 122.

2. Tom Parfitt, 'Kvas Is It? Coca-Cola Bids to Bottle the "Coke of Communism"', *Guardian* (5 February 2007).

3. Marina Koren, 'Why the Far Side of the Moon Matters So Much. China's Successful Landing Is Part of the Moon's Long Geopolitical History', *The Atlantic* (3 January 2019).

4. Chris Buckley, 'The Rise and Fall of the Goddess of Democracy', *The New York Times* (1 June 2014); Craig Calhoun, *Neither Gods Nor Emperors: Students and the Struggle for Democracy in China* (University of California Press, 1995), p. 108.

5. 'Deng's June 9 Speech: "We Faced a Rebellious Clique" and "Dregs of Society"', *The New York Times* (30 June 1989).

6. Soon after the events, curiously enough, Donald Trump expressed his admiration for the crackdown: 'When the students poured into Tiananmen Square, the Chinese government almost blew it. Then they were vicious, they were horrible, but they put it down with strength. That shows you the power of strength. Our country is right now perceived as weak . . . as being spit on by the rest of the world.' 'The 1990 Playboy Interview With Donald Trump', *Playboy* (1 March 1990).

7. Bagger describes the West German consensus on this after 1989 as follows: 'China would only be able to continue its miraculous economic rise if it introduced individual liberties. Only a free and open society could unleash the creativity that was at the core of economic innovation and success in the information age.' Thomas Bagger, 'The World According to Germany: Reassessing 1989', *Washington Quarterly* (22 January 2019), p. 55.

8. Francis Fukuyama, 'The End of History?', *National Interest* (Summer 1989), p. 12.

9. 'China is reversing the commonly held vision of technology as a great democratizer, bringing people more freedom and connecting them to the world. In China, it has brought control.' Paul Mozur, 'Inside China's Dystopian Dreams: A.I., Shame and Lots of Cameras', *The New York Times* (8 June 2018).

10. Chris Buckley and Steven Lee Myers, 'On Anniversary of China's Reforms, Xi Doubles Down on Party Power', *The New York Times* (18 December 2018).

11. Ibid.

12. Ibid.

13. Jonah Newman, 'Almost One-Third of All Foreign Students in US Are From China', *Chronicle of Higher Education* (7 February 2014).

14. Elizabeth C. Economy, *The Third Revolution: Xi Jinping and the New Chinese State* (Oxford, 2018), p. 42.

15. Xi Jinping at a conference to commemorate the fortieth anniversary of China's Reform and Opening Up Policy at the Great Hall of the People in Beijing. Cited in Yanan Wang, 'China Will "Never Seek Hegemony," Xi Says in Reform Speech', *Washington Post* (18 December 2018).

16. Kerry Brown, *The World According to Xi: Everything You Need to Know About the New China* (I. B. Tauris, 2018), pp. 46–7.

17. Chris Buckley, 'Xi Jinping Thought Explained: A New Ideology for a New Era', *The New York Times* (26 February 2018).

18. Georges Devereux and Edwin M. Loeb, 'Antagonistic Acculturation', *American Sociological Review* 8 (1943), pp. 133–47.

19. Christopher Walker *et al.*, *Sharp Power: Rising Authoritarian Influence* (International Forum for Democratic Studies, National Endowment for Democracy, December 2017); https://www.ned.org/wp-content/uploads/2017/12/Sharp-Power-Rising-Authoritarian-Influence-Full-Report.pdf.

20. Economy, *The Third Revolution*, p. 37. 'Contrary to the very essence of globalization, Xi has moved to reverse the trend of greater flows of information between China and the outside world. New regulations seek to restrict the ability of professors to use Western social science textbooks or to discuss Western ideas of governance and economics in the classroom. The party increasingly circumscribes the range of foreign television and other media content available to avoid the passive indoctrination of the Chinese people with Western values. And new restrictions on Internet content, as well technological advances, constrain the free flow of information in the cyber world.' Ibid., p. 232.

21. Mark Lander, 'Trump Has Put the US and China on the Cusp of a New Cold War', *The New York Times* (19 September 2018).

22. 'On October 13, 2013, China's Xinhua News Agency shocked the global media circuits with an unequivocal call for a 'de-americanized world' . . . in response to a debilitating fiscal fight within the US ruling elite that threatened a US debt default, risking China's $1.3 trillion US debt holdings.' Yuezhi Zhao, 'Communication, Crisis, and Global Power Shifts', *International Journal of Communication* 8 (2014), pp. 275–300.

23. Lucian W. Pye, *The Spirit of Chinese Politics* (Harvard University Press, 1992), p. 56.

24. Brown, *The World According to Xi*, pp. 81–2.

25. Fukuyama, 'The End of History?', p. 11.

26. Ibid., p. 17.

27. Pye, *The Spirit of Chinese Politics*, p. 235.

28. 'What binds the Chinese together is their sense of culture, race, and civilization, not an identification with the nation as a state.' Lucian W. Pye, 'Chinese Democracy and Constitutional Development' in Fumio Itoh

(ed.), *China in the Twenty-first Century: Politics, Economy, and Society* (United Nations University Press, 1997), p. 209.

29. Richard McGregor, *The Party: The Secret World of China's Communist Rulers* (Harper, 2010), p. 77.
30. Brown, *The World According to Xi*, p. 35.
31. Ken Jowitt, 'Setting History's Course', *Policy Review* (1 October 2009).

Index